Introduction to Data Science

Covered with R18 JNTU-H III CSE-Data Science Syllabus

Dr.J. Gladson Maria Britto

Dr. Diana Moses

Dr.MD Ashfaqul Hasan

Published by

BONFRING®
Intellectual Integrity

Introduction to Data Science

9 789392 537493 >

ISBN 978-93-92537-49-3

Authors

Dr.J. Gladson Maria Britto| Dr. Diana Moses| Dr.MD Ashfaqul Hasan

Bonfring

309, 5th Street Extension, Gandhipuram,

Coimbatore - 641 012,

Tamil Nadu, India.

E-mail: info@bonfring.org

Website: www.bonfring.org

Preface

It is becoming clear by the day that there is enormous value in data processing and analysis—and that is where a data scientist steps into the spotlight. Without the expertise of professionals who turn cutting-edge technology into actionable insights, Big Data is nothing.

This textbook aims to be an approachable introduction to the world of data science. In this book, we define data science as the process of generating insight from data through reproducible and auditable processes.

This textbook cover topic exhaustively and provides complete hands-on basic guidance using R Programming. The flow of delivery in the book starts with data preprocessing and preparation methods and proceeds to analysis, reporting and visualization. The book also highlights the interpretation of the results of all the analytic methods and empowers the reader to draw high-level refined knowledge and insights from the large sources of data. The readers would have a enriching reading experience and a challenging hands-on experience from this book.

Data science can add value to any business who can use their data well. From statistics and insights across workflows and hiring new candidates, to helping senior staff make better-informed decisions, data science is valuable to any company in any industry. As we gear-up to tapping the advantages of Data Science, this book would be a milestone in your learning journey.

> "DATA IS A PRECIOUS THING AND **WILL LAST LONGER** THAN THE SYSTEMS THEMSELVES."

Dr.J. Gladson Maria Britto

Dr. Diana Moses

Dr.MD Ashfaqul Hasan

Acknowledgement

First and foremost, I thank, the Almighty God for endowing his immense blessing that helped me in each step of my progress towards the successful completion of this text book "Introduction to Data Science".

I owe a warm debt of gratitude to my co-authors for their guidance, novel ideas, inspiration and brilliant discussions at every stage of this work. From my bottom of heart, I thank him for made this as a good research work.

It is my privilege to thank the management and Dr.M. Sreedhar Reddy, Principal, MRCE and Dr.M. Ashok, Principal, MRIET for their constant support and cooperation to complete the text book.

I whole heartedly thank God almighty for giving me knowledge, wisdom and guidance in all aspects of my life. I express my profound thanks to the Management, The Director and The Principal of Methodist college of Engineering and Technology for their support in this initiative. Furthermore, I am grateful for the strength given by my family and friends always.

Most importantly, none of this would have been possible without the love and patience of our family. Words alone cannot describe the encouragement, affection and our parent, wife and children; I thank them for all the help, care and moral support provided throughout this work.

Dr.J. Gladson Maria Britto

Dr. Diana Moses

Dr.MD Ashfaqul Hasan

This text book is devoted to Almighty God for making it all possible, our family members and our Gurus for their loving, encouraging and everlasting support.

TABLE OF CONTENTS

SYLLABUS

Unit - 1

Introduction: Definition of Data Science- Big Data and Data Science hype - and getting past the hype - Datafication - Current landscape of perspectives - Statistical Inference - Populations and samples - Statistical modeling, probability distributions, fitting a model - Over fitting. Basics of R: Introduction, R Environment Setup, Programming with R, Basic Data Types.

Unit - 2

Data Types & Statistical Description: Types of Data: Attributes and Measurement, What is an Attribute? The Type of an Attribute, The Different Types of Attributes, Describing Attributes by the Number of Values, Asymmetric Attributes, Binary Attribute, Nominal Attributes, Ordinal Attributes, Numeric Attributes, Discrete versus Continuous Attributes. Basic Statistical Descriptions of Data: Measuring the Central Tendency: Mean, Median, and Mode, Measuring the Dispersion of Data: Range, Quartiles, Variance, Standard Deviation, and Interquartile Range, Graphic Displays of Basic Statistical Descriptions of Data.

Unit - 3

Vectors: Creating and Naming Vectors, Vector Arithmetic, Vector sub setting, Matrices: Creating and Naming Matrices, Matrix Sub setting, Arrays, Class. Factors and Data Frames: Introduction to Factors: Factor Levels, Summarizing a Factor, Ordered Factors, Comparing Ordered Factors, Introduction to Data Frame, subsetting of Data Frames, Extending Data Frames, Sorting Data Frames. Lists: Introduction, creating a List: Creating a Named List, Accessing List Elements, Manipulating List Elements, Merging Lists, Converting Lists to Vectors.

Unit - 4

Conditionals and Control Flow: Relational Operators, Relational Operators and Vectors, Logical Operators, Logical Operators and Vectors, Conditional Statements. Iterative Programming in R: Introduction, While Loop, For Loop, Looping Over List. Functions in R: Introduction, writing a Function in R, Nested Functions, Function Scoping, Recursion, Loading an R Package, Mathematical Functions in R.

Unit - 5

Data Reduction: Overview of Data Reduction Strategies, Wavelet Transforms, Principal Components Analysis, Attribute Subset Selection, Regression and Log-Linear Models: Parametric Data Reduction, Histograms, Clustering, Sampling, Data Cube Aggregation. Data Visualization: Pixel-Oriented Visualization Techniques, Geometric Projection Visualization Techniques, Icon-Based Visualization Techniques, Hierarchical Visualization Techniques, Visualizing Complex Data and Relations.

UNIT - 1

CHAPTER 1

INTRODUCTION TO DATA SCIENCE

1.1. Definition of Data Science

- **Data Science** is an interdisciplinary field that focuses on extracting knowledge from data sets which are typically huge in amount. The field encompasses analysis, preparing data for analysis, and presenting findings to inform high-level decisions in an organization. As such, it incorporates skills from computer science, mathematics, statics, information visualization, graphic, and business.
- Data science is a deep study of the massive amount of data, which involves extracting meaningful insights from raw, structured, and unstructured data that is processed using the scientific method, different technologies, and algorithms.
- It is a multidisciplinary field that uses tools and techniques to manipulate the data so that you can find something new and meaningful.
- Data science uses the most powerful hardware, programming systems, and most efficient algorithms to solve the data related problems. It is the future of artificial intelligence.

In short, we can say that data science is all about:

- Asking the correct questions and analyzing the raw data.
- Modeling the data using various complex and efficient algorithms.
- Visualizing the data to get a better perspective.
- Understanding the data to make better decisions and finding the final result.

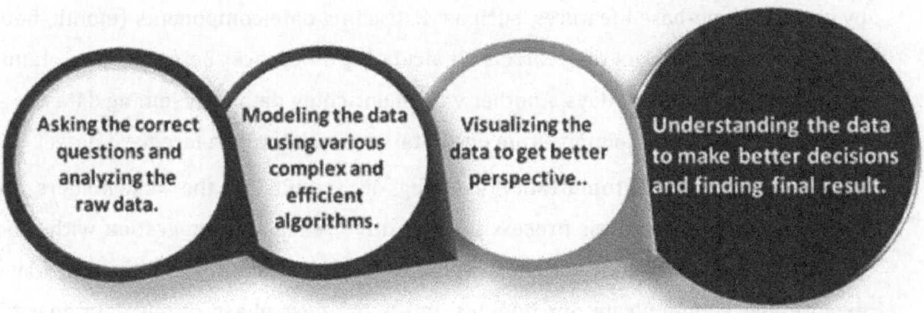

Figure 1: About Data Science

Example

Let suppose we want to travel from station A to station B by car. Now, we need to take some decisions such as which route will be the best route to reach faster at the location, in which route there will be no traffic jam, and which will be cost-effective. All these decision factors will act as input data, and we will get an appropriate answer from these decisions, so this analysis of data is called the data analysis, which is a part of data science.

Note: Few important steps to help you work more successfully with data science projects.

- **Setting the Research Goal:** Understanding the business or activity that our data science project is part of is key to ensuring its success and the first phase of any sound data analytics project. Defining the what, the why, and the how of our project in a project charter is the foremost task. Now sit down to define a timeline and concrete key performance indicators and this is the essential first step to kick-start our data initiative!
- **Retrieving Data:** Finding and getting access to the data needed in our project is the next step. Mixing and merging data from as many data sources as possible is what makes a data project great, so look as far as possible. This data is either found within the company or retrieved from a third party. So, here are a few ways to get ourselves some usable data: connecting to a database, using API's or looking for open data.
- **Data Preparation:** The next data science step is the dreaded data preparation process that typically takes up to 80% of the time dedicated to our data project. Checking and remediating data errors, enriching the data with data from other data sources, and transforming it into a suitable format for your models.
- **Data Exploration:** Now that we have clean our data, it's time to manipulate it to get the most value out of it. Diving deeper into our data using descriptive statistics and visual techniques is how we explore our data. One example of that is to enrich our data by creating time-based features, such as: Extracting date components (month, hour, day of the week, week of the year, etc.), Calculating differences between date columns or Flagging national holidays. Another way of enriching data is by joining datasets — essentially, retrieving columns from one data-set or tab into a reference data-set.
- **Presentation and Automation:** Presenting our results to the stakeholders and industrializing our analysis process for repetitive reuse and integration with other tools. When we are dealing with large volumes of data, visualization is the best way to explore and communicate our findings and is the next phase of our data analytics project.

- **Data Modeling:** Using machine learning and statistical techniques is the step to further achieve our project goal and predict future trends. By working with clustering algorithms, we can build models to uncover trends in the data that were not distinguishable in graphs and stats. These create groups of similar events (or clusters) and more or less explicitly express what feature is decisive in these results.

1.2. Big Data and Data Science Hype

- **Big Data:** This is a term related to extracting meaningful data by analyzing the huge amount of complex, variously formatted data generated at high speed, that cannot be handled, or processed by the traditional system.
- Big data refers to significant volumes of data that cannot be processed effectively with the traditional applications that are currently used. The processing of big data begins with raw data that isn't aggregated and is most often impossible to store in the memory of a single computer.
- Big data is a buzzword used to describe immense volumes of data, both unstructured and structured, that can inundate a business on a day-to-day basis.
- Big data is used to analyze insights, which can lead to better decisions and strategic business moves.

Source of Big Data

- **Social Media:** Today's world a good percent of the total world population is engaged with social media like Facebook, WhatsApp, Twitter, YouTube, Instagram, etc. Each activity on such media like uploading a photo, or video, sending a message, making comment, putting like, etc create data.
- **A Sensor Placed in Various Places:** Sensor placed in various places of the city that gathers data on temperature, humidity, etc. A camera placed beside the road gather information about traffic condition and creates data. Security cameras placed in sensitive areas like airports, railway stations, and shopping malls create a lot of data.
- **Customer Satisfaction Feedback:** Customer feedback on the product or service of the various company on their website creates data. For Example, retail commercial sites like Amazon, Walmart, Flipkart, and Myntra gather customer feedback on the quality of their product and delivery time. Telecom companies, and other service provider organizations seek customer experience with their service. These create a lot of data.

- **IoT Appliance:** Electronic devices that are connected to the internet create data for their smart functionality, examples are a smart TV, smart washing machine, smart coffee machine, smart AC, etc. It is machine-generated data that are created by sensors kept in various devices. For Example, a Smart printing machine – is connected to the internet. A number of such printing machines connected to a network can transfer data within each other. So, if anyone loads a file copy in one printing machine, the system stores that file content, and another printing machine kept in another building or another floor can print out that file hard copy. Such data transfer between various printing machines generates data.
- **E-commerce:** In e-commerce transactions, business transactions, banking, and the stock market, lots of records stored are considered one of the sources of big data. Payments through credit cards, debit cards, or other electronic ways, all are kept recorded as data.
- **Global Positioning System (GPS):** GPS in the vehicle helps in monitoring the movement of the vehicle to shorten the path to a destination to cut fuel, and time consumption. This system creates huge data on vehicle position and movement.

Applications of Big Data

- Big Data for Financial Services

  Credit card companies, retail banks, private wealth management advisories, insurance firms, venture funds, and institutional investment banks all use big data for their financial services. The common problem among them all is the massive amounts of multi-structured data living in multiple disparate systems, which big data can solve. As such, big data is used in several ways, including:

  1. Customer analytics
  2. Compliance analytics
  3. Fraud analytics
  4. Operational analytics

- Big Data in Communications

  Gaining new subscribers, retaining customers, and expanding within current subscriber bases are top priorities for telecommunication service providers. The solutions to these challenges lie in the ability to combine and analyze the masses of customer-generated data and machine-generated data that is being created every day.

- Big Data for Retail

  Whether it's a brick-and-mortar company an online retailer, the answer to staying in the game and being competitive is understanding the customer better. This requires the ability to analyze all disparate data sources that companies deal with every day, including the weblogs, customer transaction data, social media, store-branded credit card data, and loyalty program data.

Data Science	**Big Data**
Data Science is an area.	Big Data is a technique to collect, maintain and process huge information.
It is about the collection, processing, analyzing, and utilizing of data in various operations. It is more conceptual.	It is about extracting vital and valuable information from a huge amount of data.
It is a field of study just like Computer Science, Applied Statistics, or Applied Mathematics.	It is a technique for tracking and discovering trends in complex data sets.
The goal is to build data-dominant products for a venture.	The goal is to make data more vital and usable i.e. by extracting only important information from the huge data within existing traditional aspects.
Tools mainly used in Data Science include SAS, R, Python, etc.	Tools mostly used in Big Data include Hadoop, Spark, Flink, etc.
It is a superset of Big Data as data science consists of Data scrapping, cleaning, visualization, statistics, and many more techniques.	It is a sub-set of Data Science as mining activities which is in a pipeline of Data science.
It is mainly used for scientific purposes.	It is mainly used for business purposes and customer satisfaction.
It broadly focuses on the science of the data.	It is more involved with the processes of handling voluminous data.

1.3. Getting Past the Hype (Promote)

- Rachel's experience going from getting a PhD in statistics to working at Google is a great example to illustrate why we thought, in spite of the above-mentioned reasons to be doubtful, there might be some meat in the data science sandwich. In her words:
- It was clear to me pretty quickly that the stuff I was working on at Google was different than anything I had learned at school when I got my PhD in statistics. This is not to say that my degree was useless; far from it—what I'd learned in school provided a framework and way of thinking that I relied on daily, and much of the actual content provided a solid theoretical and practical foundation necessary to do my work.

1.4. Datafication

- Datafication is a buzzword ie, popular/important word.
- Datafication is the transformation of social action into online quantified data, thus allowing for real-time tracking and predictive analysis. Simply said, it is about taking previously invisible process/activity and turning it into data, that can be monitored, tracked, analysed and optimised. Latest technologies we use have enabled lots of new ways of 'datify' our daily and basic activities.
- Summarizing, datafication is a technological trend turning many aspects of our lives into computerized data using processes to transform organizations into data-driven enterprises by converting this information into new forms of value.
- Datafication refers to the fact that daily interactions of living things can be rendered into a data format and put to social use.
- Organizations require data and extract knowledge and information to perform critical business processes. An organization also uses data for decision making, strategies and other key objectives.
- Datafication needs that in a modern data-oriented landscape, an organization's survival is depending on total control over the storage, extraction, manipulation and extraction of data and associated information.
- Example

  For example, we create data every time we talk on the phone, SMS, tweet, email, use Facebook, watch a video, withdraw money from an ATM, use a credit card, or even walk past a security camera. The notion is different from digitization. In fact datafication is far broader than digitization. This astronomical amount of data has information about our identity and our behaviour.
- For example marketers are analysing Facebook and Twitter data to determine and predict sales. Companies spanning from all sectors and sizes have started to realize the big benefits of data and its analytics. They are beginning to improve their capabilities to collect and analyse data.

1.5. Current Landscape of Perspectives

The Data Science Landscape

Data science is part of the computer sciences. It comprises the disciplines of i) Analytics, ii) Statistics and iii) Machine Learning.

Data Science						
Discipline	Analytics		Statistics		Machine Learning	
Focus	"Ask better questions"		"Give better answers"		"Decision making at scale"	
Sub-Discipline	Business Analysis	Exploratory Data Analytics	Descriptive Statistics	Inferential Statistics	Supervised Machine Learning	Unsupervised Machine Learning
Tools	Spreadsheets, Visualization Tools		Statistical Packages		Programming Languages	
Process	Business Understanding > Data Collection > Data Preparation > Model Building > Evaluation > Deployment					

Figure 2: The Data Science Landscape

1.6. Analytics

- Analytics generates insights from data using simple presentation, manipulation, calculation or visualization of data. In the context of data science, it is also sometimes referred to as exploratory (trial) data analytics. It often serves the purpose to familiarize oneself with the subject matter and to obtain some initial hints for further analysis.
- Business analysis is a professional discipline of identifying business needs and determining solutions to business problems.
- Exploratory data analysis is an approach of analyzing data sets to summarize their main characteristics, often using statistical graphics and other data visualization methods.

1.7. Statistics

- Statistics is a branch of mathematics that is used for organization and interpretation of the numerical data. When it comes to the data organization, the kind of statistics we used are known as descriptive statistics.

- So descriptive statistics is basically used to describe the situation or the event, or whatever the property that we are measuring. For example, suppose we are discussing the marks obtained by the student in the examination, we might be interested in the average marks scored by the student, or the spread or division of the marks. So mean, median, standard deviation, percentile, etc. they all examples of descriptive statistics.
- **Descriptive statistics** summarizes or describes the characteristics of a data set.
- Descriptive statistics consists of three basic categories of measures: measures of central tendency, measures of variability (or spread), and frequency distribution.
- Measures of central tendency describe the center of the data set (mean, median, mode).
- Measures of variability describe the dispersion of the data set (variance, standard deviation).
- Measures of frequency distribution describe the occurrence of data within the data set (count).
- **Inferential statistics** can be defined as a field of statistics that uses analytical tools for drawing conclusions about a population by examining random samples. The goal of inferential statistics is to make generalizations about a population. In inferential statistics, a statistic is taken from the sample data (e.g., the sample mean) that used to make inferences about the population parameter (e.g., the population mean).
  - **Artificial Intelligence** is composed of two words **Artificial** and **Intelligence**, where Artificial defines *"man-made,"* and intelligence defines *"thinking power"*, hence AI means *"a man-made thinking power."*
  - "It is a branch of computer science by which we can create intelligent machines which can behave like a human, think like humans, and able to make decisions."
  - Intelligence, as we know, is the ability to acquire and apply knowledge. Knowledge is the information acquired through experience. Experience is the knowledge gained through exposure (training). Summing the terms up, we get **artificial intelligence** as the "copy of something natural (i.e., human beings) 'WHO' is capable of acquiring and applying the information it has gained through exposure."

Machine Learning

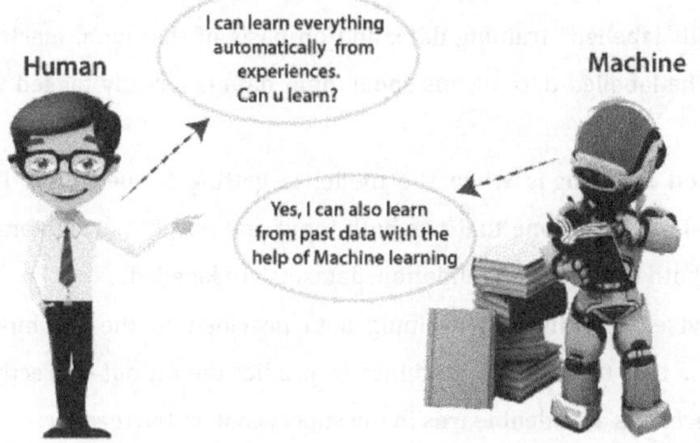

Figure 3: Understanding about Machine Learning

- Machine Learning is said as a subset of **artificial intelligence** that is mainly concerned with the development of algorithms which allow a computer to learn from the data and past experiences on their own.
- Machine learning enables a machine to automatically learn from data, improve performance from experiences, and predict things without being explicitly programmed.
- A Machine Learning system **learns from historical data, builds the prediction models, and whenever it receives new data, predicts the output for it**. The accuracy of predicted output depends upon the amount of data, as the huge amount of data helps to build a better model which predicts the output more accurately.
- Suppose we have a complex problem, where we need to perform some predictions, so instead of writing a code for it, we just need to feed the data to generic algorithms, and with the help of these algorithms, machine builds the logic as per the data and predict the output. Machine learning has changed our way of thinking about the problem.

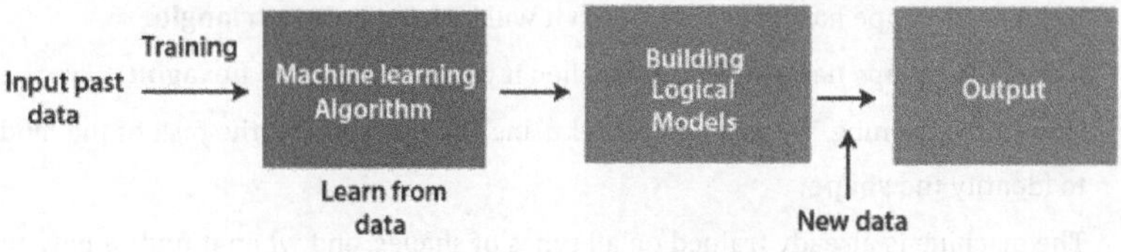

Figure 4: Process of Machine Learning System

Supervised Machine Learning

- Supervised learning is the types of machine learning in which machines are trained using well "labelled" training data, and on basis of that data, machines predict the output. The labelled data means some input data is already tagged with the correct output.
- **Supervised learning** is when the model is getting trained on a labelled dataset. A **labelled** dataset is one that has both input and output parameters. In this type of learning both training and validation, datasets are labelled.
- In supervised learning, the training data provided to the machines work as the supervisor that teaches the machines to predict the output correctly. It applies the same concept as a student learns in the supervision of the teacher.

E.G: Image classification, Fraud Detection, spam filtering, etc.

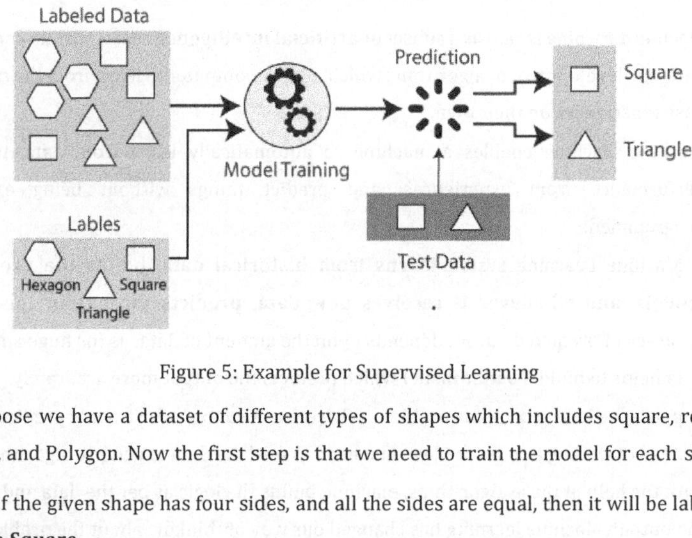

Figure 5: Example for Supervised Learning

Suppose we have a dataset of different types of shapes which includes square, rectangle, triangle, and Polygon. Now the first step is that we need to train the model for each shape.

- If the given shape has four sides, and all the sides are equal, then it will be labelled as a **Square**.
- If the given shape has three sides, then it will be labelled as a **triangle.**
- If the given shape has six equal sides then it will be labelled as **hexagon**.
- Now, after training, we test our model using the test set, and the task of the model is to identify the **shape**.
- The machine is already trained on all types of shapes, and when it finds a new shape, it classifies the shape on the bases of a number of sides, and predicts the output.

User ID	Gender	Age	Salary	Purchased
15624510	Male	19	19000	0
15810944	Male	35	20000	1
15668575	Female	26	43000	0
15603246	Female	27	57000	0
15804002	Male	19	76000	1
15728773	Male	27	58000	1
15598044	Female	27	84000	0
15694829	Female	32	150000	1
15600575	Male	25	33000	1
15727311	Female	35	65000	0
15570769	Female	26	80000	1
15606274	Female	26	52000	0
15746139	Male	20	86000	1
15704987	Male	32	18000	0
15628972	Male	18	82000	0
15697686	Male	29	80000	0
15733883	Male	47	25000	1

Figure 6.A: Classification

Temperature	Pressure	Relative Humidity	Wind Direction	Wind Speed
10.69261758	986.882019	54.19337313	195.7150879	3.278597116
13.59184184	987.8729248	48.0648859	189.2951202	2.909167767
17.70494885	988.1119385	39.11965597	192.9273834	2.973036289
20.95430404	987.8500366	30.66273218	202.0752869	2.965289593
22.9278274	987.2833862	26.06723423	210.6589203	2.798230886
24.04233986	986.2907104	23.46918024	221.1188507	2.627005816
24.41475295	985.2338867	22.25082295	233.7911987	2.448749781
23.93361956	984.8914795	22.35178837	244.3504333	2.454271793
22.68800023	984.8461304	23.7538641	253.0864716	2.418341875
20.56425726	984.8380737	27.07867944	264.5071106	2.318677425
17.76400389	985.4262085	33.54900114	280.7827454	2.343950987
11.25680746	988.9386597	53.74139903	68.15406036	1.650191426
14.37810685	989.6819458	40.70884681	72.62069702	1.553469896
18.45114201	990.2960205	30.85038484	71.70604706	1.005017161
22.54895853	989.9562988	22.81738811	44.66042709	0.264133632
24.23155922	988.796875	19.74790765	318.3214111	0.329656571

Figure 6.B: Regression

Both the above figures have labelled data set as follows:

- **Figure A:** It is a dataset of a shopping store that is useful in predicting whether a customer will purchase a particular product under consideration or not based on his/her gender, age, and salary.
  Input: Gender, Age, Salary.
  Output: Purchased i.e. 0 or 1; 1 means yes the customer will purchase and 0 means that the customer won't purchase it.

- **Figure B:** It is a Meteorological dataset that serves the purpose of predicting wind speed based on different parameters.
- **Input:** Dew Point, Temperature, Pressure, Relative Humidity, Wind Direction.
- **Output:** Wind Speed.

Training the system: While training the model, data is usually split in the ratio of 80:20 i.e. 80% as training data and the rest as testing data. In training data, we feed input as well as output for 80% of data. The model learns from training data only. We use different machine learning algorithms to build our model. Learning means that the model will build some logic of its own.

Once the model is ready then it is good to be tested. At the time of testing, the input is fed from the remaining 20% of data that the model has never seen before, the model will predict some value and we will compare it with the actual output and calculate the accuracy.

Unsupervised Learning

- *Unsupervised learning is a type of machine learning in which models are trained using unlabeled dataset and are allowed to act on that data without any supervision.*

Example: Suppose the unsupervised learning algorithm is given an input dataset containing images of different types of cats and dogs. The algorithm is never trained upon the given dataset, which means it does not have any idea about the features of the dataset. The task of the unsupervised learning algorithm is to identify the image features on their own. Unsupervised learning algorithm will perform this task by clustering the image dataset into the groups according to similarities between images.

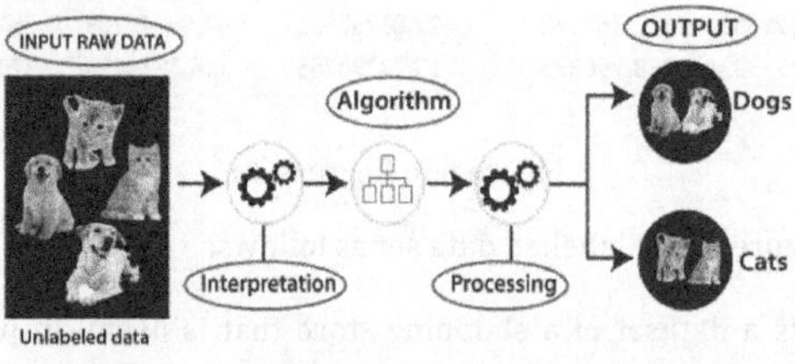

Figure 7: Example for Unsupervised Learning

- Here, we have taken an unlabeled input data, which means it is not categorized and corresponding outputs are also not given. Now, this unlabeled input data is fed to the machine learning model in order to train it. Firstly, it will interpret the raw data to find the hidden patterns from the data and then will apply suitable algorithms such as k-means clustering, Decision tree, etc.

- Once it applies the suitable algorithm, the algorithm divides the data objects into groups according to the similarities and difference between the objects.

1.8. Statistical Inference

- Statistics is a branch of Mathematics, that deals with the collection, analysis, interpretation, and the presentation of the numerical data. In other words, it is defined as the collection of quantitative data.
- The main purpose of Statistics is to make an accurate conclusion using a limited sample about a greater population.

Types of Statistics

Statistics can be classified into two different categories. The two different types of Statistics are:

- Descriptive Statistics.
- Inferential Statistics.
- **Descriptive statistics** summarizes or describes the characteristics of a data set.
- Descriptive statistics consists of three basic categories of measures: measures of central tendency, measures of variability (or spread), and frequency distribution.
- Measures of central tendency describe the center of the data set (mean, median, mode).
- Measures of variability describe the dispersion of the data set (variance, standard deviation).
- Measures of frequency distribution describe the occurrence of data within the data set (count).
- **Inferential statistics** can be defined as a field of statistics that uses analytical tools for drawing conclusions about a population by examining random samples. The goal of inferential statistics is to make generalizations about a population. In inferential statistics, a statistic is taken from the sample data (e.g., the sample mean) that used to make inferences about the population parameter (e.g., the population mean).
  - In Statistics, **descriptive statistics** describe the data, whereas **inferential statistics** help you make predictions from the data. In inferential statistics, the data are taken from the sample and allows you to generalize the population.
  - In general, inference means "guess", which means making inference about something. So, statistical inference means, making inference about the population. To take a conclusion about the population, it uses various statistical analysis techniques.

1.9. Populations and Samples

Population

- A complete collection of the objects or measurements is called the population or else everything in the group we want to learn about will be termed as population or else In statistics population is the entire set of items from which data is drawn in the statistical study.
- It can be a group of individuals or a set of items.

Figure 8: Example for Population

Population is the entire group you want to draw conclusions about.

- The population is usually denoted with **N.**
- The number of citizens living in the State of Rajasthan represents a population of the state.
- The number of planets in the entire universe represents the planet population of the entire universe.
- The types of candies and chocolates are made in India.
- Population mean is usually denoted by the Greek letter μ.

$$\mu \text{ (population mean)} = \sum_{i=1}^{N}(x_i) \, / \, N\text{(total population)}$$

For Example: Let us assume that there are 5 employees in my company, So 5 people is a complete set hence it will represent the population of my company.

If I want to find the average age of my company then I will simply add their ages and divide it by N which is the number of population.

$$\text{ages} = \{23,45,12,34,22\}$$

$$\mu = \sum_{i=1}^{5}(x_i)/5$$

$$= (23 + 45 + 12 + 34 + 22) \, / \, 5$$

The results say that the average age of my company is 27.2 years.

So this is what we call the **population mean.**

Sample

- A sample represents a group of the interest of the population which we will use to represent the data. The sample is an unbiased (balanced) subset of the population in which we represent the whole data.
- A sample is a group of the elements actually participating in the survey or study.
- A sample is the representation of the manageable size.
- Samples are collected and stats are calculated from the sample so one can make interferences or extrapolations from the sample.
- This process of collecting information from the sample is called **sampling.**

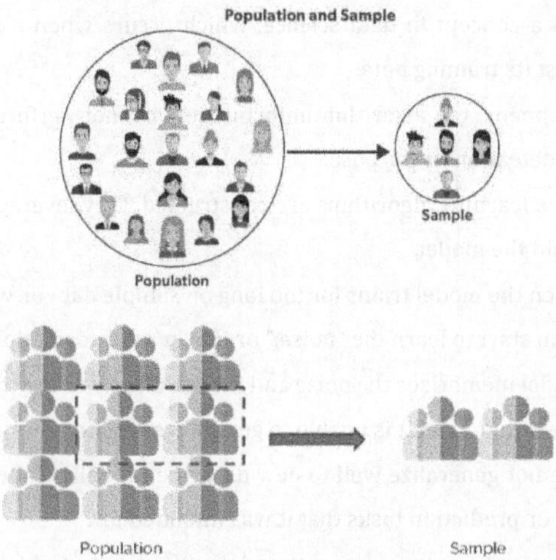

Figure 9: Understanding about Population & Sample

- *The sample is denoted by the **n**.*
- 500 people from a total population of the Rajasthan state will be considered as a sample.
- 143 total chess players from all total number of chess players will be considered as a sample.
- Sample mean is denoted by x.

$$x \text{ (sample mean)} = \sum_{i=1}^{n} (x_i)/n \text{ (total sample)}$$

Example: Let us assume the population of India is 10 million, and recent elections were conducted in India between two parties 'party A ' and 'party B' now researchers want to find which party is winning so here we will create a group of few people lets say 10,000 from different regions and age groups so that sample is not biased. Then ask them who they voted we can get the exit poll. This is the thing which most of our media do during the elections, and show stats such as there 55% chances of party A winning the elections.

Samples are Used When

- The population is too large to collect data.
- The data collected is not reliable.
- The population is hypothetical (Proposed) and is unlimited in size.

1.10. Fitting a Model – Over Fitting

- Overfitting is a concept in data science, which occurs when a statistical model fits exactly against its training data.
- When this happens, the algorithm unfortunately cannot perform accurately against unseen data, defeating its purpose.
- When machine learning algorithms are constructed, they leverage (control) a sample dataset to train the model.
- However, when the model trains for too long on sample data or when the model is too complex, it can start to learn the "noise," or irrelevant information, within the dataset.
- When the model memorizes the noise and fits too closely to the training set, the model becomes "overfitted," and it is unable to generalize well to new data.
- If a model cannot generalize well to new data, then it will not be able to perform the classification or prediction tasks that it was intended for.
- If the training data has a low error rate and the test data has a high error rate, it signals overfitting.

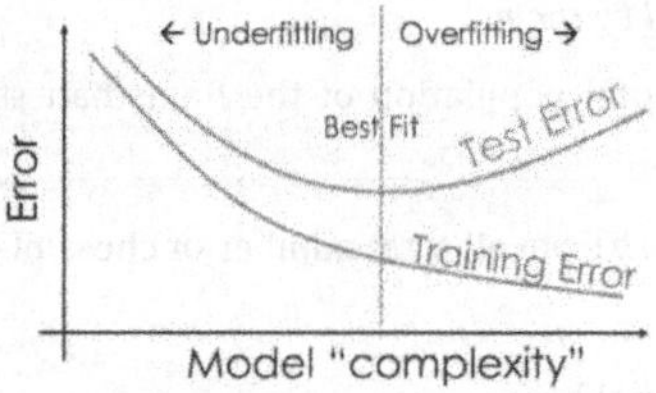

Figure 10: Depicts Overfitting

How to Avoid Overfitting

- **Early Stopping:** This method seeks to pause training before the model starts learning the noise within the model.
- **Train with More Data:** Expanding the training set to include more data can increase the accuracy of the model. This is a more effective method when clean, relevant data is injected into the model.
- **Data Augmentation:** While it is better to inject clean, relevant data into your training data, sometimes noisy data is added to make a model more stable.
- Which is used to increase the amount of data by adding slightly modified copies of already existing data or newly created synthetic data from existing data. It acts as a regularizer and helps reduce overfitting when training a machine learning model.
- However, this method should be done sparingly (In a restricted or in small quantities).
- **Regularization:** If overfitting occurs when a model is too complex, it makes sense for us to reduce the number of features.
- But what if we don't know which inputs to eliminate during the feature selection process. So certain If we don't know which features to remove from our model, **regularization methods** can be particularly helpful.
- E.G L1 regularization (Lasso regularization).

1.11. Statistical Modeling

- Statistical Modelling is a process of using data to construct a mathematical or algorithmic device to measure the probability of some observation.
- **Training:** Using an set of observations to learn parameters of a model or construct the decision making process.
- **Evaluation:**
- Determining the probability of a new observation.
    - Statistical Modelling is simply the method of implementing statistical analysis to a dataset.
- Where a Statistical Model is a mathematical representation of observed data."
- Statistical modeling refers to the data science process of applying statistical analysis to datasets.

Statistical Modeling Techniques

- The first step in developing a statistical model is gathering data, which may be sourced from spreadsheets, databases, data lakes, or the cloud.
- The most common statistical modeling methods for analyzing this data are categorized as either supervised learning or unsupervised learning.
- Some **popular statistical model examples** include logistic regression, time-series, clustering, and decision trees.

Supervised Learning Techniques Include Regression Models and Classification Models

Ex:

- Prediction of rain using temperature and other factors.
- Determining Market trends.

1.12. Terminologies Related to the Regression Analysis

- **Dependent Variable (Target Variable):** The main factor in Regression analysis which we want to predict or understand is called the dependent variable. It is also called **target variable**.
- **EX: A test score** could be a dependent variable because it could change depending on several factors such as how much you studied, how much sleep you got the night before you took the test, or even how hungry you were when you took it.
- **Independent Variable:** The factors which affect the dependent variables or which are used to predict the values of the dependent variables are called independent variable, also called as a **predictor**.
- **EX:** It is a variable that stands alone and isn't changed by the other variables you are trying to measure. For example, someone's age might be an independent variable. Other factors (such as what they eat, how much they go to school, how much television they watch) aren't going to change a person's age.
- **Underfitting and Overfitting:** If our algorithm works well with the training dataset but not well with test dataset, then such problem is called **Overfitting**. And if our algorithm does not perform well even with training dataset, then such problem is called **underfitting**.

- Regression is a process of finding the correlations between dependent and independent variables. It helps in predicting the continuous variables such as prediction of **Market Trends**, prediction of House prices, etc.
- The task of the Regression algorithm is to find the mapping function to map the input variable(x) to the continuous output variable(y).

Example: Suppose we want to do weather forecasting, so for this, we will use the Regression algorithm. In weather prediction, the model is trained on the past data, and once the training is completed, it can easily predict the weather for future days.

Types of Regression Algorithm

- Simple Linear Regression
- Multiple Linear Regression
- Polynomial Regression
- Support Vector Regression
- Decision Tree Regression
- Random Forest Regression

Purpose of Regression Analysis

- Regression analysis helps in the prediction of a continuous variable.
- There are various scenarios in the real world where we need some future predictions such as weather condition, sales prediction, marketing trends, etc., for such case we need some technology which can make predictions more accurately.
    - So for such case we need Regression analysis which is a statistical method and used in machine learning and data science.
    - Regression estimates the relationship between the target and the independent variable.

Reasons

- It is used to find the trends in data.
- It helps to predict real/continuous values.
- By performing the regression, we can confidently determine the **most important factor, the least important factor, and how each factor is affecting the other factors**.

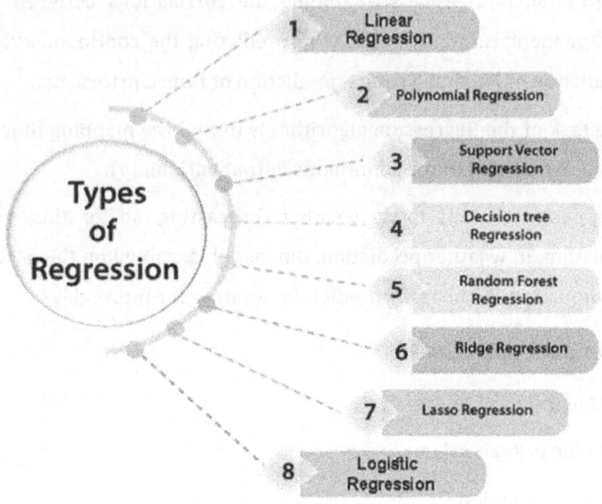

Figure 11: Types of Regression

Linear Regression

- Regression is a process of finding the correlations between dependent and independent variables. It helps in predicting the continuous variables such as prediction of Market Trends, prediction of House prices, etc.
- The task of the Regression algorithm is to find the mapping function to map the input variable(x) to the continuous output variable(y).
- **Example:** Suppose we want to do weather forecasting, so for this, we will use the Regression algorithm. In weather prediction, the model is trained on the past data, and once the training is completed, it can easily predict the weather for future days.
  - Linear regression is a statistical regression method which is used for predictive analysis. Linear regression is a machine learning concept that is used to build or train the models (mathematical models or equations) for solving **supervised learning problems** related to predicting **continuous numerical value.**
  - It is one of the very simple and easy algorithms which works on regression and shows the relationship between the continuous variables.
  - It is used for solving the regression problem in machine learning.
  - Linear regression analysis is used to predict the value of a variable based on the value of another variable.

- The variable you want to predict is called the dependent variable. The variable you are using to predict the other variable's value is called the independent variable.
- Linear regression shows the linear relationship between the independent variable (X-axis) and the dependent variable (Y-axis), hence called linear regression.
- If there is only one input variable (x), then such linear regression is called **simple linear regression**. And if there is more than one input variable, then such linear regression is called **multiple linear regression**.
- The relationship between variables in the linear regression model can be explained using the below image. Here we are predicting the salary of an employee on the basis of **the year of experience**.

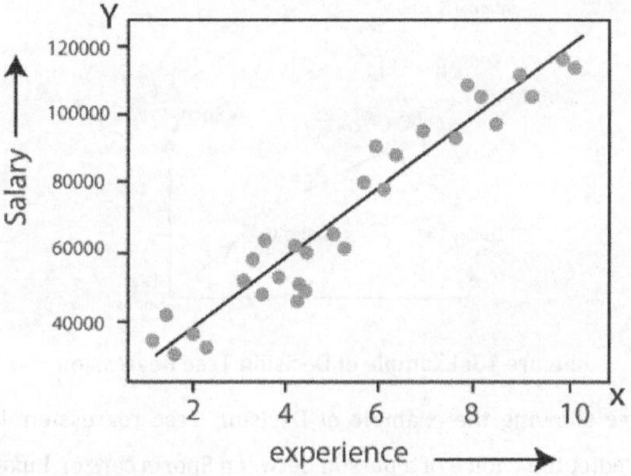

Figure 12: Example for Linear Regression

- Below is the mathematical equation for Linear regression:

1. Y= aX+b

- Here, Y = Dependent variables (target variables), X = Independent variables (predictor variables), a and b are the linear coefficients.
- Some popular applications of linear regression are:
  - Analyzing trends and sales estimates
  - Salary forecasting
  - Real estate prediction

Decision Tree Regression

- Decision Tree is a supervised learning algorithm which can be used for solving both classification and regression problems.
- It can solve problems for both categorical and numerical data.
- Decision Tree regression builds a tree-like structure in which each internal node represents the "test" for an attribute, each branch represent the result of the test, and each leaf node represents the final decision or result.
- A decision tree is constructed starting from the root node/parent node (dataset), which splits into left and right child nodes (subsets of dataset). These child nodes are further divided into their children node, and themselves become the parent node of those nodes. Consider the below image.

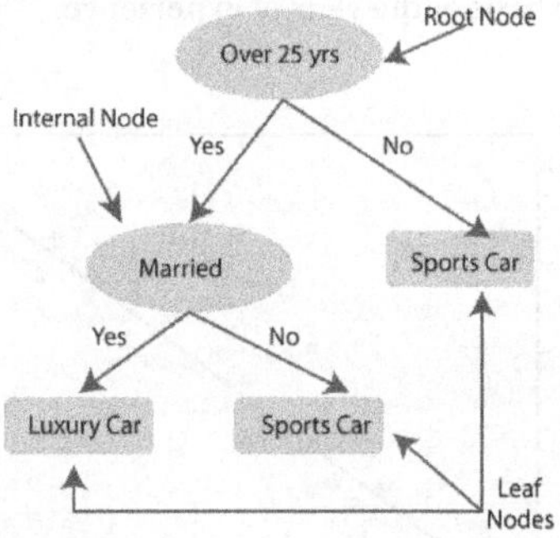

Figure 13: Example of Decision Tree Regression

- Above image showing the example of Decision Tree regression, here, the model is trying to predict the choice of a person between Sports cars or Luxury car.

1.13. Notes Additional

- Regression and Classification algorithms are Supervised Learning algorithms. Both the algorithms are used for prediction in Machine learning and work with the labeled datasets. But the difference between both is how they are used for different machine learning problems.
- The main difference between Regression and Classification algorithms that Regression algorithms are used to **predict the continuous** values such as price, salary, age, etc. and Classification algorithms are used to **predict/Classify the discrete values** such as Male or Female, True or False, Spam or Not Spam, etc.

Consider the Below Diagram

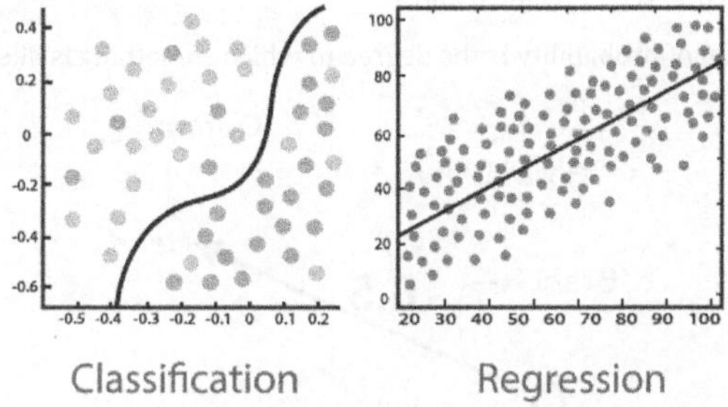

Figure 14: Example of Classification/ Regression

Classification

- Classification is a process of finding a function which helps in dividing the dataset into classes based on different parameters. In Classification, a computer program is trained on the training dataset and based on that training, it categorizes the data into different classes.

Example: The best example to understand the Classification problem is Email Spam Detection. The model is trained on the basis of millions of emails on different parameters, and whenever it receives a new email, it identifies whether the email is spam or not. If the email is spam, then it is moved to the Spam folder.

Types of ML Classification Algorithms

Classification Algorithms can be further divided into the following types:

- Logistic Regression
- K-Nearest Neighbours
- Support Vector Machines
- Kernel SVM
- Naïve Bayes
- Decision Tree Classification
- Random Forest Classification

Probability

- The word 'Probability' means the chance of occurring of a particular event.
- Probability denotes the possibility of something happening.

- It is a mathematical concept that predicts how likely events are to occur. The probability values are expressed between 0 and 1.
- The definition of probability is the degree to which something is likely to occur.

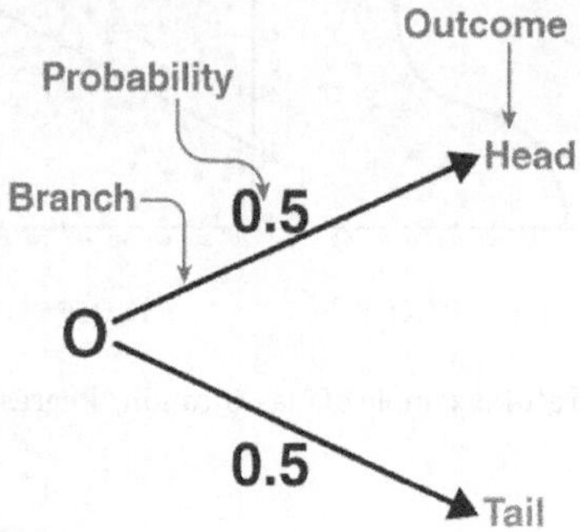

Important Terms Related to Probability

1. **Trial and Event:** The **performance of an experiment** is called a trial, and the set of its outcomes is termed an event.

   Example: Tossing a coin and getting head is a trial. Then the event is {HT, TH; HH}.
2. **Random Experiment:** It is an experiment in which all the possible outcomes of the experiment are known in advance. But the exact outcomes of any specific performance are not known in advance.

Example

1. Tossing a Coin.
2. Rolling a dice.
3. Drawing a card from a pack of 52 cards.
4. Drawing a ball from a bag.

3. **Outcome:** The result of a random experiment is called an Outcome.

   Example:

   1. Tossing a coin is an experiment and getting head is called an outcome.
   2. Rolling a dice and getting 6 is an outcome.
4. **Sample Space:** The set of all possible outcomes of an experiment is called sample space and is denoted by S.

   Example: When a dice is thrown, sample space is S = {1, 2, 3, 4, 5, 6} It consists of six outcomes 1, 2, 3, 4, 5, 6.

Probability Distribution

- Probability distribution is a function that is used to give the **probability of all the possible values that a random variable can take.**
- A **probability distribution** is a mathematical function that describes the **probability of different possible values of a variable**.
- Probability distributions are often depicted using **graphs or probability tables**.
- Probability distribution gives the **possibility of each outcome of a random experiment or event.**
- It provides the probabilities of **different possible occurrences.**
- A probability distribution is a statistical function that **describes all the possible values and probabilities for a random variable within a given range.**
- This range will be bound by the minimum and maximum possible values, but where the possible value would be plotted on the probability **distribution will be determined by a number of factors.**

Types of Probability Distribution

The probability distribution is divided into two parts:

- Discrete Probability Distributions.
- Continuous Probability Distributions.

1. Discrete Probability Distributions

- A discrete probability distribution can be defined as a probability distribution giving the probability that a discrete random variable will have a specified value.
- Such a distribution will represent data that has a finite countable number of outcomes.

Discrete Probability Distribution Example

- **EX:1** A discrete distribution has a range of values that are countable. For example, the numbers on birthday cards have a possible range from 0 to 122 (122 is the age of Jeanne the oldest person who ever lived).
- **EX:2** Suppose a fair dice is rolled and the discrete probability distribution has to be created. The possible outcomes are {1, 2, 3, 4, 5, 6}.
- Thus, the total number of outcomes will be 6. All numbers have a fair chance of turning up.
- This means that the probability of getting any one number is 1 / 6. Using this data the discrete probability distribution table for a dice roll can be given as follows.

x	1	2	3	4	5	6
P(X = x)	1 / 6	1 / 6	1 / 6	1 / 6	1 / 6	1/6

2. Continuous Probability Distributions

- A continuous distribution has a range of values that are infinite, and therefore uncountable.
- For example, time is infinite: you could count from 0 seconds to a billion seconds...a trillion seconds...and so on.

CHAPTER 2

2.1. Basics of R: Introduction

- R is an open-source programming language that is widely used as a statistical software and data analysis tool. R generally comes with the Command-line interface. R is available across widely used platforms like Windows, Linux, and macOS. Also, the R programming language is the latest cutting-edge tool.
- It was designed by Ross Ihaka and Robert Gentleman at the University of Auckland, New Zealand, and is currently developed by the R Development Core Team. R programming language is an implementation of the S programming language. It also combines with lexical scoping semantics inspired by Scheme. Moreover, the project conceives in 1992, with an initial version released in 1995 and a stable beta version in 2000.

Why R Programming Language?

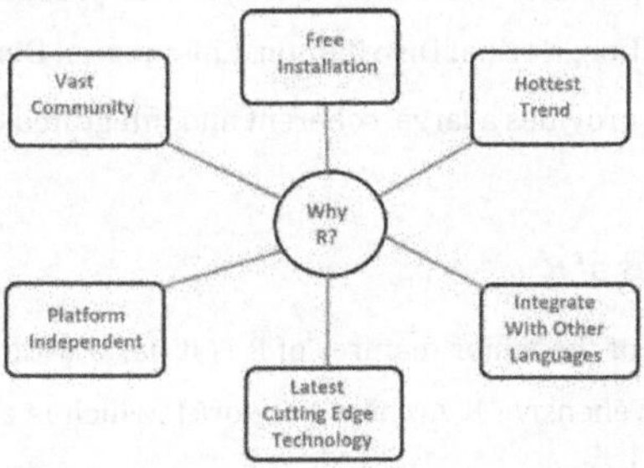

Figure 15: Features of R Programming

- R programming is used as a leading tool for machine learning, statistics, and data analysis. Objects, functions, and packages can easily be created by R.
- It's a platform-independent language. This means it can be applied to all operating system.
- It's an open-source free language. That means anyone can install it in any organization without purchasing a license.
- R programming language is not only a statistic package but also allows us to integrate with other languages (C, C++). Thus, you can easily interact with many data sources and statistical packages.

- The R programming language has a vast community of users and it's growing day by day.
- R is currently one of the most requested programming languages in the Data Science job market that makes it the hottest trend nowadays.

Features of R Programming Language

Statistical Features of R

- **Basic Statistics:** The most common basic statistics terms are the mean, mode, and median. These are all known as "Measures of Central Tendency." So using the R language we can measure central tendency very easily.
- **Static Graphics:** R is rich with facilities for creating and developing interesting static graphics. R contains functionality for many plot types including graphic maps, mosaic plots, biplots, and the list goes on.
- **Probability Distributions:** Probability distributions play a vital role in statistics and by using R we can easily handle various types of probability distribution such as Binomial Distribution, Normal Distribution, Chi-squared Distribution and many more.
- **Data Analysis:** It provides a large, coherent and integrated collection of tools for data analysis.

Programming Features of R

- **R Packages:** One of the major features of R is it has a wide availability of libraries. R has CRAN (Comprehensive R Archive Network), which is a repository holding more than 10, 0000 packages.
- **Distributed Computing:** Distributed computing is a model in which components of a software system are shared among multiple computers to improve efficiency and performance. Two new packages ddR and multidplyr used for distributed programming in R were released in November 2015.
    - **Programming in R:**
    - Since R is much similar to other widely used languages syntactically, it is easier to code and learn in R. Programs can be written in R in any of the widely used IDE like **R Studio, Rattle, Tinn-R**, etc. After writing the program save the file with the extension.r. To run the program use the following command on the command line.
    - R file_name.r.

Advantages of R

- R is the most comprehensive statistical analysis package. As new technology and concepts often appear first in R.
- As R programming language is an open source. Thus, you can run R anywhere and at any time.
- R programming language is suitable for GNU/Linux and Windows operating system.
- R programming is cross-platform which runs on any operating system.
- In R, everyone is welcome to provide new packages, bug fixes, and code enhancements.

Disadvantages of R

- In the R programming language, the standard of some packages is less than perfect.
- Although, R commands give little pressure to memory management. So R programming language may consume all available memory.
- In R basically, nobody to complain if something doesn't work.
- R programming language is much slower than other programming languages such as Python and MATLAB.

Applications of R

- We use R for Data Science. It gives us a broad variety of libraries related to statistics. It also provides the environment for statistical computing and design.
- R is used by many quantitative analysts as its programming tool. Thus, it helps in data importing and cleaning.
- R is the most prevalent language. So many data analysts and research programmers use it. Hence, it is used as a fundamental tool for finance.
- Tech giants like Google, Facebook, bing, Twitter, Accenture, Wipro and many more **using** R nowadays.

Note: "R is an interpreted computer programming language which was created by Ross Ihaka and Robert Gentleman at the University of Auckland, New Zealand." The *R Development Core Team* currently develops R. It is also a software environment used to analyze statistical information, graphical representation, reporting, and data modeling.

2.2. R - Environment Setup

- **R programming** is a very popular language and to work on that we have to install two things, i.e., R and RStudio. R and RStudio works together to create a project on R.

- Installing R to the local computer is very easy. First, we must know which operating system we are using so that we can download it accordingly.
- The official site https://cloud.r-project.org provides binary files for major operating systems including Windows, Linux, and Mac OS. In some Linux distributions, R is installed by default, which we can verify from the console by entering R.
- To install R, either we can get it from the site https://cloud.r-project.org or can use commands from the terminal.

Install R in Windows

There are following steps used to install the R in Windows:

Step 1

First, we have to download the R setup from https://cloud.r-project.org/bin/windows/base/.

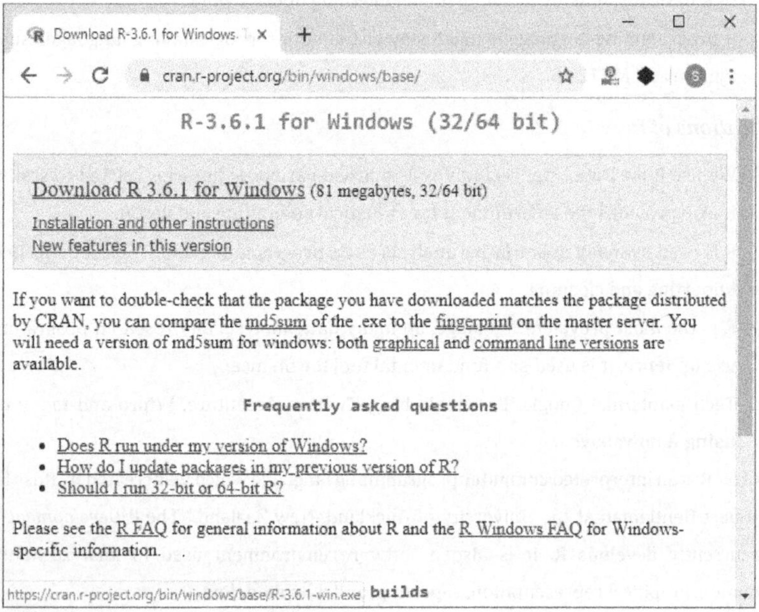

Step 2

When we click on **Download R 3.6.1 for windows**, our downloading will be started of R setup. Once the downloading is finished, we have to run the setup of R in the following way.

1. Select the path where we want to download the R and proceed to Next.

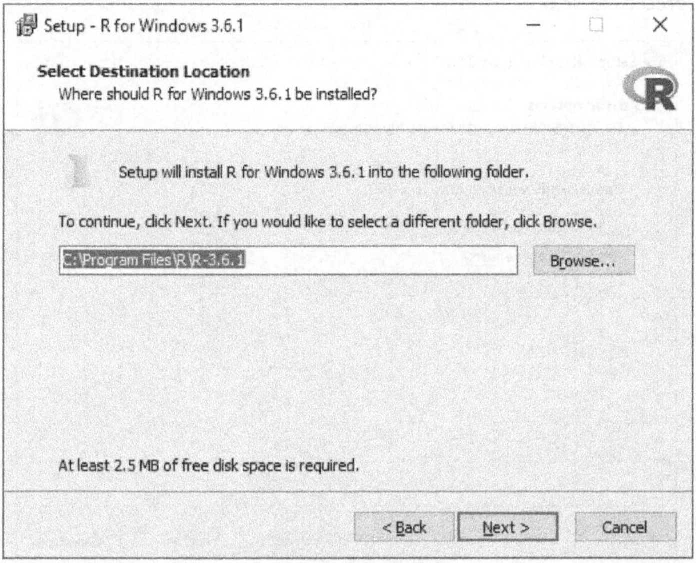

2. Select all components which we want to install, and then we will proceed to **Next**.

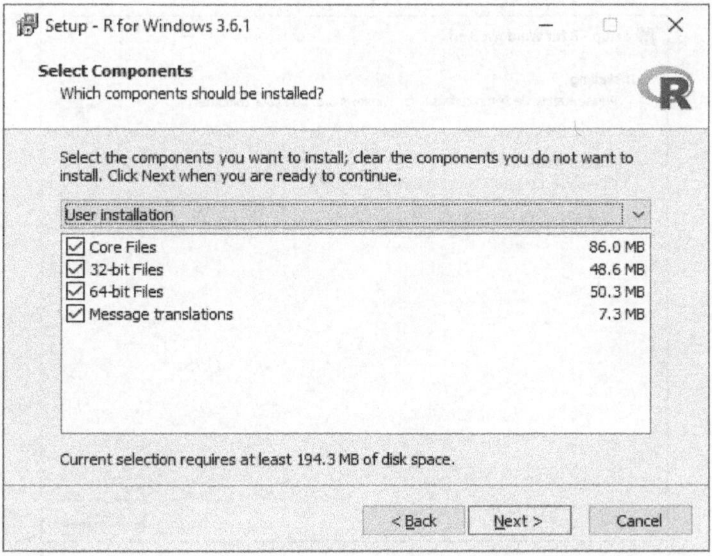

3. In the next step, we have to select either customized startup or accept the default, and then we proceed to **Next**.

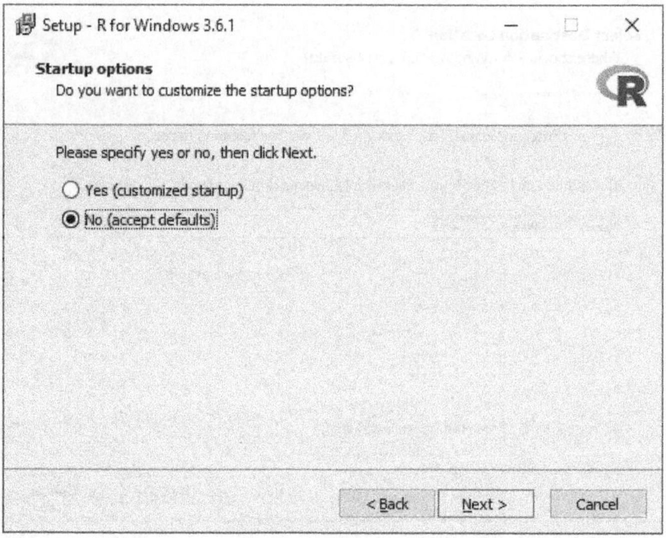

4. When we proceed to next, our installation of R in our system will get started.

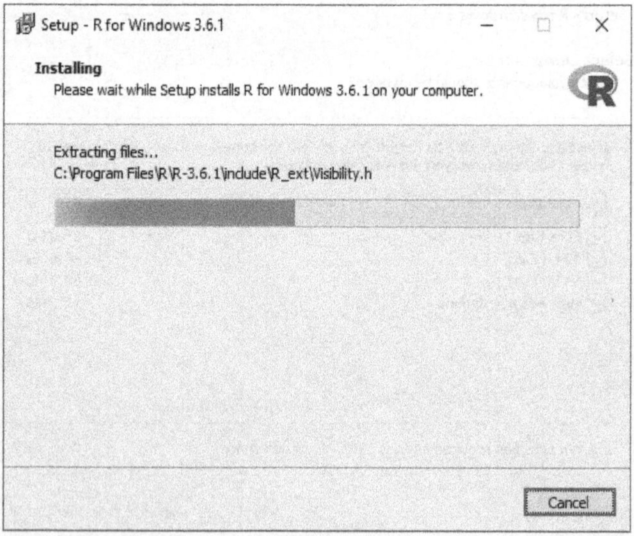

5. In the last, we will click on finish to successfully install R in our system.

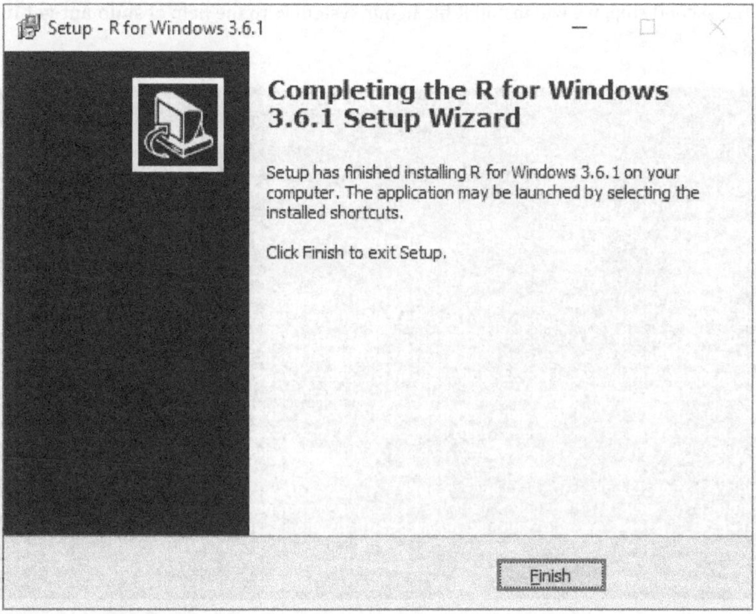

2.3. Install R in Linux

There are only three steps to install R in Linux.

Step 1

In the first step, we have to update all the required files in our system using **sudo apt-get update** command as:

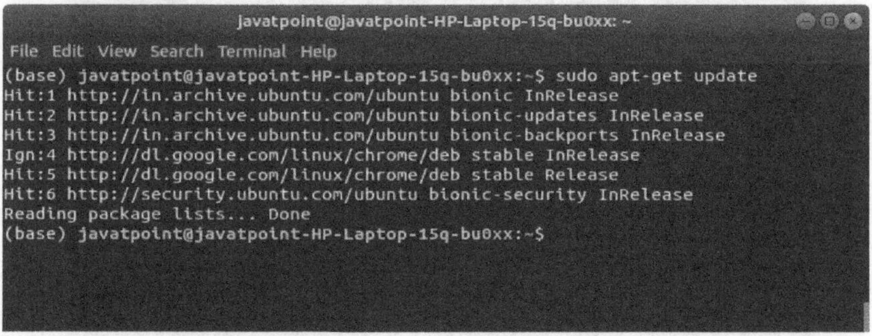

Step 2

In the second step, we will install R file in our system with the help of **sudo apt-get install r-base** as:

```
javatpoint@javatpoint-HP-Laptop-15q-bu0xx: ~
File  Edit  View  Search  Terminal  Help
Reading package lists... Done
(base) javatpoint@javatpoint-HP-Laptop-15q-bu0xx:~$ sudo apt-get install r-base
Reading package lists... Done
Building dependency tree
Reading state information... Done
The following package was automatically installed and is no longer required:
  libllvm7
Use 'sudo apt autoremove' to remove it.
The following additional packages will be installed:
  autoconf automake autopoint autotools-dev bzip2-doc cdbs debhelper
  dh-autoreconf dh-strip-nondeterminism dh-translations gfortran gfortran-7
  gir1.2-harfbuzz-0.0 icu-devtools intltool jq libarchive-cpio-perl
  libblas-dev libblas3 libbz2-dev libcurl4 libfile-stripnondeterminism-perl
  libfile-which-perl libgfortran-7-dev libgfortran4 libglib2.0-dev
  libglib2.0-dev-bin libgraphite2-dev libharfbuzz-dev libharfbuzz-gobject0
  libicu-dev libicu-le-hb-dev libicu-le-hb0 libiculx60 libjpeg-dev
  libjpeg-turbo8-dev libjpeg8-dev libjq1 liblapack-dev liblapack3 libltdl-dev
  liblzma-dev libmail-sendmail-perl libncurses5-dev libonig4 libpcre16-3
  libpcre3-dev libpcre32-3 libpcrecpp0v5 libpng-dev libpng-tools
  libreadline-dev libsigsegv2 libsys-hostname-long-perl libtcl8.6 libtinfo-dev
  libtk8.6 libtool m4 pkg-config po-debconf python3-scour r-base-core
  r-base-dev r-base-html r-cran-boot r-cran-class r-cran-cluster
  r-cran-codetools r-cran-foreign r-cran-kernsmooth r-cran-lattice r-cran-mass
  r-cran-matrix r-cran-mgcv r-cran-nlme r-cran-nnet r-cran-rpart
```

Step 3

In the last step, we type R and press enter to work on R editor.

```
javatpoint@javatpoint-HP-Laptop-15q-bu0xx: ~
File  Edit  View  Search  Terminal  Help
Processing triggers for libglib2.0-0:amd64 (2.56.4-0ubuntu0.18.04.4) ...
Setting up libharfbuzz-dev:amd64 (1.7.2-1ubuntu1) ...
Setting up libicu-le-hb-dev:amd64 (1.0.3+git161113-4) ...
(base) javatpoint@javatpoint-HP-Laptop-15q-bu0xx:~$ R

R version 3.4.4 (2018-03-15) -- "Someone to Lean On"
Copyright (C) 2018 The R Foundation for Statistical Computing
Platform: x86_64-pc-linux-gnu (64-bit)

R is free software and comes with ABSOLUTELY NO WARRANTY.
You are welcome to redistribute it under certain conditions.
Type 'license()' or 'licence()' for distribution details.

  Natural language support but running in an English locale

R is a collaborative project with many contributors.
Type 'contributors()' for more information and
'citation()' on how to cite R or R packages in publications.

Type 'demo()' for some demos, 'help()' for on-line help, or
'help.start()' for an HTML browser interface to help.
Type 'q()' to quit R.

>
```

RStudio IDE

RStudio is an integrated development environment which allows us to interact with R more readily. RStudio is similar to the standard RGui, but it is considered more user-friendly. This IDE has various drop-down menus, Windows with multiple tabs, and so many customization processes. The first time when we open RStudio, we will see three Windows. The fourth Window will be hidden by default. We can open this hidden Window by clicking the **File** drop-down menu, then **New File** and then **R Script**.

RStudio Windows/Tabs	**Location**	**Description**
Console Window	Lower-left	The location where commands are entered and output is printed.
Source Tabs	Upper-left	Built-in test editor
Environment Tab	Upper-left	An interactive list of loaded R objects.
History Tab	Upper-left	List of keystrokes entered into the console.
Files Tab	Lower-right	File explorer to navigate C drive folders.
Plots Tab	Lower-right	Output location for plots.
Packages Tab	Lower-right	List of installed packages.
Help Tab	Lower-right	Output location for help commands and help search Window.
Viewer Tab	Lower-right	Advanced tab for local web content.

Installation of RStudio

RStudio Desktop is available for both Windows and Linux. The open-source RStudio Desktop installation is very simple to install on both operating systems. The licensed version of RStudio has some more features than open-source. Before installing RStudio, let's see what are the additional features in the license version of RStudio.

Factor	**Open-Source**	**Commercial License**
Overview	1) Access RStudio locally	All of the features of open-source are include with 1) There is a commercial license for organizations which are not able to use AGPL software. 2) It provides access to priority support.
	2) Code completion, syntax highlighting, and smart indentation	
	3) Can execute R code directly from the source editor	
	4) Quickly jump to function definitions.	
	5) Easily manage multiple working directories using projects.	
	6) Integrated R help and documentation.	
	7) Provide interactive debugger to diagnose and fix errors quickly.	
	8) Extensive package deployment tools.	
Support	It supports for community forums only.	1) It supports priority email. 2) It supports for an 8-hour response during business hour.
License	AGPL v3	RStudio License Agreement
Pricing	Free	$995/year

Installation on Windows/Linux

- On Windows and Linux, it is quite simple to install RStudio. The process of installing RStudio in both the OS is the same. There are the following steps to install RStudio in our Windows/Linux.

Step 1

In the first step, we visit the RStudio official site and click on **Download RStudio**.

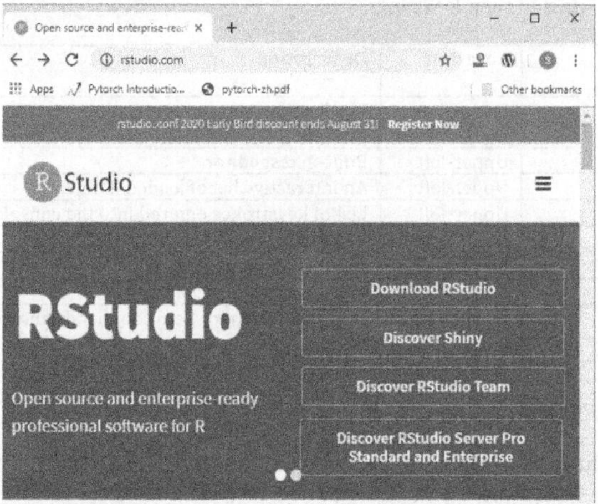

Step 2

In the next step, we will select the RStudio desktop for open-source license and click on download.

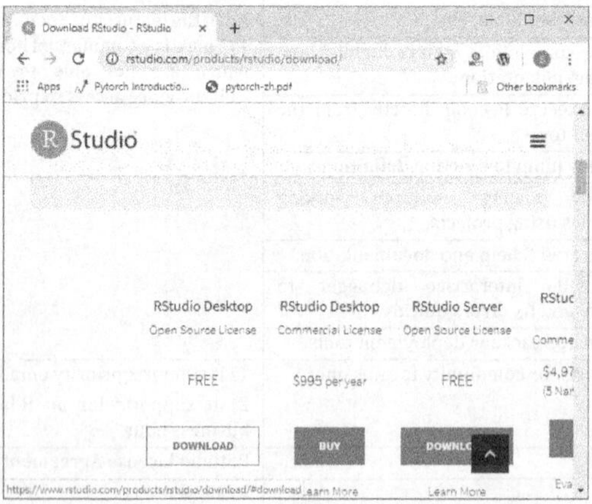

Step 3

In the next step, we will select the appropriate installer. When we select the installer, our downloading of RStudion setup will start.

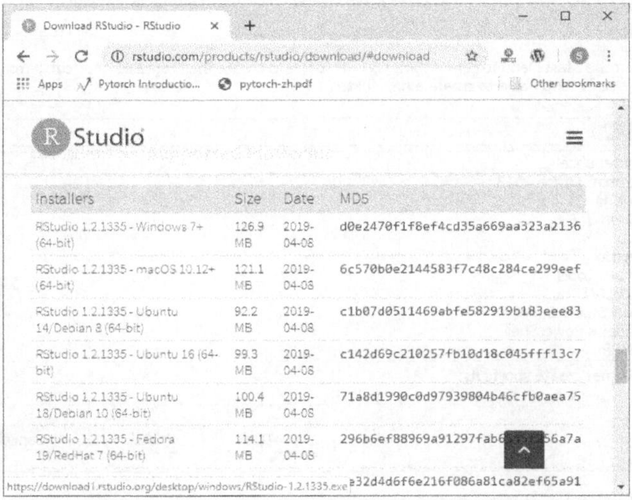

Step 4

In the next step, we will run our setup in the following way:

1. Click on Next.

2. Click on Install.

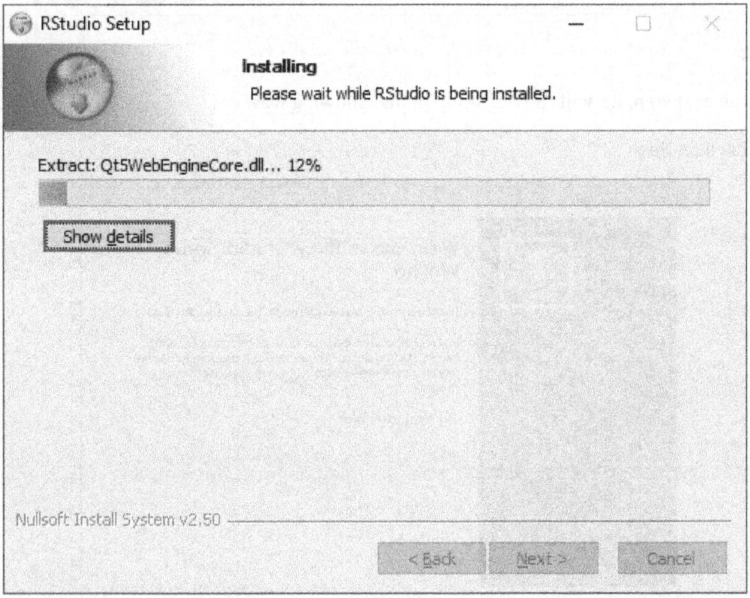

3. Click on finish.

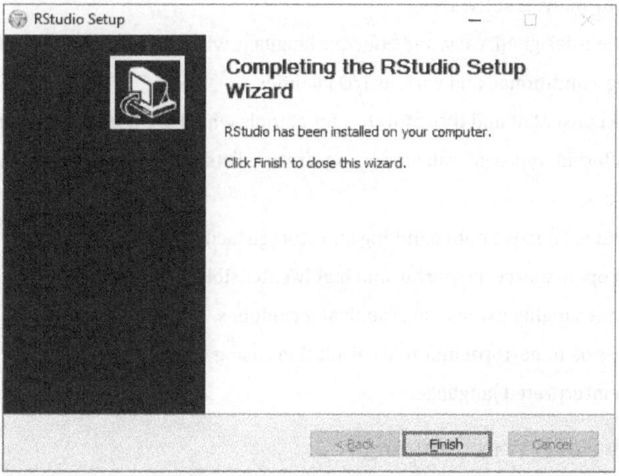

4. RStudio is ready to work.

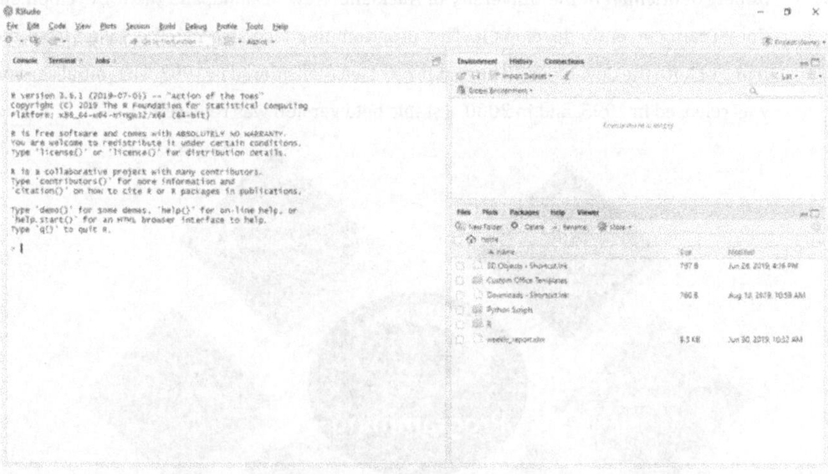

2.4. Features of R Programming

R is a domain-specific programming language which aims to do data analysis. It has some unique features which make it very powerful. The most important arguably being the notation of vectors. These vectors allow us to perform a complex operation on a set of values in a single command. There are the following features of R programming.

1. It is a simple and effective programming language which has been well developed.
2. It is data analysis software.
3. It is a well-designed, easy, and effective language which has the concepts of user-defined, looping, conditional, and various I/O facilities.
4. It has a consistent and incorporated set of tools which are used for data analysis.
5. For different types of calculation on arrays, lists and vectors, R contains a suite of operators.
6. It provides effective data handling and storage facility.
7. It is an open-source, powerful, and highly extensible software.
8. It provides highly extensible graphical techniques.
9. It allows us to perform multiple calculations using vectors.
10. R is an interpreted language.

2.5. History of R Programming

1. The history of R goes back about 20-30 years ago. R was developed by Ross lhaka and Robert Gentleman in the University of Auckland, New Zealand, and the R Development Core Team currently develops it. This programming language name is taken from the name of both the developers. The first project was considered in 1992. The initial version was released in 1995, and in 2000, a stable beta version was released.

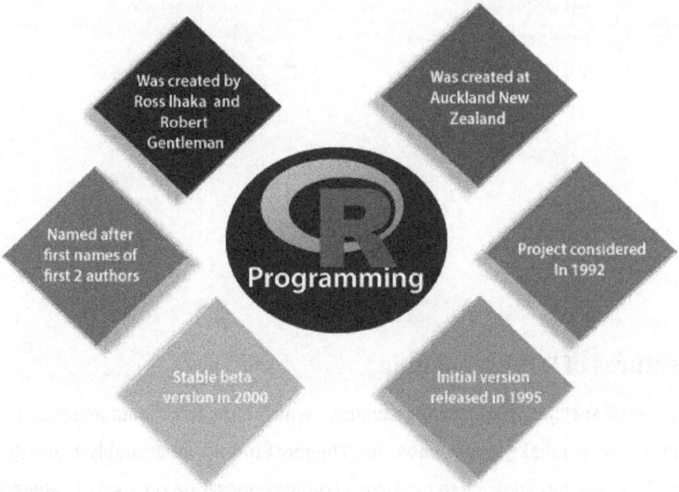

Figure 16: History of R Programming

The following table shows the release date, version, and description of R language.

Version-Release	Date	Description
0.49	1997-04-23	First time R's source was released, and CRAN (Comprehensive R Archive Network) was started.
0.60	1997-12-05	R officially gets the GNU license.
0.65.1	1999-10-07	update.packages and install.packages both are included.
1.0	2000-02-29	The first production-ready version was released.
1.4	2001-12-19	First version for Mac OS is made available.
2.0	2004-10-04	The first version for Mac OS is made available.
2.1	2005-04-18	Add support for UTF-8 encoding, internationalization, localization etc.
2.11	2010-04-22	Add support for Windows 64-bit systems.
2.13	2011-04-14	Added a function that rapidly converts code to byte code.
2.14	2011-10-31	Added some new packages.
2.15	2012-03-30	Improved serialization speed for long vectors.
3.0	2013-04-03	Support for larger numeric values on 64-bit systems.
3.4	2017-04-21	The just-in-time compilation (JIT) is enabled by default.
3.5	2018-04-23	Added new features such as compact internal representation of integer sequences, serialization format etc.

Why Use R Programming?

- There are several tools available in the market to perform data analysis. Learning new languages is time taken. The data scientist can use two excellent tools, i.e., R and Python. We may not have time to learn them both at the time when we get started to learn data science. Learning statistical modeling and algorithm is more important than to learn a programming language. A programming language is used to compute and communicate our discovery.
- The important task in data science is the way we deal with the data: clean, feature engineering, feature selection, and import. It should be our primary focus. Data scientist job is to understand the data, manipulate it, and expose the best approach. For machine learning, the best algorithms can be implemented with R. **Keras** and **TensorFlow** allow us to create high-end machine learning techniques. R has a package to perform **Xgboost**. Xgboost is one of the best algorithms for **Kaggle competition**.
- R communicate with the other languages and possibly calls Python, Java, C++. The big data world is also accessible to R. We can connect R with different databases like **Spark** or **Hadoop**.

- In brief, R is a great tool to investigate and explore the data. The elaborate analysis such as clustering, correlation, and data reduction are done with R.

Comparison between R and Python

- Data science deals with identifying, extracting, and representing meaningful information from the data source. R, Python, SAS, SQL, Tableau, MATLAB, etc. are the most useful tools for data science. R and Python are the most used ones. But still, it becomes confusing to choose the better or the most suitable one among the two, R and Python.

Comparison Index	**R**	**Python**
Overview	"R is an interpreted computer programming language which was created by Ross Ihaka and Robert Gentleman at the University of Auckland, New Zealand." The R Development Core Team currently develops R. R is also a software environment which is used to analyze statistical information, graphical representation, reporting, and data modeling.	Python is an Interpreted high-level programming language used for general-purpose programming. Guido Van Rossum created it, and it was first released in 1991. Python has a very simple and clean code syntax. It emphasizes the code readability and debugging is also simple and easier in Python.
Specialties for data science	R packages have advanced techniques which are very useful for statistical work. The CRAN text view is provided by many useful R packages. These packages cover everything from Psychometrics to Genetics to Finance.	For finding outliers in a data set both R and Python are equally good. But for developing a web service to allow peoples to upload datasets and find outliers, Python is better.
Functionalities	For data analysis, R has inbuilt functionalities	Most of the data analysis functionalities are not inbuilt. They are available through packages like Numpy and Pandas
Key domains of application	Data visualization is a key aspect of analysis. R packages such as ggplot2, ggvis, lattice, etc. make data visualization easier.	Python is better for deep learning because Python packages such as Caffe, Keras, OpenNN, etc. allows the development of the deep neural network in a very simple way.
Availability of packages	There are hundreds of packages and ways to accomplish needful data science tasks.	Python has few main packages such as viz, Sccikit learn, and Pandas for data analysis of machine learning, respectively.

Applications of R

There are several-applications available in real-time. Some of the popular applications are as follows:

- Facebook
- Google
- Twitter

- HRDAG
- Sunlight Foundation
- RealClimate
- NDAA
- XBOX ONE
- ANZ
- FDA

Syntax of R Programming

- R Programming is a very popular programming language which is broadly used in data analysis. The way in which we define its code is quite simple. The "Hello World!" is the basic program for all the languages, and now we will understand the syntax of R programming with "Hello world" program. We can write our code either in command prompt, or we can use an R script file.

R Command Prompt

- It is required that we have already installed the R environment set up in our system to work on the R command prompt. After the installation of R environment setup, we can easily start R command prompt by typing R in our Windows command prompt. When we press enter after typing R, it will launch interpreter, and we will get a prompt on which we can code our program.

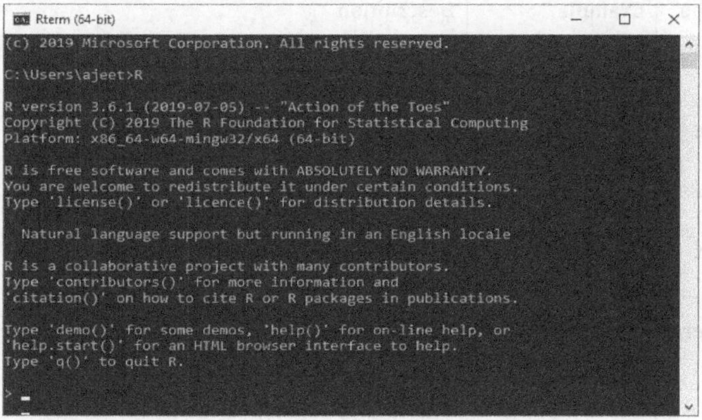

Hello, World!" Program

The code of "Hello World!" in R programming can be written as.

2.6. Data Types in R Programming

- In programming languages, we need to use various variables to store various information. Variables are the reserved memory location to store values. As we create a variable in our program, some space is reserved in memory.
- In R, there are several data types such as integer, string, etc. The operating system allocates memory based on the data type of the variable and decides what can be stored in the reserved memory.
- There are the following data types which are used in R programming.

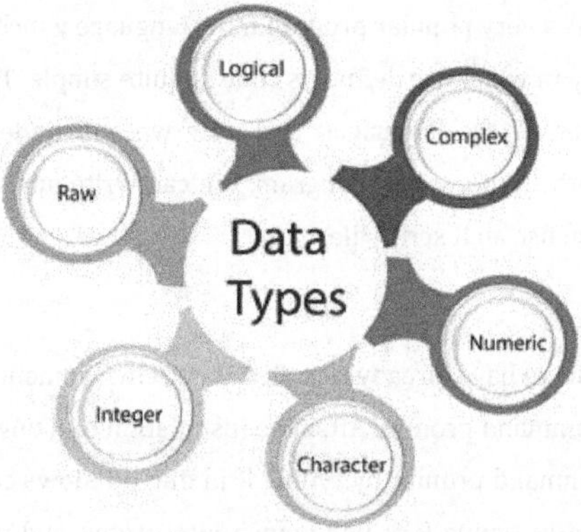

Figure 17: Data Types in R

Data Type	Example	Description
Logical	True, False	It is a special data type for data with only two possible values which can be construed as true/false.
Numeric	12,32,112,5432	Decimal value is called numeric in R, and it is the default computational data type.
Integer	3L, 66L, 2346L	Here, L tells R to store the value as an integer.
Complex	Z=1+2i, t=7+3i	A complex value in R is defined as the pure imaginary value i.
Character	'a', '"good"', "TRUE", '35.4'	In R programming, a character is used to represent string values. We convert objects into character values with the help of as.character() function.
Raw		A raw data type is used to holds raw bytes.

Data Type

- A variable can store different types of values such as numbers, characters etc. These different types of data that we can use in our code are called **data types**. For example,

```
x <- 123L
```

Here, `123L` is an integer data. So the data type of the variable `x` is `integer`.

We can verify this by printing the class of `x`.

```
x <- 123L

# print value of x
X<-123
print(x)

# print type of x
print(class(x))
```

Output

```
[1] 123
[1] "integer"
```

Here, `x` is a variable of data type `integer`.

Different Types of Data Types

In R, there are 6 basic data types:

- `logical`
- `numeric`
- `integer`
- `complex`
- `character`
- `raw`

1. Logical Data Type

The `logical` data type in R is also known as **boolean** data type. It can only have two values: `TRUE` and `FALSE`. For example,

```
bool1 <- TRUE

print(bool1)
print(class(bool1))

bool2 <- FALSE

print(bool2)
print(class(bool2))
```

Output

```
[1] TRUE
[1] "logical"
[1] FALSE
[1] "logical"
```

In the above example,

- `bool1` has the value `TRUE`.
- `bool2` has the value `FALSE`.

Here, we get `"logical"` when we check the type of both variables.

Note: You can also define logical variables with a single letter - `T` for `TRUE` or `F` for `FALSE`.

For example,

```
is_weekend <- F
print(class(is_weekend)) # "logical"
```

2. Numeric Data Type

- In R, the `numeric` data type represents all real numbers with or without decimal values.

  For example,

```
# floating point values
weight <- 63.5

print(weight)
print(class(weight))

# real numbers
height <- 182

print(height)
print(class(height))
```

Output

```
[1] 63.5
[1] "numeric"
[1] 182
[1] "numeric"
```

- Here, both *weight* and *height* are variables of numeric type.

3. Integer Data Type

- The integer data type specifies real values without decimal points. We use the suffix L to specify integer data. For example,

```
integer_variable <- 186L
print(class(integer_variable))
```

Output

```
[1] "integer"
```

- Here, 186L is an integer data. So we get "integer" when we print the class of *integer_variable*.

4. Complex Data Type

- The complex data type is used to specify purely imaginary values in R. We use the suffix i to specify the imaginary part. For example,

```
# 2i represents imaginary part
complex_value <- 3 + 2i

# print class of complex_value
print(class(complex_value))
```

Output

```
[1] "complex"
```

Here, 3 + 2i is of complex data type because it has an imaginary part 2i.

5. Character Data Type

- The character data type is used to specify character or string values in a variable.
- In programming, a string is a set of characters. For example, 'A' is a single character and "Apple" is a string.

- You can use single quotes '' or double quotes "" to represent strings. In general, we use:
  - '' for character variables
  - "" for string variables

For example,

```
# create a string variable
fruit <- "Apple"

print(class(fruit))

# create a character variable
my_char <- 'A'

print(class(my_char))
```

Output

```
[1] "character"
[1] "character"
```

Here, both the variables - *fruit* and *my_char* - are of character data type.

6. Raw Data Type

A raw data type specifies values as raw bytes. You can use the following methods to convert character data types to a raw data type and vice-versa:

- charToRaw() - converts character data to raw data.
- rawToChar() - converts raw data to character data.

For example,

```
# convert character to raw
raw_variable <- charToRaw("Welcome ")


print(raw_variable)
print(class(raw_variable))

# convert raw to character
char_variable <- rawToChar(raw_variable)


print(char_variable)
print(class(char_variable))
```

```
# convert character to raw
raw_variable <- charToRaw("Welcome")
print(raw_variable)
print(class(raw_variable))
raw_variable <- rawToChar(raw_variable)
print(raw_variable)
```

Output

```
[1] 57 65 6c 63 6f 6d 65 20 74 6f 20 50 72 6f 67 72 61 6d 69 7a
[1] "raw"
[1] "Welcome "
[1] "character"
```

In this program,

- We have first used the charToRaw() function to convert the string "Welcome to Programming" to raw bytes.

  This is why we get "raw" as output when we print the class of *raw_variable*.
- Then, we have used the rawToChar() function to convert the data in *raw_variable* back to character form.

  This is why we get "character" as output when we print the class of *char_variable.*

Basic Programs

How to the User Input in 'R'

There are two methods in R.

- Using **readline()** method
- Using **scan() method**

Using readline() method

- In R language **readline()** method takes input in string format. If one inputs an integer then it is inputted as a string, lets say, one wants to input **255**, then it will input as **"255"**, like a string.
- So one needs to convert that inputted value to the format that he needs. In this case, string **"255"** is converted to integer 255. To convert the inputted value to the desired data type, there are some functions in R.

- **as.integer(n)**; —> convert to integer
- **as.numeric(n)**; —> convert to numeric type (float, double etc)
- **as.complex(n)**; —> convert to complex number (i.e 3+2i)
- **as.Date(n)** —> convert to date ..., etc

Syntax

var = readline();

var = as.integer(var);

Note that one can use "<-" instead of "="

UNIT - 2

CHAPTER 3

3.1. Data

It is how the data objects and their attributes are stored.

- A data object represents an entity—in a sales database, the objects may be customers, store items, and sales; in a medical database, the objects may be patients; in a university database, the objects may be students, professors, and courses. Data objects are typically described by attributes.
- An **attribute** is an object's property or characteristics. For example. A person's hair colour, air humidity etc.
- An attribute set defines an **object**. The **object** is also referred to as a record of the instances or entity.
- For example, a sales data object may represent customers, sales, or purchases. When a data object is listed in a database they are called data tuples.
- **<u>Attribute:</u>**

  It can be seen as a data field that represents the characteristics or features of a data object. For a customer, object attributes can be customer Id, address, etc. We can say that a **set of attributes used to describe a given object are known as attribute vector or feature vector.**
- An attribute is a data field, representing a characteristic or feature of a data object. The nouns attribute, dimension, feature, and variable are often used interchangeably.
- The term dimension is commonly used in data warehousing. Machine learning literature tends to use the term feature, while statisticians prefer the term variable. Data mining and database professionals commonly use the term attribute.
- Attributes describing a customer object can include, for example, customer ID, name, and address. Observed values for a given attribute are known as observations. A set of attributes used to describe a given object is called an attribute vector (or feature vector).

3.2. Type of Attributes

- This is the First step of Data-preprocessing. We differentiate between different types of attributes and then preprocess the data. So here is the description of attribute types.

- Qualitative (Nominal (N), Ordinal (O), Binary (B)).
- Quantitative (Numeric, Discrete, Continuous).

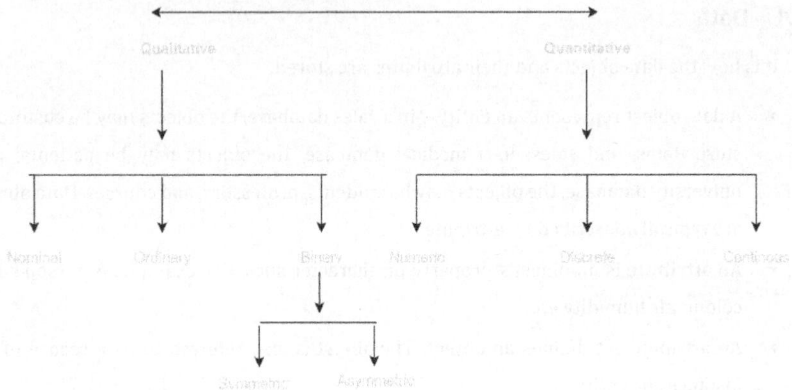

3.3. Qualitative Attributes

1. **Nominal Attributes – Related to Names:** The values of a Nominal attribute are names of things, some kind of symbols. Values of Nominal attributes represents some category or state and that's why nominal attribute also referred as categorical attributes and there is no order (rank, position) among values of the nominal attribute.
2. Nominal means "relating to names." The values of a nominal attribute are symbols or names of things. Each value represents some kind of category, code, or state, and so nominal attributes are also referred to as categorical. The values do not have any meaningful order. In computer science, the values are also known as **enumerations**.

Example

- **Nominal Attributes:** Suppose that hair color and marital status are two attributes describing person objects. In our application, possible values for hair color are black, brown, blond, red, auburn, gray, and white. The attribute marital status can take on the values single, married, divorced, and widowed. Both hair color and marital status are nominal attributes. Another example of a nominal attribute is occupation, with the values teacher, dentist, programmer, farmer, and so on.

Attribute	Values
Colours	Black, Brown, White

Categorical Data	Lecturer, Professor, Assistant Professor

3. **Ordinal Attributes:** The Ordinal Attributes contains values that have a meaningful sequence or ranking (order) between them, but the magnitude between values is not actually known, the order of values that shows what is important but don't indicate how important it is.
   - Suppose that drink size corresponds to the size of drinks available at a fast-food restaurant. This nominal attribute has three possible values: small, medium, and large. The values have a meaningful sequence (which corresponds to increasing drink size).
   - For example, assistant, associate, and full for professors Customer satisfaction had the following ordinal categories: 0: very dissatisfied, 1: Somewhat dissatisfied, 2: Neutral, 3: Satisfied, and 4: Very satisfied.

Attribute	Value
Grade	A,B,C,D,E,F
Basic pay scale	16,17,18

4. **Binary Attributes:** Binary data has only 2 values/states. For Example yes or no, affected or unaffected, true or false.

   A binary attribute is a nominal attribute with only two categories or states: 0 or 1, where 0 typically means that the attribute is absent, and 1 means that it is present. Binary attributes are referred to as Boolean if the two states correspond to true and false.

- **Symmetric:** Both values are equally important (Gender).
   - A binary attribute is symmetric if both of its states are equally valuable and carry the same weight; that is, there is no preference on which outcome should be coded as 0 or 1. One such example could be the attribute gender having the states male and female.
- **Asymmetric:** Both values are not equally important (Result).
   - A binary attribute is asymmetric if the outcomes of the states are not equally important, such as the positive and negative outcomes of a medical test for HIV. By convention, we code the most important outcome, which is usually the rarest one, by 1 (e.g., HIV positive) and the other by 0 (e.g., HIV negative).

Attribute	Values
Gender	Male, Female
Attribute	**Values**
Cancer Detected	Yes, No
Result	Pass, Fail

3.4. Quantitative Attributes

1. **Numeric:** A numeric attribute is quantitative because, it is a measurable quantity, represented in integer or real values. Numerical attributes are of 2 types, **interval**, and **ratio.**
2. **Ex: e.g., height, weight, temperature, blood glucose,...)**

Numeric Attributes

- A numeric attribute is quantitative; that is, it is a measurable quantity, represented in integer or real values. Numeric attributes can be interval-scaled or ratio-scaled.

Interval-Scaled Attributes

- Interval-scaled attributes are measured on a scale of equal-size units. The values of interval-scaled attributes have order and can be positive, 0, or negative. Thus, in addition to providing a ranking of values, such attributes allow us to compare and quantify the difference between values.
- An **interval-scaled** attribute has values, whose differences are interpretable, but the numerical attributes do not have the correct reference point, or we can call zero points. Data can be added and subtracted at an interval scale but cannot be multiplied or divided. Consider an example of temperature in degrees Centigrade. If a day's temperature of one day is twice of the other day we cannot say that one day is twice as hot as another day.
- **Eg:** An interval scale is one where there is order and the difference between two values is meaningful. Examples of interval variables include: **temperature (Farenheit), temperature (Celcius),**
- A **ratio-scaled** attribute is a numeric attribute with a fix zero-point. If a measurement is ratio-scaled, we can say of a value as being a multiple (or ratio) of another value. The values are ordered, and we can also compute the difference between values, and the mean, median, mode, Quantile-range, and Five number summary can be given.

E.g: height, money, age, weight etc.

3. **Discrete:** Discrete data have finite values it can be numerical and can also be in categorical form. These attributes has finite or countably infinite set of values.

Example

Attribute	Value
Profession	Teacher, Business man, Peon
ZIP Code	301701, 110040

4. **Continuous**: Continuous data have an infinite no of states. Continuous data is of float type. There can be many values between 2 and 3.

Example

Attribute	Value
Height	5.4, 6.2 ...etc
weight	50.33 ....etc

3.5. Basic Statistical Descriptions of Data

- **Statistical Analysis:** In statistics, data is collected, analyzed, explored, and presented to identify patterns and trends. Alternatively, it is referred to as quantitative analysis.
    - **Descriptive Statistics:** The purpose of descriptive statistics is to organize data and identify the main characteristics of that data. Graphs or numbers summarize the data. Average, Mode, SD (Standard Deviation), and Correlation are some of the commonly used descriptive statistical methods.
    - **Inferential Statistics:** The process of drawing conclusions based on probability theory and generalizing the data. By analyzing sample statistics, you can infer parameters about populations and make models of relationships within data.

CHAPTER 4

4.1. Measure of Central Tendency

- A measure of central tendency is a single value that attempts to describe a set of data by identifying the central position within that set of data.
- As such, measures of central tendency are sometimes called measures of central location.
- They are also classed as summary statistics. The mean (often called the average) is most likely the measure of central tendency that you are most familiar with, but there are others, such as the median and the mode.
- The central tendency is defined as the statistical measure that can be used to represent the entire distribution or a dataset using a single value called a measure of central tendency.

The mean, median and mode are all valid measures of central tendency.

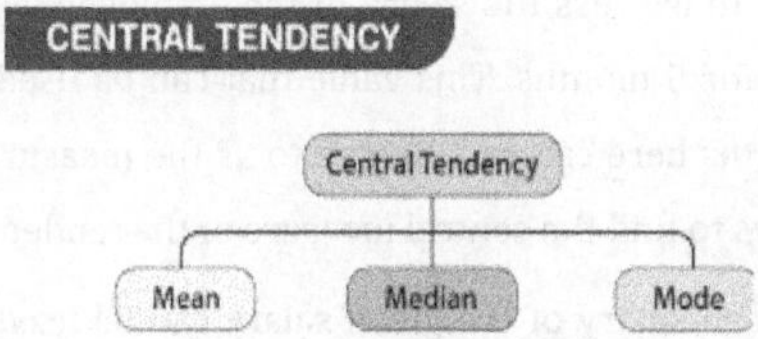

Figure 18: Measure of Central Tendency

- In statistics, the mean, median, and mode are the three most common measures of central tendency.
- Each one calculates the central point using a different method. Choosing the best measure of central tendency depends on the type of data you have.
- Measures of central tendency are summary statistics that represent the center point or typical value of a dataset.
- Examples of these measures include the mean, median, and mode. These statistics indicate where most values in a distribution fall and are also referred to as the central location of a distribution.
- Measures of central tendency are summary statistics that represent the center point or typical value of a dataset.
- Examples of these measures include the mean, median, and mode. These statistics indicate where most values in a distribution fall and are also referred to as the central location of a distribution.

4.2. Measures of Central Tendency Example

Example. The monthly salary of an employee for the 5 months is given in the table below.

Month	Salary
January	$105
February	$95
March	$105
April	$105
May	$100

- Suppose, we want to express the salary of the employee using a single value and not 5 different values for 5 months. This value that can be used to represent the data for salaries for 5 months here can be referred to as the measure of central tendency. The three possible ways to find the central measure of the tendency for the above data are:
    - **Mean:** The mean salary of the given salary can be used as on of the measures of central tendency, i.e., $\bar{x} = (105 + 95 + 105 + 105 + 100)/5 = \$102$.
    - **Mode:** If we use the most frequently occurring value to represent the above data, i.e., $105, the measure of central tendency would be mode.
    - **Median:** If we use the central value, i.e., $105 for the ordered set of salaries, given as, $95, $100, $105, $015, $105, then the measure of central tendency here would be median.

4.3. Measuring the Central Tendency: Mean, Median, and Mode

- Mean is the average of the given numbers and is calculated by dividing the sum of given numbers by the total number of numbers.

Mean = (Sum of all the observations/Total number of observations)

Example

What is the mean of 2, 4, 6, 8 and 10?

Solution

First, add all the numbers.

2 + 4 + 6 + 8 + 10 = 30

Now divide by 5 (total number of observations).

Mean = 30/5 = 6

Mean Symbol (X Bar)

- The symbol of mean is usually given by the symbol '$\bar{x}$'. The bar above the letter x, represents the mean of x number of values.
- $\bar{X}$ = (Sum of values ÷ Number of values)
- $\bar{X} = (x_1 + x_2 + x_3 + ... + x_n)/n$

Mean = Sum of the Given Data/Total number of Data

- **To calculate the arithmetic mean of a set of data we must first add up (sum) all of the data values (x) and then divide the result by the number of values (n). Since ∑ is the symbol used to indicate that values are to be summed (see Sigma Notation) we obtain the following formula for the mean ($\bar{x}$).**
- $\bar{x}=\sum x/n$

Example

In a class there are 20 students and they have secured a percentage of 88, 82, 88, 85, 84, 80, 81, 82, 83, 85, 84, 74, 75, 76, 89, 90, 89, 80, 82, and 83.

Find the mean percentage obtained by the class.

Solution

Mean = Total of percentage obtained by 20 students in class/Total number of students

= [88 + 82 + 88 + 85 + 84 + 80 + 81 + 82 + 83 + 85 + 84 + 74 + 75 + 76 + 89 + 90 + 89 + 80 + 82 + 83]/20

= 1660/20

= 83

Hence, the **mean percentage of each student in the class is 83%.**

Median

- A Median is a middle value for a sorted data. The sorting of the data can be done either in ascending order or in descending order. A median divides the data into two halves.

The Formula for Median

- If the number of values (n value) in the data set is odd then the formula to calculate median is:

$$\textbf{Median} = ((n + 1)/2)^{th} \textbf{ term}$$

If the number of values (n value) in the data set is even then the formula to calculate median is:

$$\textbf{Median} = [(n/2)^{th} \textbf{ term} + \{(n/2) + 1\}^{th} \textbf{ term}] / 2$$

Median

- The median is the mid-value or average of a data set. The data set must be sorted either in ascending or descending order.
- In other words, it is a middle value of a sorted data set. We find mean or average by using the median.

How to Find Median

To determine the median of a data set, the values of the data set must be sorted or arranged in either ascending or descending order. The data may be in two formats:

- Ungrouped Frequency Distribution.
- Grouped Frequency Distribution.

Ungrouped Frequency Distribution

In an ungrouped frequency distribution, the data may of two types:

- When an odd number of the frequency distribution is given.
- When even number of the frequency distribution is given.

When an Odd Number of the Frequency Distribution is Given

- To find the median of odd frequency distribution follow the steps given below. But remember that data must be sorted. After sorting the data, use the following formula:

$$\text{Median} = \left(\frac{n+1}{2}\right) \text{th item}$$

Where **n** is the total number of items in the data set.

Another quick method to find the median is:

- First, sort the values or items.
- Pick the middle value as the median.

Example 1: Find the Median of 23, 2, 12, 33, 65, 45, and 9.

Solution:

First, we sort the given data set.

2, 9, 12, **23**, 33, 45, 65

There is a total of 7 values, so the mid-value (4th) will be median, i.e. 23.

Similarly, we can find the median using the formula:

$$\text{Median} = \left(\frac{n+1}{2}\right) \text{th item}$$

Putting the value of n in the formula, we get:

$$\text{Median} = \left(\frac{7+1}{2}\right) \text{th item}$$

$$\text{Median} = 4\text{th item}$$

The 4th item or value will be median, i.e. 23.

Hence, the median of the given data set is 23.

When even number of the frequency distribution is given.

- To find the median of the data set that contains even number of frequency distribution, we must follow the steps given below.
- Sort the values of the data set.
- Find the middle pair and its values.
- Sum up the values and divide it by 2.
- The value that we get on dividing is the median of the given data set.
- We can also write the above steps in terms of the formula.

$$\text{Median} = \frac{\left(\frac{N}{2}\right) \text{th item} + \left(\frac{N}{2}\right) + 1 \text{ th item}}{2}$$

Where **N** is the total number of items in the data set.

Let's understand the example of even frequency distribution.

Example 2: Find the Median of the Following List

1, 5, 77, 32, 65, 12, 44, 21, 90, 34, 8, 56, 4, 99

Solution:

Step 1: Sort the given list.

1, 4, 5, 8, 12, 21, **32, 34,** 44, 56, 65, 77, 90, 99

There are total 14 values in the list.

Step 2: Find the middle pair and its values.

The middle pair terms of the list are **7th** and **8th** and its values are **32** and **34,** respectively.

Step 3: Sum up the values and divide it by 2.

$$\frac{32 + 34}{2} = \frac{66}{2} = 33$$

- A point to be noticed here is that **33** is not in the list. But it indicates that half values in the list are less than 33, and half values are greater than 33.
- Let's find the median through the formula which we have learned above.

$$\text{Median} = \frac{\left(\frac{N}{2}\right)\text{th item} + \left(\frac{N}{2}\right) + 1\text{ th item}}{2}$$

$$\text{Median} = \frac{\left(\frac{14}{2}\right)\text{th item} + \left(\frac{14}{2}\right) + 1\text{ th item}}{2}$$

$$\text{Median} = \frac{7\text{th item} + (7) + 1\text{ th item}}{2}$$

$$\text{Median} = \frac{7\text{th item} + 8\text{th item}}{2}$$

Count the **7th** and **8th** item in the list and put the values.

$$\text{Median} = \frac{32 + 34}{2} = \frac{66}{2} = 33$$

Hence, the median of the given list is 33.

Example 1

The median of the data 30, 40, 10, 20, 50 is:

Step 1: Order the given data in ascending order as:

10, 20, 30, 40, 50

Step 2: Check n (number of terms of data set) is even or odd and find the median of the data with respective 'n' value.

Step 3: Here, n = 5 (odd) then Median = $[(n + 1)/2]^{th}$ term 10, 20, 30, 40, 50.

The median of the data is $[(5 + 1)/2]^{th}$ term is 30.

Example 2

25, 12, 5, 24, 15, 22, 23, 25

Step 1: Order the given data in ascending order as:

5, 12, 15, 22, 23, 24, 25, 25

Step 2: Check n (number of terms of data set) is even or odd and find the median of the data with respective 'n' value.

Step 3: Here, n = 8 (even) then,

Median = $[(n/2)^{th}$ term + $\{(n/2) + 1)^{th}$ term] / 2

Median = $[(8/2)^{th}$ term + $\{(8/2) + 1\}^{th}$ term] / 2 = (22+23) / 2 = 22.5

4.4. Mode

A mode is the most frequent value or item of the data set. A data set can generally have one or more than one mode value. If the data set has one mode then it is called "Uni-modal". Similarly, If the data set contains 2 modes then it is called "Bimodal" and if the data set contains 3 modes then it is known as "Trimodal". If the data set consists of more than one mode then it is known as "multi-modal" (can be bimodal or trimodal). There is no mode for a data set if every number appears only once.

Example 1

If the data set is {1, 2, 2, 3, 3, 4, 5} then it has 2 modes i.e, 2 and 3 (bi-modal). Since, both the values 2 and 3 are repeating twice in the data set.

Example 2

If the data set is {15, 42, 65, 65, 95} then the mode is 65 (uni-modal). Since 65 is the only repeating value in the data set.

Range

It is the difference between the highest value and the lowest value. It is a way to understand how the numbers are spread in a data set. Formula to find Range is:

Range = Highest value – Lowest Value

Example

If the data set is {12, 19, 6, 2, 15, 4} then the lowest value is 2 and the highest value is 19.

So the range is 19 – 2 = 17.

Reading Bar Charts: Putting it Together with Central Tendency.

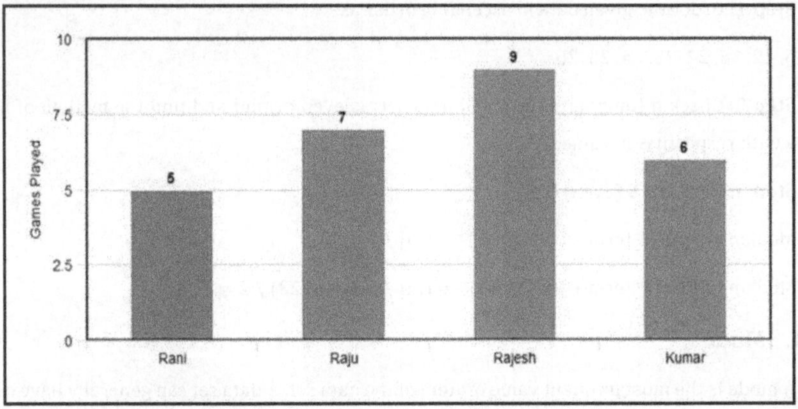

Question 1. Finding Mean for the above Bar Chart:

Mean = (sum of all data values) / (number of values)

Mean = (5 + 7 + 9 + 6) / 4 = 27 / 2 = 6.75

Question 2. Finding the Median for the above Bar Chart:

Order the given data in ascending order as: 5, 6, 7, 9

Here, n = 4 (number of students which is even)

Median = $[(n/2)^{th}$ term + $\{(n/2) + 1\}^{th}$ term] / 2

Median = (6 + 7) / 2 = 6.5

Question 3. Finding Mode for the above Bar Chart:

Mode = most frequent value = 9 (highest value)

Question 4. Finding the Range for the above Bar Chart:

Range = highest value – lowest value

Range = 9 – 5 = 4

4.5. Measuring the Dispersion of Data: Range, Quartiles, Variance, Standard Deviation, and Interquartile Range

- Dispersion or variability describes how items are distributed (scattered) from each other and the centre of a distribution.
- Example: Height of students.
- In statistics, dispersion helps to understand the distribution of the data.
- Dispersion in statistics is a way of describing how to spread out a set of data is. Dispersion is the state of data getting dispersed, stretched, or spread out in different categories. It involves finding the size of distribution values that are expected from the set of data for the specific variable. The meaning of dispersion in statistics is "numeric data that is likely to vary at any instance of average value assumption".

Measures of Dispersion

- Statistical methods that help to know about the distribution or the spread of the data points in the datasets are known as Measures of Dispersion.
- There are 4 methods to measures the dispersion of the data.
    - Range
    - Interquartile Range
    - Variance
    - Standard Deviation

Range

- The range is the easiest measure of dispersion. It is simply calculated by subtracting the highest value from the lowest value.

Range = Highest Value – Lowest Value

Ex:

- Problem Statement:
- Let there be 5 students in the class having heights of 150cm, 160cm, 175cm, 190cm and 200 cm.
- Calculate the range of heights?

  Range = 200cm – 150cm

  Hence, Range = 50cm

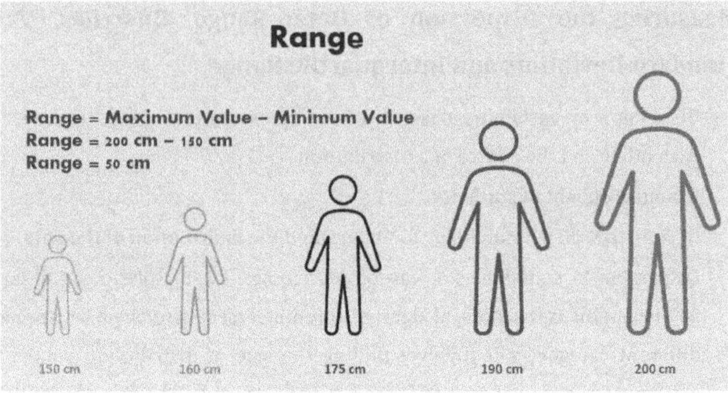

Figure 19: Depicts Range

Range for Ungrouped Data

Question 1: Find Out the Range for the Following Observations

20, 24, 31, 17, 45, 39, 51, 61

Solution

The largest value in the given observations is 61 and the smallest value is 17. The Range is 61 – 17 = 44.

Range for Grouped Data

Question 2: Find out the range for the following frequency distribution table for the marks scored by class 10 students.

Marks Intervals	Number of Students
0-10	5
10-20	8
20-30	15
30-40	9

Solution

For the largest value – Take higher limit of the highest class = 40

For the smallest value – Take lower limit of the lowest class = 0

Range = 40 – 0

Range = 40

Interquartile Range

- Before defining the interquartile range, let's discuss the quartiles and five-number summary.

Quartiles: Quartiles divide the set into 4 equal parts.

There are three quartiles Q1, Q2 and Q3, where Q2 is the median of the distribution.

Five Number Summary

Every dataset can be described using these 5 numbers.

- Lowest value
- Q1: 25 percentile
- Q2: Median
- Q3: 75 Percentile
- Highest Value

Interquartile Range

Interquartile Range: Interquartile range is defined as the range between 75 percentile (Q3) and 25 percentile (Q1).

$$IQR = Q3 - Q1$$

Let's understand Q1, Q2, Q3 and the Interquartile range by an example.

Problem Statement

Let there are 8 numbers between 10 and 90 which are equally distributed.

Define the five-number summary and find the Interquartile Range?

- Lowest value : 10
- Q1 (25 percentile) : 25
- Q2 (50 percentile) : 50
- Q3 (75 percentile) : 75
- Highest value : 90
- Interquartile Range(IQR) = Q3 – Q1 = 75 – 25 = 50

Interquartile Range = 50

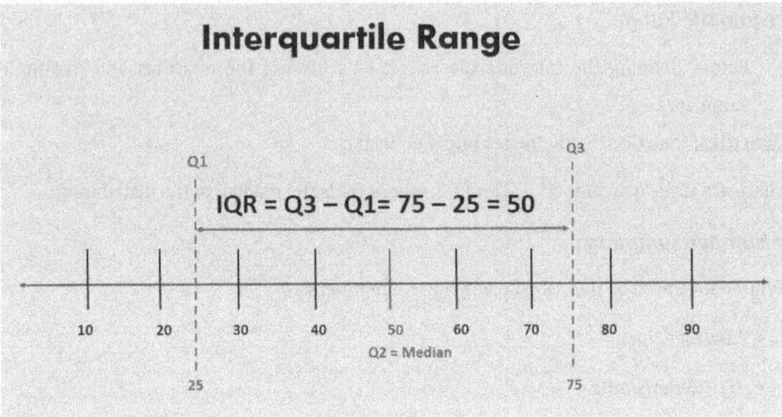

Ex: 2

Example:

a) Odd number of elements

4, 8, 3, 3, 7, 2, 9

Sort the values

2, 3, 3, 4, 7, 8, 9

Divide into four equal parts

2	3	3	4	7	8	9

P1 Q1 P2 Q2 P3 Q3 P4

Quartile 1 (Q1) = **3**

Quartile 2 (Q2) or Median = **4**

Quartile 3 (Q3) = **8**

P1, P2, P3, P4 are four parts.

b) Even number of elements

7, 8, 4, 6, 5, 6, 3, 3

Sort the values

3, 3, 4, 5, 6, 6, 7, 8

Divide into four equal parts

3	3	4	5	6	6	7	8

P1 Q1 P2 Q2 P3 Q3 P4

Quartile 1 (Q1) = **3**

Quartile 2 (Q2) or Median =5+6/2 ⟹ **5.5**

Quartile 3 (Q3) = **7**

P1, P2, P3, P4 are four parts.

4.6. Variance

Definition

- Variance is a measure of how data points differ from the mean. According to Layman, a variance is a measure of how far a set of data (numbers) are spread out from their mean (average) value.
- Variance means to find the expected difference of deviation from actual value. Therefore, variance depends on the standard deviation of the given data set.

Ex:

How to Calculate Variance

Variance can be calculated easily by following the steps given below:

- Find the mean of the given data set. Calculate the average of a given set of values.
- Now subtract the mean from each value and square them.
- Find the average of these squared values, that will result in variance.

Say if $x_1, x_2, x_3, x_4, \ldots, x_n$ are the given values.

Therefore, the mean of all these values is:

$$\bar{x} = (x_1+x_2+x_3+\ldots+x_n)/n$$

Now subtract the mean value from each value of the given data set and square them.

$$(x_1-\bar{x})^2, (x_2-\bar{x})^2, (x_3-\bar{x})^2, \ldots\ldots, (x_n-\bar{x})^2$$

Find the average of the above values to get the variance.

$$\text{Var}(X) = [(x_1-\bar{x})^2 + (x_2-\bar{x})^2 + (x_3-\bar{x})^2 + \ldots\ldots + (x_n-\bar{x})^2]/n$$

Hence, the variance is calculated.

Example of Variance

Let's say the heights (in mm) are 610, 450, 160, 420, 310.

Mean and Variance is interrelated. The first step is finding the mean which is done as follows,

Mean = (610+450+160+420+310)/ 5 = 390

So the mean average is 390 mm.

To calculate the Variance, compute the difference of each from the mean, square it and find then find the average once again.

So for this particular case the variance is:

$= (220^2 + 60^2 + (-230)^2 + 30^2 + (-80)^2)/5$

$= (48400 + 3600 + 52900 + 900 + 6400)/5$

Final answer: Variance = 22440

Example: Find the variance of the numbers 3, 8, 6, 10, 12, 9, 11, 10, 12, 7.

Solution:

Given,

3, 8, 6, 10, 12, 9, 11, 10, 12, 7

Step 1: Compute the mean of the 10 values given.

Mean = (3+8+6+10+12+9+11+10+12+7) / 10 = 88 / 10 = 8.8.

Step 2: Make a table with three columns, one for the X values, the second for the deviations and the third for squared deviations. As the data is not given as sample data so we use the formula for population variance. Thus, the mean is denoted by μ.

Value X	X – μ	$(X – \mu)^2$
3	-5.8	33.64
8	-0.8	0.64
6	-2.8	7.84
10	1.2	1.44
12	3.2	10.24
9	0.2	0.04
11	2.2	4.84
10	1.2	1.44
12	3.2	10.24
7	-1.8	3.24
Total	0	73.6

Step 3:

σ2=∑(X−μ)2N

= 73.6 / 10

= 7.36

Standard Deviation

- **Standard deviation is a metric that represents the amount to which various values of a statistical series tend to fluctuate or disperse from its mean or median. It describes how the values are distributed over the data sample and is a measure of the data points' deviation from the mean.**
- **The square root of the variance of a sample, statistical population, random variable, data collection, or probability distribution is its standard deviation.**

Steps to Calculate Standard Deviation

- Find the mean, which is the arithmetic mean of the observations.
- Find the squared differences from the mean. (The data value - mean)^2
- Find the average of the squared differences. (Variance = The sum of squared differences ÷ the number of observations).
- Find the square root of variance. (Standard deviation = √Variance).

Ex: 1

Consider the data set: 2, 1, 3, 2, 4. The mean and the sum of squares of deviations of the observations from the mean will be 2.4 and 5.2, respectively. Thus, the standard deviation will be √(5.2/5) = 1.01.

Ex: 2

For example: Take the values 2, 1, 3, 2 and 4.

1. Determine the mean (average):

2 + 1 +3 + 2 + 4 = 12

12 ÷ 5 = **2.4 (mean)**

2. Subtract the mean from each value:

2 - 2.4 = **-0.4**

1 - 2.4 = **-1.4**

3 - 2.4 = **0.6**

2 - 2.4 = **-0.4**

4 - 2.4 = **1.6**

3. Square each of those differences:

-0.4 x -0.4 = **0.16**

-1.4 x -1.4 = **1.96**

0.6 x 0.6 = **0.36**

-0.4 x -0.4 = **0.16**

1.6 x 1.6 = **2.56**

4. Determine the average of those squared numbers to get the variance.

0.16 + 1.96 + 0.36 + 0.16 + 2.56 = **5.2**

5.2 ÷ 5 = **1.04 (variance)**

5. Find the square root of the variance.

Square root of 1.04 = **1.01**

The standard deviation of the values 2, 1, 3, 2 and 4 is **1.01.**

Ex: 3

A class of students took a math test. Their teacher wants to know whether most students are performing at the same level, or if there is a high standard deviation.

1. The scores for the test were 85, 86, 100, 76, 81, 93, 84, 99, 71, 69, 93, 85, 81, 87, and 89. When the teacher adds them together, she gets 1279. She divides by the number of scores (15) to get the mean score.

1279 ÷ 15 =**85.2 (mean)**

2. 85.2 is a high score, but is everyone performing at that level? To find out, the teacher subtracts the mean from every test score.

85 - 85.2 = **-0.2**

86 - 85.2 = **0.8**

100 - 85.2 = **14.8**

76 - 85.2 = **-9.2**

81 - 85.2 = **-4.2**

93 - 85.2 = **7.8**

84 - 85.2 = **-1.2**

99 - 85.2 = **13.8**

71 - 85.2 = **-14.2**

69 - 85.2 = **-16.2**

93 - 85.2 = **7.8**

85 - 85.2 = -**0.2**

81 - 85.2 = **-4.2**

87 - 85.2 = **1.8**

89 - 85.2 = **3.8**

3. She squares each difference:

-0.2 x -0.2 = **0.04**

0.8 x 0.8 = **0.64**

14.8 14.8 = **219.04**

-9.2 x -9.2 = **84.64**

-4.2 x -4.2 = **17.64**

7.8 x 7.8 = **60.84**

-1.2 x -1.2 = **1.44**

13.8 x 13.8 = **190.44**

-14.2 x -14.2 = **201.64**

-16.2 x -16.2 = **262.44**

7.8 x 7.8 = **60.84**

-0.2 x -0.2 = **0.04**

-4.2 x -4.2 = **17.64**

1.8 x 1.8 = **3.24**

3.8 x 3.8 = **14.44**

4. The teacher finds the variance, which is the average of the squares:

0.04 + 0.64 + 219.04 + 84.64 + 17.64 + 60.84 +1.44 +190.44 +201.64 +262.44 + 60.84 + 0.04 + 17.64 + 3.24 + 14.44 = 1135

830.64 ÷ 15 = **75.6 (variance)**

5. Last, the teacher finds the square root of the variance:

Square root of 75.6 = **8.7 (standard deviation)**

The standard deviation of these tests is **8.7** points out of 100. Since the variance is somewhat low, the teacher knows that most students are performing around the same level.

Ex: 4

A market researcher is analyzing the results of a recent customer survey that ranks a product from 1 to 10. He wants to have some measure of the reliability of the answers received in the survey in order to predict how a larger group of people might answer the same questions. Because this is a sample size, the researcher needs to subtract 1 from the total number of values in step 4.

1. The scores for the survey are 9, 7, 10, 8, 9, 7, 8, and 9. The mean is **8.4.**
2. The researcher subtracts the mean from every score (differences: 0.6, -1.4, 1.6, -0.4, 0.6, -1.4, -0.4, 0.6).
3. He squares each number (0.36, 1.96, 2.56, 0.16, 0.36, 1.96, 0.16, 0.36).
4. Because this is a sample of responses, the researcher subtracts one from the number of values (8 values -1 = 7) to average squares and find the variance: **1.12 (variance)**
5. Last, the researcher finds the square root of the variance: **1.06 (standard deviation)**

The standard deviation is 1.06, which is somewhat low. The researcher now knows that the results of the sample size are probably reliable.

4.7. Graphic Displays of Basic Statistical Descriptions of Data

Graphical Representation of Data

- In today's world of the internet and connectivity, there is a lot of data available and some or the other method is needed for looking at large data, the patterns, and trends in it.
- There is an entire branch in mathematics dedicated to dealing with collecting, analyzing, interpreting, and presenting the numerical data in visual form in such a way that it becomes easy to understand and the data becomes easy to compare as well, the branch is known as **Statistics**.
- There are two ways of representing data.
- **Tables.**
- **Pictorial Representation through graphs.**
- They say, "A picture is worth the thousand words". It's always better to represent data in graphical format.
- Study the graphic displays of basic statistical descriptions.
- These include.
    - **Quantile plots.**
    - **Quantile–quantile plots, (Q-Q).**
    - **Histograms.**
    - **And scatter plots.**

Such graphs are helpful for the visual inspection of data, which is useful for data preprocessing.

Scatter Plot Chart

- Scatter Plot refers to a two-dimensional chart that visually represents supplied data in real-time.
- Generally, the scatter plot visualizes two sets of data on the X and Y axis that are co-related.
- This type of chart displays many points on vertical and horizontal axes as per the supplied data sets, and it is mainly used to show relationships between two variables.
- A scatter plot works by placing one variable on the vertical axis and a different variable on the horizontal axis.
- Each piece of data is then plotted as a discrete point on the chart. Both the X and Y axis display values in a scatter plot, which means that the scatter chart has no category axis.
- By convention, the X-axis represents arbitrary values that do not depend on another variable, called the independent variable. Besides, Y values are placed on the vertical axis and represent the dependent variable.

These charts are also known by many other names, such as '**Scatter Graphs, Scatter Charts, Scattergrams, Scatter Diagrams, XY Graph,** etc.'

Components of Scatter Plot Chart

There are mainly five components in a Scatter Plot Chart, as listed below:

- **Plot Area:** A graphical form/area within the sheet where the data is drawn is called the Plot Area.
- **Chart Title:** A chart title represents the subject of the plotted chart that primarily helps determine the chart's topic or motive. The text in the chart title can be edited, and the position can be arranged accordingly.
- **Vertical Axis:** An axis that lies vertically in the chart window is called the vertical axis, and it is located on the bottom area of the plot area. Since the vertical axis typically represents the measurement values across X-axis, it is known as the X-axis.
- **Horizontal Axis:** An axis that lies horizontally in the chart window is called the horizontal axis, and it is located on the left side of the plot area. Since the horizontal axis represents the different data categories across Y-axis, it is also known as the Y-axis. We can group series data on the horizontal axis.
- **Legend:** The legend is another useful component of the chart that helps list and distinguish various data groups. We can move the legend or change the legend's position accordingly, and it can be placed on any side in the chart window.

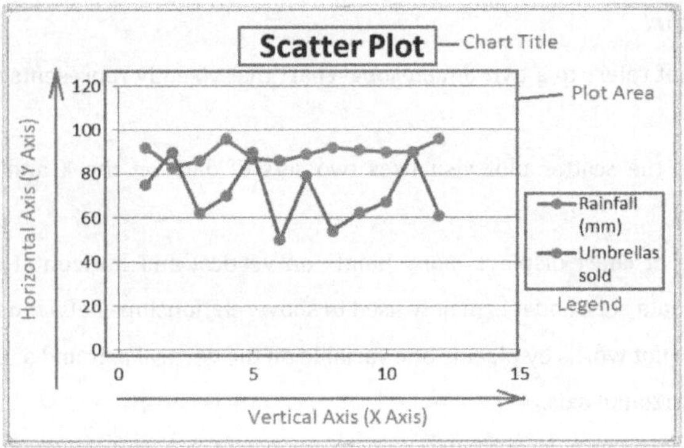

Figure 20: Example for Scatter Charts

Advantages of Using Scatter Plots

- The scatter charts help determine the relationship between two or more variables, and they mainly showcase the relationship of one variable concerning another.
- The scatter plots can show correlations visually.
- It is easy to analyze the maximum and minimum values (high and low) in scatter charts on the data flow range.
- The scatter charts are used for various scientific analyses because plotting these charts is moderately easy, and perception and readings are accurate.

Histogram

- A **histogram** is a graphical representation of the frequency distribution of **continuous** series using rectangles.
- The **x-axis of the graph represents the class interval**, and the **y-axis shows the various frequencies corresponding to different class intervals.**
- A histogram is a **two-dimensional diagram** in which the width of the rectangles shows the **width** of the class intervals, and the length of the rectangles depicts the corresponding frequency.
- There are no gaps between two consecutive rectangles based on the fact that histograms can be drawn when data are in the form of the frequency distribution of **continuous series.**
  - **Question:** The following table gives the lifetime of 400 neon lamps. Draw the histogram for the below data.

Lifetime (in hours)	Number of lamps
300 – 400	14
400 – 500	56
500 – 600	60
600 – 700	86
700 – 800	74
800 – 900	62
900 – 1000	48

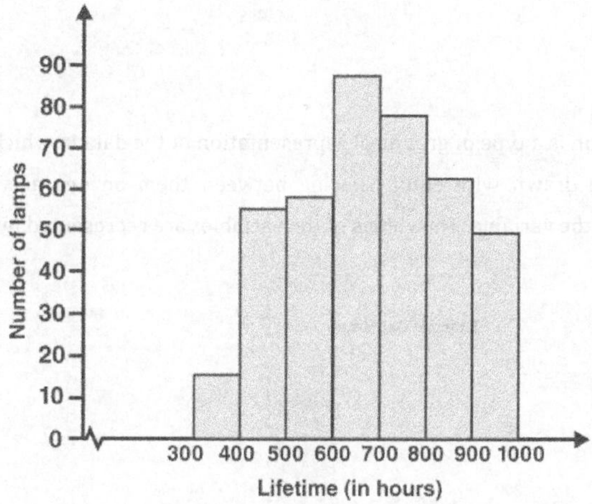

Example

Present the following information in the form of a Histogram:

Marks	0-10	10-20	20-30	30-40	40-50
Number of students	16	36	70	50	28

Solution

- It is visible that the set of data given is of the equal class interval; i.e., the difference between the upper limit and the lower limit of each class interval is 10. So, drawing a Histogram is feasible.
- The X-axis represents the marks (class intervals), and Y-axis represents the number of students (frequency distribution).

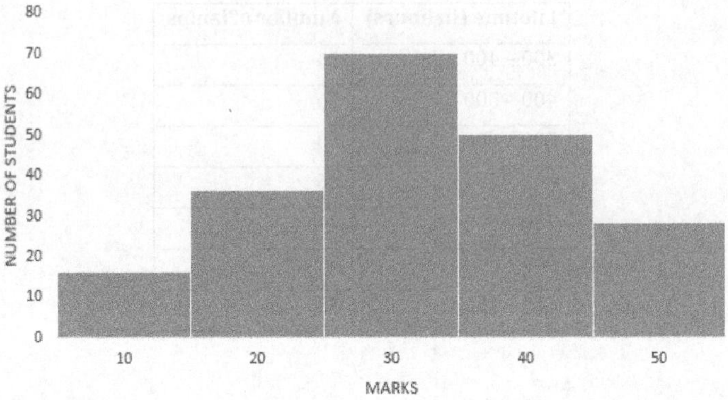

Bar Graph

- A bar graph is a type of graphical representation of the data in which bars of uniform width are drawn with equal spacing between them on one axis (x-axis usually), depicting the variable. The values of the variables are represented by the height of the bars.

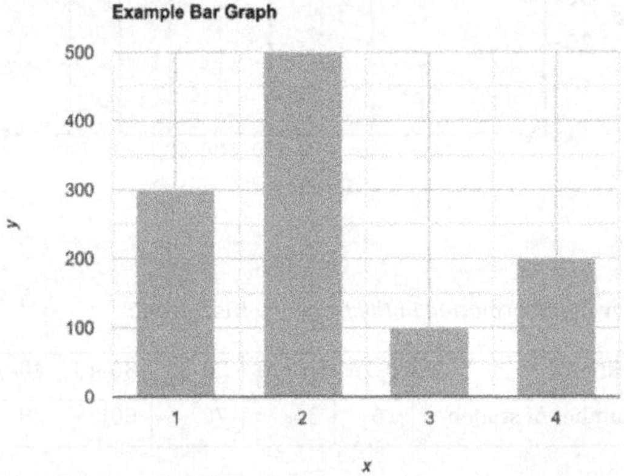

Histograms

"Histos" means pole or mast, and "gram" means chart, so a histogram is a chart of poles. Plotting histograms is a graphical method for summarizing the distribution of a given attribute.

This is similar to bar graphs, but it is based frequency of numerical values rather than their actual values. The data is organized into intervals and the bars represent the frequency of the values in that range. That is, it counts how many values of the data lie in a particular range.

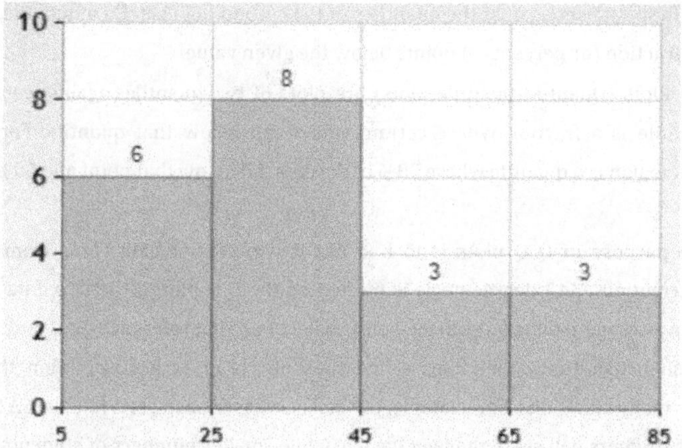

Box and Whisker Plot

- These plots divide the data into four parts to show their summary. They are more concerned about the spread, average, and median of the data.

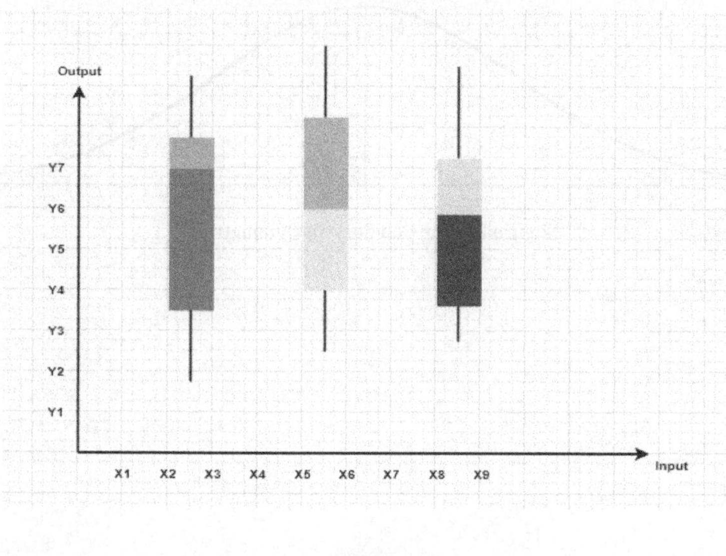

Quantile-quantile (q-q) Plot

- The quantile-quantile plot is a graphical method for determining whether two samples of data came from the same population or not. A q-q plot is a plot of the quantiles of the first data set against the quantiles of the second data set. By a quantile, we mean the fraction (or percent) of points below the given value.
- Q Q Plots (Quantile-Quantile plots) are plots of two quantiles against each other. A quantile is a fraction where certain values fall below that quantile. For example, the median is a quantile where 50% of the data fall below that point and 50% lie above it.
- The purpose of Q Q plots is to find out if two sets of data come from the same distribution. A 45 degree angle is plotted on the Q Q plot; if the two data sets come from a common distribution, the points will fall on that reference line.

A normal distribution, sometimes called the bell curve, is a distribution that occurs naturally in many situations. For example, the bell curve is seen in tests like the SAT and GRE. The bulk of students will score the average (C), while smaller numbers of students will score a B or D. An even smaller percentage of students score an F or an A. This creates a distribution that resembles a bell (hence the nickname). The bell curve is symmetrical. Half of the data will fall to the left of the mean; half will fall to the right.

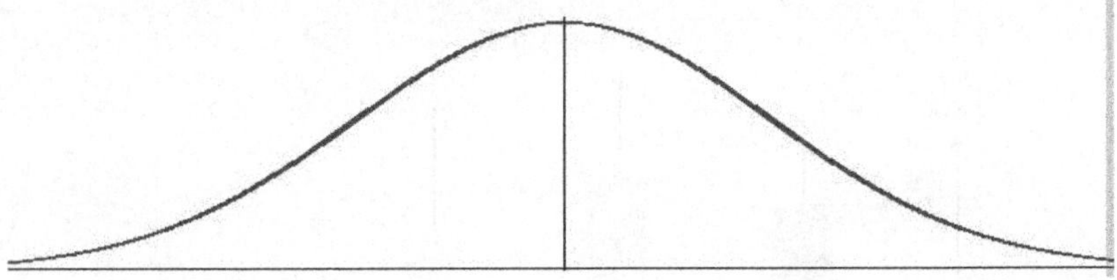

Figure 21: The Bell Curve is Symmetrical

UNIT - 3

CHAPTER 5

5.1. Vectors

- A vector is simply a list of items that are of the same type.
- A **vector** is a basic data structure which plays an important role in R programming.
- In R, a sequence of elements which share the same data type is known as vector. A vector supports logical, integer, double, character, complex, or raw data type. The elements which are contained in vector known as **components** of the vector. We can check the type of vector with the help of the **type of ()** function.
- To combine the list of items to a vector, use the c () function and separate the items by a comma.
- Vectors in R are the same as the arrays in C language which are used to hold multiple data values of the same type. One major key point is that in R the indexing of the vector will start from '1' and not from '0'. We can create numeric vectors and character vectors as well.
- The length is an important property of a vector. A vector length is basically the number of elements in the vector, and it is calculated with the help of the length () function.

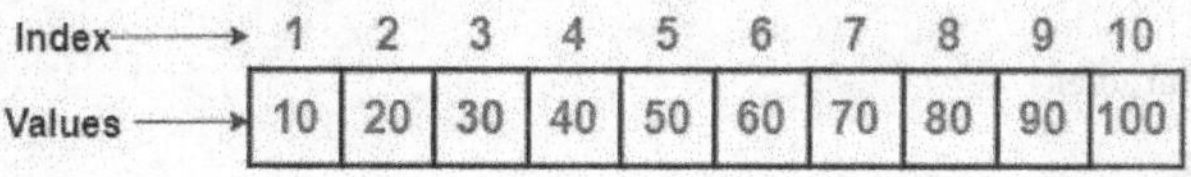

Types of Vectors

- Vectors are of different types which are used in R.

1. Numeric Vectors

Numeric vectors are those which contain numeric values such as integer, float, etc.

Example 1

```
# R program to create numeric Vectors
  # creation of vectors using c() function.
v1 <- c(4, 5, 6, 7)
  # display type of vector
typeof(v1)
```

```
# by using 'L' we can specify that we want integer values.
v2 <- c(1L, 4L, 2L, 5L)
# display type of vector
typeof(v2)
```

O/P: [1] "double"

[1] "integer"

Example 2

- ***Character Vectors***

Character vectors contain alphanumeric values and special characters.

```
# R program to create Character Vectors
# by default numeric values
# are converted into characters
v1 <-c('geeks', '2', 'hello', 57)
# Displaying type of vector
typeof(v1)
```

Output

- [1] "character"

Example 3

- ***Logical Vectors***

Logical vectors contain boolean values such as TRUE, FALSE and NA for Null values.

```
# R program to create Logical Vectors

# Creating logical vector
# using c() function
v1 <-c(TRUE, FALSE, TRUE, NA)

# Displaying type of vector
typeof(v1)
```

Output

- [1] "logical"

5.2. Creating and Naming Vectors

- We use c() function to create a vector. This function returns a one-dimensional array or simply vector. The c() function is a generic function which combines its argument.
- All arguments are restricted with a common data type which is the type of the returned value. There are various other ways also there.

Types

1. Using c() Function
2. Using the colon(:) operator
3. Using the seq() function
4. Using assign() function

1. Using c() Function

- The c function in R programming stands for 'combine. ' This function is used to get the output by giving parameters inside the function.

Example 1

```
# R program to create Vectors

# we can use the c function
# to combine the values as a vector.
# By default the type will be double

X <-c(61, 4, 21, 67, 89, 2)
cat('using c function', X)

# print the vales option 1
X
# print the vales option 2
# print(X)

O/P: using c function 61 4 21 67 89 2
```

2. Using the colon(:) operator

- Colon operator (":") in R is **a function that generates regular sequences**. It is most commonly used in for loops, to index and to create a vector with increasing or decreasing sequence. It is a binary operator i.e. it takes two arguments.

Syntax: z<- x:y

Example 1

```
# Vector with numerical values in a sequence
numbers <- 1:10
numbers
```

Example 2

```
# Vector with numerical decimals in a sequence
numbers1 <- 1.5:6.5
numbers1
```

3. *Using the Seq() Function*

- In R, we can create a vector with the help of the seq() function. A sequence function creates a sequence of elements as a vector.
- The seq() function is used in two ways, i.e., by setting step size with? by' parameter or specifying the length of the vector (sequence) with the 'length.out' feature.

Example 1

```
seq_vec<-seq(1,4,by=0.5)
seq_vec
class(seq_vec)
```

Output

```
[1] 1.0 1.5 2.0 2.5 3.0 3.5 4.0
[1] "numeric"
```

Example 2

```
seq_vec<-seq(1,4,length.out=10)
seq_vec
class(seq_vec)
```

Output

```
[1] 1.000000 1.333333 1.666667 2.000000 2.333333 2.666667 3.000000 3.333333
[9] 3.666667 4.000000
[1] "numeric"
```

Example 3

```
seq_vec<-seq(1,4,length.out=5)
seq_vec
class(seq_vec)
```

Output

```
[1] 1.00 1.75 2.50 3.25 4.00
[1] "numeric"
```

Example 4

```
# Creating a sequence from 5 to 13.
v <-5:13
print(v)
# Creating a sequence from 6.6 to 12.6.
v <-6.6:12.6
print(v)
```

Example 5

```
# R program to illustrate
# Assigning vectors

# Assigning a vector using
# seq() function
V = seq(1, 3, by=0.2)

# Printing the vector
print(V)
```

Output

```
[1] 1.0 1.2 1.4 1.6 1.8 2.0 2.2 2.4 2.6 2.8 3.0
```

4. *Using Assign() Function*

- The assign() function takes the following mandatory parameter values: **x : This represents the variable name that is given as a character string. value : This is the value to be assigned to the x variable**.

Example 1

```
assign("vec2",c(6,7,8,9,10))
vec2
```

Output

```
[1] 6 7 8 9 10
```

5.3. Vector Arithmetic Operations

- We can perform arithmetic operations on vectors, like addition, subtraction, multiplication and division.
- Please note that the two vectors should be of same length and same type. Or one of the vectors can be an atomic value of same type.
- If the vectors are not of same length, then **Vector Recycling** happens implicitly.
- **Vector Recycling:**
- If two vectors are of unequal length, the shorter one will be recycled in order to match the longer vector. For example, the following vectors u and v have different lengths, and their sum is computed by recycling values of the shorter vector u.

```
> u = c(10, 20, 30)
> v = c(1, 2, 3, 4, 5, 6, 7, 8, 9)
> u + v
[1] 11 22 33 14 25 36 17 28 39
```

Types

1. Addition

- Addition operator takes two vectors as operands, and returns the result of sum of two vectors.

$$a + b$$

Example

In the following program, we create two integer vectors and add them using Addition Operator.

Example 1

```
a <- c(10, 20, 30, 40, 50)
b <- c(1, 3, 5, 7, 9)
result <- a + b
print(result)
```

Output

```
[1] 11 23 35 47 59
```

2. *Subtraction*

- Subtraction operator takes two vectors as operands, and returns the result of difference of two vectors.

a - b

Example

In the following program, we create two integer vectors and find their different using Subtraction Operator.

Example 1

```
a <- c(10, 20, 30, 40, 50)
b <- c(1, 3, 5, 7, 9)
result <- a - b
print(result)
```

Output

```
[1] 9 17 25 33 41
```

3. *Multiplication*

- Multiplication operator takes two vectors as operands, and returns the result of product of two vectors.

a * b

Example

- In the following program, we create two integer vectors and find their product using Multiplication Operator.

Example 1

```
a <- c(10, 20, 30, 40, 50)
b <- c(1, 3, 5, 7, 9)
result <- a * b
print(result)
```

Output

```
[1] 10 60 150 280 450
```

4. *Division*

- Division operator takes two vectors are operands, and returns the result of division of two vectors.

a + b

Example

In the following program, we create two integer vectors and divide them using Division Operator.

Example.R

```
a <- c(10, 20, 30, 40, 50)
b <- c(1, 3, 5, 7, 9)
result <- a / b
print(result)
```

Output

```
[1] 10.000000 6.666667 6.000000 5.714286 5.555556
```

5.4. Accessing Elements of Vectors

We can access the elements of a vector with the help of vector indexing. Indexing denotes the position where the value in a vector is stored. Indexing will be performed with the help of integer, character, or logic.

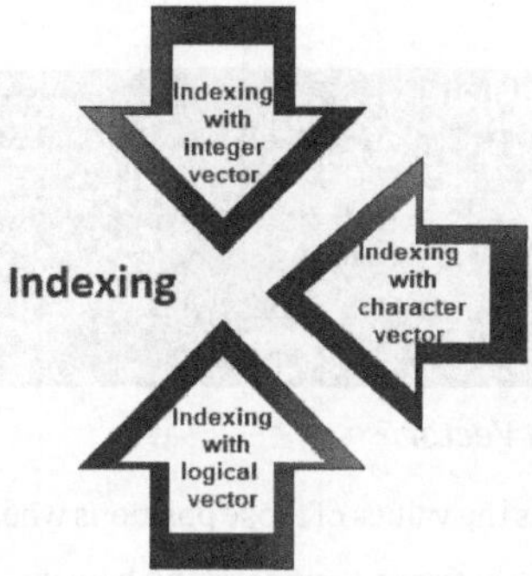

Figure 22: Depicts Accessing Elements of Vectors using Indexing

1. Indexing with Integer Vector

On integer vector, indexing is performed in the same way as we have applied in C, C++, and java. There is only one difference, i.e., in C, C++, and java the indexing starts from 0, but in R, the indexing starts from 1. Like other programming languages, we perform indexing by specifying an integer value in square braces [] next to our vector.

Example

```
seq_vec<-seq(1,4,length.out=6)
seq_vec
seq_vec[2]
```

Output

```
[1] 1.0 1.6 2.2 2.8 3.4 4.0
[1] 1.6
```

2. Indexing with a Character Vector

In character vector indexing, we assign a unique key to each element of the vector. These keys are uniquely defined as each element and can be accessed very easily. Let's see an example to understand how it is performed.

Example

```
char_vec<-c("shubham"=22,"arpita"=23,"vaishali"=25)
char_vec
char_vec["arpita"]
```

Output

```
shubhamarpitavaishali
 22  23  25
arpita
 23
```

3. *Indexing with a Logical Vector*

In logical indexing, it returns the values of those positions whose corresponding position has a logical vector TRUE. Let see an example to understand how it is performed on vectors.

Example

1. a<-**c**(1,2,3,4,5,6)
2. a[c(TRUE, FALSE,TRUE,TRUE,FALSE,TRUE)]

Output

```
[1] 1 3 4 6
```

5.5. Vector Sub Setting

- **Vectors** are basic objects in R and they can be sub setted using the **[operator]**.

Example

```
> x <-c("a", "b", "c", "c", "d", "a")
>x[1]   ## Extract the first element
[1] "a"
```

Example

```
>x[2]   ## Extract the second element
[1] "b"
```

- **The [operator** can be used to extract multiple elements of a vector by passing the operator an integer sequence. Here we extract the first four elements of the vector.

```
>x[1:4]
[1] "a""b""c""c"
```

- The sequence does not have to be in order; you can specify any arbitrary integer vector.

Example

```
>x[c(1, 3, 4)]
[1] "a""c""c"
```

5.6. Matrices: Creating and Naming Matrices

- In R, a two-dimensional rectangular data set is known as a matrix. A matrix is created with the help of the vector input to the matrix function. On R matrices, we can perform addition, subtraction, multiplication, and division operation.
- In the R matrix, elements are arranged in a fixed number of rows and columns. The matrix elements are the real numbers. In R, we use matrix function, which can easily reproduce the memory representation of the matrix. In the R matrix, all the elements must share a common basic type.
- **To create a matrix in R you need to use the function called matrix()**. The arguments to this matrix() are the set of elements in the vector.
- You have to pass how many numbers of rows and how many numbers of columns you want to have in your matrix. Note: By default, matrices are in column-wise order.
- Matrices are the R objects in which the elements are arranged in a two-dimensional rectangular layout. They contain elements of the same atomic types. Though we can create a matrix containing only characters or only logical values, they are not of much use. We use matrices containing numeric elements to be used in mathematical calculations.
- A Matrix is created using the matrix() function.

Syntax

- The basic syntax for creating a matrix in R is,

matrix(data, nrow, ncol, byrow, dimnames).

Note

Following is the Description of the Parameters Used

- **data** is the input vector which becomes the data elements of the matrix.
- **nrow** is the number of rows to be created.
- **ncol** is the number of columns to be created.

- **byrow** is a logical clue. If TRUE then the input vector elements are arranged by row. (byrow is a logical variable. Matrices are by default column-wise. By setting byrow as TRUE, we can arrange the data row-wise in the matrix).
- **dimname** is the names assigned to the rows and columns (takes two-character arrays as input for row names and column names).

5.7. How to Create a Matrix in R

- Like vector and list, R provides a function which creates a matrix. R provides the matrix() function to create a matrix. This function plays an important role in data analysis. There is the following syntax of the matrix in R:

1. *matrix (data, nrow, ncol, byrow, dim_name)*

data

The first argument in matrix function is data. It is the input vector which is the data elements of the matrix.

nrow

The second argument is the number of rows which we want to create in the matrix.

ncol

The third argument is the number of columns which we want to create in the matrix.

byrow

The byrow parameter is a logical clue. If its value is true, then the input vector elements are arranged by row.

dim_name

The dim_name parameter is the name assigned to the rows and columns.

Example to understand how matrix function is used to create a matrix and arrange the elements sequentially by row or column.

Example

```
P <- matrix(c(5:16), nrow = 4, byrow = TRUE)
print(P)
```

Output

```
     [,1] [,2] [,3]
[1,] 5    6    7
[2,] 8    9    10
[3,] 11   12   13
[4,] 14   15   16
```

```
# Arranging elements sequentially by column.
Q <- matrix(c(3:14), nrow = 4, byrow = FALSE)
print(Q)
```

```
     [,1] [,2] [,3]
[1,] 3    7    11
[2,] 4    8    12
[3,] 5    9    13
[4,] 6    10   14
```

```
# Defining the column and row names.
row_names = c("row1", "row2", "row3", "row4")
col_names = c("col1", "col2", "col3")
R <- matrix(c(3:14), nrow = 4, byrow = TRUE, dimnames = list(row_names, col_names))
print(R)
```

```
     col1 col2 col3
row1 3    4    5
row2 6    7    8
row3 9    10   11
row4 12   13   14
```

5.8. Accessing Matrix Elements in R

There are three ways to access the elements from the matrix.

1. We can access the element which presents on nth row and mth column.
2. We can access all the elements of the matrix which are present on the nth row.
3. We can also access all the elements of the matrix which are present on the mth column.

Example

```
# Defining the column and row names.
row_names = c("row1", "row2", "row3", "row4")
col_names = c("col1", "col2", "col3")
#Creating matrix
R <-
matrix(c(5:16), nrow = 4, byrow = TRUE, dimnames = list(row_names, col_names))
print(R)

#Accessing element present on 3rd row and 2nd column
print(R[3,2])

#Accessing element present in 3rd row
print(R[3,])

#Accessing element present in 2nd column
print(R[,2])
```

Output

```
      col1  col2 col3
row1   5    6    7
row2   8    9    10
row3   11   12   13
row4   14   15   16

[1] 12

col1  col2  col3
11    12    13

row1  row2  row3  row4
6     9     12    15
```

5.9. Modification of the Matrix

R allows us to do modification in the matrix. There are several methods to do modification in the matrix, which are as follows.

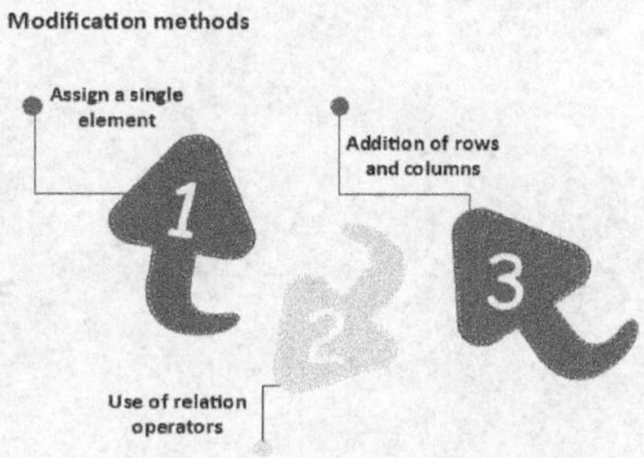

Figure 23: Shows Modification of the Matrix in R

Assign a Single Element

- In matrix modification, the first method is to assign a single element to the matrix at a particular position. By assigning a new value to that position, the old value will get replaced with the new one. This modification technique is quite simple to perform matrix modification. The basic syntax for it is as follows:

1. ***matrix[n, m]**<-y*

Here, n and m are the rows and columns of the element, respectively. And, y is the value which we assign to modify our matrix.

Example

```
# Defining the column and row names.
row_names = c("row1", "row2", "row3", "row4")
ccol_names = c("col1", "col2", "col3")

R <-
  matrix(c(5:16), nrow = 4, byrow = TRUE, dimnames = list(row_names, col_names))
print(R)

#Assigning value 20 to the element at 3d roe and 2nd column
R[3,2]<-20
print(R)
```

Output

```
        col1  col2  col3
row1  5      6      7
row2  8      9      10
row3  11     12     13
row4  14     15     16

        col1  col2  col3
row1  5      6      7
row2  8      9      10
row3  11     20     13
row4  14     15     16
```

Use of Relational Operator

- R provides another way to perform matrix modication. In this method, we used some relational operators like >, <, ==. Like the first method, the second method is quite simple to use. Let see an example to understand how this method modifies the matrix.

Example 1

```
# Defining the column and row names.
row_names = c("row1", "row2", "row3", "row4")
ccol_names = c("col1", "col2", "col3")

R <-
 matrix(c(5:16), nrow = 4, byrow = TRUE, dimnames = list(row_names, col_names))
print(R)

#Replacing element that equal to the 12
R[R==12]<-0
print(R)
```

Output

```
        col1  col2  col3
row1  5     6     7
row2  8     9     10
row3  11    12    13
row4  14    15    16

        col1  col2  col3
row1  5     6     7
row2  8     9     10
row3  11    0     13
row4  14    15    16
```

Example 2

```
# Defining the column and row names.
row_names = c("row1", "row2", "row3", "row4")
ccol_names = c("col1", "col2", "col3")

R <-
  matrix(c(5:16), nrow = 4, byrow = TRUE, dimnames = list(row_names, col_names))
print(R)

#Replacing elements whose values are greater than 12
R[R>12]<-0
print(R)
```

Output

```
        col1  col2  col3
row1  5     6     7
row2  8     9     10
row3  11    12    13
row4  14    15    16

        col1  col2  col3
row1  5     6     7
row2  8     9     10
row3  11    12    0
row4  0     0     0
```

Addition of Rows and Columns

- The third method of matrix modification is through the addition of rows and columns using the cbind() and rbind() function. The cbind() and rbind() function are used to add a column and a row respectively. Let see an example to understand the working of cbind() and rbind() functions.

Example 1

```
# Defining the column and row names.
row_names = c("row1", "row2", "row3", "row4")
ccol_names = c("col1", "col2", "col3")

R <-
  matrix(c(5:16), nrow = 4, byrow = TRUE, dimnames = list(row_names, col_names))
print(R)

#Adding row
rbind(R,c(17,18,19))

#Adding column
cbind(R,c(17,18,19,20))

#transpose of the matrix using the t() function:
t(R)

#Modifying the dimension of the matrix using the dim() function
dim(R)<-c(1,12)
print(R)
```

Output

```
      col1  col2  col3
row1  5     6     7
row2  8     9     10
row3  11    12    13
row4  14    15    16

      col1  col2  col3
row1  5     6     7
row2  8     9     10
row3  11    12    13
row4  14    15    16
      17    18    19

      col1  col2  col3
row1  5     6     7     17
row2  8     9     10    18
row3  11    12    13    19
row4  14    15    16    20

     row1  row2  row3  row4
col1  5     8     11    14
col2  6     9     12    15
col3  7     10    13    16

  [,1] [,2] [,3] [,4] [,5] [,6] [,7] [,8] [,9] [,10] [,11] [,12]
[1,]  5    8   11   14    6    9   12   15    7    10    13    16
```

5.10. Matrix Operations

- In R, we can perform the mathematical operations on a matrix such as addition, subtraction, multiplication, etc. For performing the mathematical operation on the matrix, it is required that both the matrix should have the same dimensions.

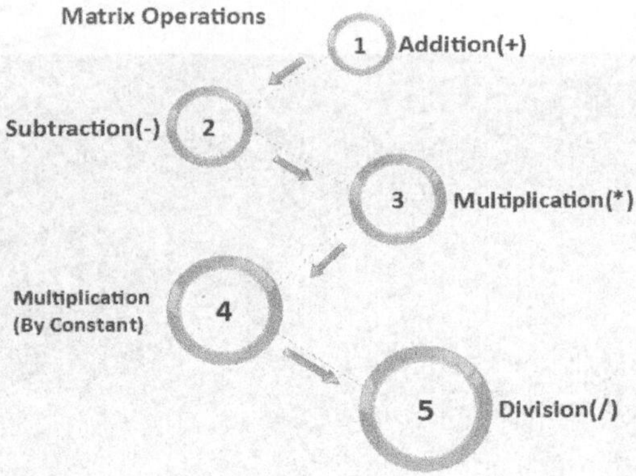

Example 1

```
R <- matrix(c(5:16), nrow = 4,ncol=3)
S <- matrix(c(1:12), nrow = 4,ncol=3)
 R
S
#Addition
sum<-R+S
print(sum)

#Subtraction
sub<-R-S
print(sub)

#Multiplication
mul<-R*S
print(mul)

#Multiplication by constant
mul1<-R*12
print(mul1)

#Division
div<-R/S
print(div)
```

Output

```
     [,1]  [,2] [,3]
[1,] 6    14  22
[2,] 8    16  24
[3,] 10   18  26
[4,] 12   20  28

     [,1]  [,2]  [,3]
[1,] 4    4     4
[2,] 4    4     4
[3,] 4    4     4
[4,] 4    4     4

     [,1]  [,2]  [,3]
[1,] 5    45    117
[2,] 12   60    140
[3,] 21   77    165
[4,] 32   96    192

     [,1]  [,2]  [,3]
[1,] 60   108   156
[2,] 72   120   168
[3,] 84   132   180
[4,] 96   144   192

     [,1]         [,2]          [,3]
[1,] 5.000000 1.800000 1.444444
[2,] 3.000000 1.666667 1.400000
[3,] 2.333333 1.571429 1.363636
[4,] 2.000000 1.500000 1.333333
```

Applications of Matrix

1. In geology, Matrices takes surveys and plot graphs, statistics, and used to study in different fields.
2. Matrix is the representation method which helps in plotting common survey things.
3. In robotics and automation, Matrices have the topmost elements for the robot movements.
4. Matrices are mainly used in calculating the gross domestic products in Economics, and it also helps in calculating the capability of goods and products.
5. In computer-based application, matrices play a crucial role in the creation of realistic seeming motion.

Subset Matrix by Row Names

- The row names (mat) method in R is used to set the names for rows of the matrix.
- A similar approach is used to check for the presence of row names of the matrix in the vector or list of specified row names.

```
# creating matrix
matr<- matrix(1:12, nrow = 4)
print("Original Matrix")
print(matr)
 # assigning row names to data frame
rownames(matr) <- c("row1","row2","row3","row4")
# getting rows
rows<- c("row1","row3")
```

5.11. Matrix Sub Setting

- A matrix is subset with two arguments within single brackets, [], and separated by a comma. The first argument specifies the rows, and the second the columns.

Example 1

```
a <- matrix(1:9, nrow = 3)
a
colnames(a) <- c("A", "B", "C")
a[1:2, ]
```

Output

```
     [,1] [,2] [,3]
[1,] 1    4    7
[2,] 2    5    8
[3,] 3    6    9
     A B C
[1,] 1 4 7
[2,] 2 5 8
```

Example 2

```
a <- matrix(1:9, nrow = 3)
a
colnames(a) <- c("A", "B", "C")
a[1:3, ]
```

Output

```
    [,1] [,2] [,3]
[1,] 1    4    7
[2,] 2    5    8
[3,] 3    6    9
     A B C
[1,] 1 4 7
[2,] 2 5 8
[3,] 3 6 9
```

5.12. Class in R Programming

- Classes and Objects are basic concepts of Object-Oriented Programming that revolve around the real-life entities.
- Everything in R is an object. An **object** is simply a data structure that has some methods and attributes. A **class** is just a blueprint or a sketch of these objects.
- It represents the set of properties or methods that are common to all objects of one type.

Unlike most other programming languages, **R has a three-class system**. These are **S3, S4, and Reference Classes**.

1. S3 Class in R

- S3 class is the most popular class in the R programming language. Most of the classes that come predefined in Rare of this type. S3 refers to a class system built into R. The system governs how R handles objects of different classes. Certain R functions will look up an object's S3 class, and then behave differently in response.
- First we create a list with various components then we create a class using the **class()** function. For example,

```
# create a list with required components
student1 <- list(name = "John", age = 21, GPA = 3.5)

# name the class appropriately
class(student1) <- "Student Info"

# create and call an object
student1
```

Output

```
$name
[1] "John"

$age
[1] 21

$GPA
[1] 3.5

attr(,"class")
[1] "student"
```

In the above example, we have created a list named `student1` with three components. Notice the creation of class,

```
class(student1) <- "Student_Info"
```

Here, `Student_Info` is the name of the class. And to create an object of this class, we have passed the `student1` list inside `class()`.

Finally, we have created an object of the `Student_Info` class and called the object `student1`.

2. S4 Class in R

S4 class is an improvement over the S3 class. They have a formally defined structure which helps in making objects of the same class look more or less similar.

In R, we use the `set Class()` function to define a class. For example,

```
set Class("Student_Info", slots=list(name="character", age="numeric",
GPA="numeric"))
```

Here, we have created a class named `Student_Info` with three slots (member variables): `name`, `age`, and `GPA`.

Now to create an object, we use the `new()` function. For example,

```
student1 <- new("Student_Info", name = "John", age = 21, GPA = 3.5)
```

Here, inside `new()`, we have provided the name of the class `"Student_Info"` and value for all three slots.

We have successfully created the object named `student1`.

Example: S4 Class in R

```
# create a class "Student_Info" with three member variables
setClass("Student_Info", slots=list(name="character", age="numeric",
GPA="numeric"))

# create an object of class
student1 <- new("Student_Info", name = "John", age = 21, GPA = 3.5)

# call student1 object
student1
```

Output

```
An object of class "Student_Info"
Slot "name":
[1] "John"

Slot "age":
[1] 21

Slot "GPA":
[1] 3.5
```

Here, we have created an S4 class named Student_Info using the setClass() function and an object named student1 using the new() function.

3. *Reference Class in R*

Reference classes were introduced later, compared to the other two. It is more similar to the object-oriented programming we are used to seeing in other major programming languages.

Defining a reference class is similar to defining a S4 class. Instead of setClass() we use the setRefClass() function. For example,

```
# create a class "Student_Info" with three member variables
Student_Info<- setRefClass("Student_Info",
fields = list(name = "character", age = "numeric", GPA = "numeric"))

# Student_Info() is our generator function which can be used to create new objects
student1 <- Student_Info(name = "John", age = 21, GPA = 3.5)

# call student1 object
student1
```

Output

```
Reference class object of class "Student_Info"
Field "name":
[1] "John"
Field "age":
[1] 21
Field "GPA":
[1] 3.5
```

In the above example, we have created a reference class named `Student_Info` using the `setRefClass()` function.

Comparison between S3 vs S4 vs Reference Class

S3 Class	**S4 Class**	**Reference Class**
Lacks formal definition	Class defined using `setClass()`	Class defined using `setRefClass()`
Objects are created by setting the class attribute	Objects are created using `new()`	Objects are created using generator functions
Attributes are accessed using `$`	Attributes are accessed using `@`	Attributes are accessed using `$`
Methods belong to generic function	Methods belong to generic function	Methods belong to the class
Follows copy-on-modify semantics	Follows copy-on-modify semantics	Does not follow copy-on-modify semantics

CHAPTER 6

6.1. R Factors

- The factor is a data structure which is used for fields which take only predefined finite number of values.
- These are the variable which takes a limited number of different values.
- These are the data objects which are used to categorize the data and to store it on multiple levels.
- It can store both integers and strings values, and are useful in the column that has a limited number of unique values.

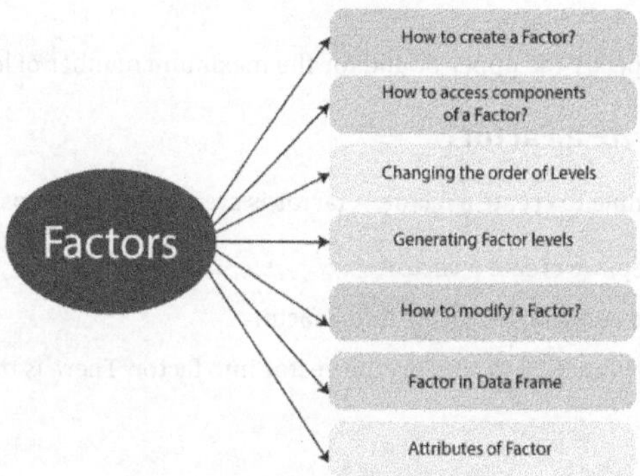

Figure 24: Shows R Factors Basics

- Factors have labels which are associated with the unique integers stored in it. It contains predefined set value known as levels and by default R always sorts levels in alphabetical order.

6.2. Attributes of a Factor

There are the following attributes of a factor in R.

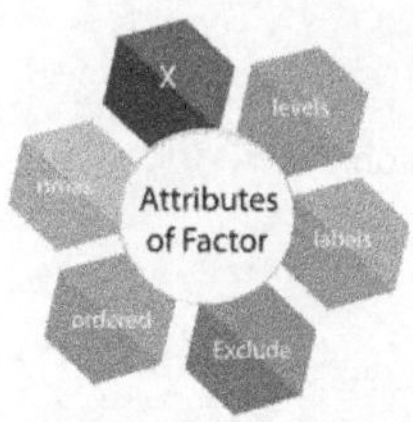

Figure 25: Attributes of a Factor in R

a. **X**

It is the input vector which is to be transformed into a factor.

b. **Levels**

It is an input vector that represents a set of unique values which are taken by x.

c. **Labels**

It is a character vector which corresponds to the number of labels.

d. **Exclude**

It is used to specify the value which we want to be excluded.

e. **Ordered**

It is a logical attribute which determines if the levels are ordered.

f. **Nmax**

It is used to specify the upper bound for the maximum number of level.

6.3. How to Create a Factor?

In R, it is quite simple to create a factor. A factor is created in two steps.

1. In the first step, we create a vector.
2. Next step is to convert the vector into a factor.

R provides factor() function to convert the vector into factor. There is the following syntax of factor() function.

```
factor_data<- factor(vector)
```

Example

```
# Creating a vector as input.
data <-
c("Shubham","Nishka","Arpita","Nishka","Shubham","Sumit","Nishka","Shubham","Sumit","Arpita","Sumit")
print(data)
print(is.factor(data))
# Applying the factor function.
factor_data<- factor(data)
print(factor_data)
print(is.factor(factor_data))
```

Output

```
[1] "Shubham" "Nishka"  "Arpita"  "Nishka"  "Shubham" "Sumit"  "Nishka"
 [8] "Shubham" "Sumit"   "Arpita"  "Sumit"
[1] FALSE
 [1] Shubham Nishka Arpita NishkaShubham Sumit Nishka Shubham Sumit
[10] Arpita Sumit
Levels: Arpita Nishka Shubham Sumit
[1] TRUE
```

6.4. Accessing Components of Factor

- Like vectors, we can access the components of factors. The process of accessing components of factor is much more similar to the vectors. We can access the element with the help of the indexing method or using logical vectors.

Example

```
# Creating a vector as input.
data <-
c("Shubham","Nishka","Arpita","Nishka","Shubham","Sumit","Nishka","Shubham","Sumit","
Arpita","Sumit")

# Applying the factor function.
factor_data<- factor(data)
 #Printing all elements of factor
print(factor_data)
 #Accessing 4th element of factor
print(factor_data[4])
 #Accessing 5th and 7th element
print(factor_data[c(5,7)])
 #Accessing all elemcent except 4th one
print(factor_data[-4])
```

Output

```
[1] Shubham Nishka Arpita Nishka Shubham Sumit Nishka Shubham Sumit
[10] Arpita Sumit
Levels: Arpita Nishka Shubham Sumit
[1] Nishka
Levels: Arpita Nishka Shubham Sumit
[1] Shubham Nishka
Levels: Arpita Nishka Shubham Sumit
 [1] Shubham Nishka Arpita Shubham Sumit Nishka Shubham Sumit Arpita
[10] Sumit
Levels: Arpita Nishka Shubham Sumit
```

6.5. Modification of Factor

- Like data frames, R allows us to modify the factor. We can modify the value of a factor by simply re-assigning it.
- In R, we cannot choose values outside of its predefined levels means we cannot insert value if it's level is not present on it.
- For this purpose, we have to create a level of that value, and then we can add it to our factor.

Example

```
# Creating a vector as input.
data <-
 c("Shubham","Nishka","Arpita","Nishka","Shubham")
 # Applying the factor function.
factor_data<- factor(data)
 #Printing all elements of factor
print(factor_data)
  #Change 4th element of factor with sumit
factor_data[4] <-"Arpita"
print(factor_data)
    #change 4th element of factor with "G"
    factor_data[4] <- "G"    # cannot assign values outside levels
```

```
print(factor_data)
#Adding the value to the level
levels(factor_data) <- c(levels(factor_data),"G")#Adding new level
factor_data[4] <- "G"
print(factor_data)
```

Output

```
[1] Shubham Nishka Arpita Nishka Shubham
Levels: Arpita Nishka Shubham
[1] Shubham Nishka Arpita Arpita Shubham
Levels: Arpita Nishka Shubham
Warning message:
In `[<-.factor`(`*tmp*`, 4, value = "G") :
invalid factor level, NA generated
[1] Shubham Nishka Arpita Shubham
Levels: Arpita Nishka Shubham
[1] Shubham Nishka Arpita G Shubham
Levels: Arpita Nishka Shubham G
```

6.6. Generating Factor Levels

- R provides gl() function to generate factor levels.
- This function takes three arguments i.e., n, k, and labels.
- Here, n and k are the integers which indicate how many levels we want and how many times each level is required.

There is the following syntax of gl() function which is as follows.

1. *gl(n, k, labels)*

1. n indicates the number of levels.
2. k indicates the number of replications.
3. labels is a vector of labels for the resulting factor levels.

Example

```
gen_factor<- gl(3,5, labels=c("BCA","MCA","B.Tech"))
  gen_factor
```

Output

```
[1] BCA BCABCABCABCA MCA MCAMCAMCAMCA
[11] B.Tech B.Tech B.Tech B.Tech B.Tech
Levels: BCA MCA B.Tech
```

6.7. R – Level Ordering of Factors

- Factors are data objects used to categorize data and store it as levels.
- They can store a string as well as an integer.
- They represent columns as they have a limited number of unique values. Factors in R can be created using **factor()** function. It takes a vector as input. **c() function** is used to create a vector with explicitly provided values.

Example

```
x <- c("Pen", "Pencil", "Brush", "Pen",
       "Brush", "Brush", "Pencil", "Pencil")
print(x)
print(is.factor(x))
# Apply the factor function.
factor_x = factor(x)
levels(factor_x)
```

Output

```
[1] "Pen"    "Pencil" "Brush" "Pen"    "Brush" "Brush" "Pencil" "Pencil"
[1] FALSE
[1] "Brush" "Pen" "Pencil"
```

- In the above code, x is a vector with 8 elements.
- To convert it to a factor the function **factor()** is used.
- Here there are 8 factors and 3 levels.
- Levels are the unique elements in the data. Can be found using **levels()** function.

6.8. Ordering Factor Levels

- Ordered factors is an extension of factors. It arranges the levels in increasing order. We use two functions: **factor()** along with argument **ordered()**.

1. **Syntax:** factor(data, levels =c(""), ordered =TRUE)
2. **Parameter:**
3. **data:** input vector with explicitly defined values.
4. **Levels ():** Mention the list of levels in c function.
5. **ordered:** It is set true for enabling ordering.

Example

```
# creating size vector
size = c("small", "large", "large", "small",
        "medium", "large", "medium", "medium")
 # converting to factor
size_factor<- factor(size)
print(size_factor)
# ordering the levels

ordered.size<- factor(size, levels = c(
  "small", "medium", "large"), ordered = TRUE)
print(ordered.size)
```

Output

```
[1] small  large  large  small  medium large  medium medium
Levels: large medium small
[1] small  large  large  small  medium large  medium medium
Levels: small < medium < large
```

- In the above code, size vector is created using c function. Then it is converted to a factor. And for ordering factor() function is used along with the arguments described above. Thus the sizes arranged in order.

The same can be done using the ordered function. The example for the same is as shown below.

Example

```
# creating vector size
size = c("small", "large", "large", "small",
      "medium", "large", "medium", "medium")
sizes <- ordered(c("small", "large", "large",
             "small", "medium"))
 # ordering the levels
sizes <- ordered(sizes, levels = c("small", "medium", "large"))
print(sizes)
```

Output

```
[1] small  large large  small  medium
Levels: small < medium < large
```

Comparing Ordered Factors using is.ordered () Function

- **is.ordered() function in R Programming Language** is used to check if the passed factor is an ordered factor.
- ***Syntax:*** *is.ordered(factor)*
- ***Parameters:***
- ***factor:*** *Factor to be checked*

Example 1

```
# creating vector size
size = c("small", "large", "large", "small",
      "medium", "large", "medium", "medium")
sizes <- ordered(c("small", "large", "large",
             "small", "medium"))
# ordering the levels
sizes <- ordered(sizes, levels = c("small", "medium",  "large"))

# Checking if the factor is ordered
# using is.ordered() function
is.ordered(sizes)
```

Output

- [1] TRUE

Example 2

```
# Creating a vector
x<-c("female", "male", "male", "female")
 # Converting vector into factor
gender <- factor(x)
 # Using is.ordered() Function
# to check if a factor is ordered
is.ordered(gender)
```

Output

```
[1] FALSE
```

6.9. Introduction to Data Frame

R Data Frame

- A data frame is a two-dimensional array-like structure or a table in which a column contains values of one variable, and rows contains one set of values from each column. A data frame is a special case of the list in which each component has equal length.
- A data frame is used to store data table and the vectors which are present in the form of a list in a data frame, are of equal length.
- In a simple way, it is a list of equal length vectors. A matrix can contain one type of data, but a data frame can contain different data types such as numeric, character, factor, etc.

R Data Frame-characteristics

- A data frame is a two-dimensional array-like structure or a table in which a column contains values of one variable, and rows contains one set of values from each column. A data frame is a special case of the list in which each component has equal length.
- A data frame is used to store data table and the vectors which are present in the form of a list in a data frame, are of equal length.
- In a simple way, it is a list of equal length vectors. A matrix can contain one type of data, but a data frame can contain different data types such as numeric, character, factor, etc.

There are following characteristics of a data frame.

6.10. Create Data Frame

- In R, the data frames are created with the help of frame() function of data. This function contains the vectors of any type such as numeric, character, or integer. In below example, we create a data frame that contains employee id (integer vector), employee name (character vector), salary (numeric vector), and starting date (Date vector).

In R, we use the data.frame() function to create a Data Frame.

The syntax of the data.frame() function is,

```
dataframe1<- data.frame(
first_col =c(val1, val2, ...),
second_col = c(val1, val2, ...),
...
)
```

Here,

- first_col - a vector with values val1, val2, ... of same data type.
- second_col - another vector with values val1, val2, ... of same data type and so on.

```
# Create a data frame
dataframe1 <- data.frame (
 Name = c("Juan", "Alcaraz", "Simantha"),
 Age = c(22, 15, 19),
 Vote = c(TRUE, FALSE, TRUE)
)

print(dataframe1)
```

Output

```
    Name     Age  Vote
1  Juan      22   TRUE
2  Alcaraz   15   FALSE
3  Simantha  19   TRUE
```

- In the above example, we have used the data.frame() function to create a data frame named dataframe1. Notice the arguments passed inside data.frame().

```
data.frame (
 Name = c("Juan", "Alcaraz", "Simantha"),
 Age = c(22, 15, 19),
 Vote = c(TRUE, FALSE, TRUE)
)
```

- Here, Name, Age, and Vote are column names for vectors of String, Numeric, and Boolean type respectively.
- And finally the datas represented in tabular format are printed.

6.11. Access Data Frame Columns

- There are different ways to extract columns from a data frame. We can use [ ], [[ ]], or $ to access specific column of a data frame in R. For example,

```
# Create a data frame
dataframe1 <- data.frame (
 Name = c("Juan", "Alcaraz", "Simantha"),
 Age = c(22, 15, 19),
 Vote = c(TRUE, FALSE, TRUE)
)

# pass index number inside [ ]
print(dataframe1[1])

# pass column name inside [[ ]]
print(dataframe1[["Name"]])

# use $ operator and column name
print(dataframe1$Name)
```

Output

```
    Name
1    Juan
2  Alcaraz
3 Simantha
[1] "Juan"     "Alcaraz" "Simantha"
[1] "Juan"     "Alcaraz" "Simantha"
```

- In the above example, we have created a data frame named *dataframe1* with three columns *Name*, *Age*, *Vote*.
- Here, we have used different operators to access *Name* column of *dataframe1*.
- Accessing with [[ ]] or $ is similar. However, it differs for [ ], [ ] will return us a data frame but the other two will reduce it into a vector and return a vector.

6.12. Combine Data Frames

In R, we use the rbind() and the cbind() function to combine two data frames together.

- rbind() - combines two data frames vertically.
- cbind() - combines two data frames horizontally.

Combine Vertically Using rbind()

If we want to combine two data frames vertically, the column name of the two data frames must be the same. For example,

```
# create a data frame
dataframe1<- data.frame (
Name = c("Juan", "Alcaraz"),
Age = c(22, 15)
)

# create another data frame
dataframe2<- data.frame (
Name = c("Yiruma", "Bach"),
Age = c(46, 89)
)

# combine two data frames vertically
updated<- rbind(dataframe1, dataframe2)
print(updated)
```

Output

```
     Name    Age
1    Juan    22
2  Alcaraz   15
3   Yiruma   46
4    Bach    89
```

Here, we have used the rbind() function to combine the two data frames: dataframe1 and dataframe2 vertically.

Combine Horizontally Using cbind()

The cbind() function combines two or more data frames horizontally. For example,

```
# create a data frame
dataframe1<- data.frame (
Name = c("Juan", "Alcaraz"),
Age = c(22, 15)
)

# create another data frame
dataframe2<- data.frame (
Hobby = c("Tennis", "Piano")
)

# combine two data frames horizontally
updated<- cbind(dataframe1, dataframe2)
print(updated)
```

Output

```
    Name    Age  Hobby
1   Juan     22   Tennis
2  Alcaraz   15   Piano
```

Here, we have used cbind() to combine two data frames horizontally.

Note: The number of items on each vector of two or more combining data frames must be equal otherwise we will get an error: arguments imply differing number of rows or columns.

Length of a Data Frame in R

In R, we use the length() function to find the number of columns in a data frame. For example,

```
# Create a data frame
dataframe1 <- data.frame (
 Name = c("Juan", "Alcaraz", "Simantha"),
 Age = c(22, 15, 19),
 Vote = c(TRUE, FALSE, TRUE)
)

cat("Total Elements:", length(dataframe1))
```

Output

```
Total Elements: 3
```

Here, we have used length() to find the total number of columns in *dataframe1*. Since there are **3** columns, the length() function returns **3**.

Note: Additional

Extracting the Specific Columns from a Data Frame

Example

```
# Creating the data frame.
emp.data<- data.frame(
employee_id = c (1:5),
employee_name= c("Shubham","Arpita","Nishka","Gunjan","Sumit"),
sal = c(623.3,515.2,611.0,729.0,843.25),

starting_date = as.Date(c("2012-01-01", "2013-09-23", "2014-11-15", "2014-05-11",
    "2015-03-27")),
stringsAsFactors = FALSE
)
# Extracting specific columns from a data frame
final <- data.frame(emp.data$employee_id,emp.data$sal)
print(final)
```

Output

```
emp.data.employee_idemp.data.sal
1                    1   623.30
2                    2   515.20
3                    3   611.00
4                    4   729.00
5                    5   843.25
```

Extracting the Specific Rows from a Data Frame

Example

```
# Creating the data frame.
emp.data<- data.frame(
employee_id = c (1:5),
employee_name = c("Shubham","Arpita","Nishka","Gunjan","Sumit"),
sal = c(623.3,515.2,611.0,729.0,843.25),

starting_date = as.Date(c("2012-01-01", "2013-09-23", "2014-11-15", "2014-05-11",
    "2015-03-27")),
stringsAsFactors = FALSE
)
# Extracting first row from a data frame
final <- emp.data[1,]
print(final)
# Extracting last two row from a data frame
final <- emp.data[4:5,]
print(final)
```

Output

```
employee_idemployee_namesalstarting_date
1    1    Shubham    623.3    2012-01-01


employee_idemployee_namesalstarting_date
4    4    Gunjan    729.00    2014-05-11
5    5    Sumit     843.25    2015-03-27
```

Extracting Specific Rows Corresponding to Specific Columns

Example

```
# Creating the data frame.
emp.data<- data.frame(
employee_id = c (1:5),
employee_name = c("Shubham","Arpita","Nishka","Gunjan","Sumit"),
sal = c(623.3,515.2,611.0,729.0,843.25),

starting_date = as.Date(c("2012-01-01", "2013-09-23", "2014-11-15", "2014-05-11",
    "2015-03-27")),
stringsAsFactors = FALSE
)
# Extracting 2nd and 3rd row corresponding to the 1st and 4th column
final <- emp.data[c(2,3),c(1,4)]
print(final)
```

Output

```
employee_idstarting_date
2    2      2013-09-23
3    3      2014-11-15
```

6.13. Modification in Data Frame

- R allows us to do modification in our data frame. Like matrices modification, we can modify our data frame through re-assignment. We cannot only add rows and columns, but also we can delete them. The data frame is expanded by adding rows and columns.

We can,

1. Add a column by adding a column vector with the help of a new column name using cbind() function.
2. Add rows by adding new rows in the same structure as the existing data frame and using rbind() function
3. Delete the columns by assigning a NULL value to them.
4. Delete the rows by re-assignment to them.

Let's see an example to understand how rbind() function works and how the modification is done in our data frame.

Example: Adding Rows and Columns

```
# Creating the data frame.
emp.data<- data.frame(
employee_id = c (1:5),
employee_name = c("Shubham","Arpita","Nishka","Gunjan","Sumit"),
sal = c(623.3,515.2,611.0,729.0,843.25),

starting_date = as.Date(c("2012-01-01", "2013-09-23", "2014-11-15", "2014-05-11",
    "2015-03-27")),
stringsAsFactors = FALSE
)
print(emp.data)

#Adding row in the data frame
x <- list(6,"Vaishali",547,"2015-09-01")
rbind(emp.data,x)

#Adding column in the data frame
y <- c("Moradabad","Lucknow","Etah","Sambhal","Khurja")
cbind(emp.data,Address=y)
```

Output

```
employee_idemployee_namesalstarting_date
1   1        Shubham   623.30      2012-01-01
2   2        Arpita    515.20      2013-09-23
3   3        Nishka    611.00      2014-11-15
4   4        Gunjan    729.00      2014-05-11
5   5        Sumit     843.25      2015-03-27
employee_idemployee_namesalstarting_date
1   1        Shubham   623.30      2012-01-01
2   2        Arpita    515.20      2013-09-23
3   3        Nishka    611.00      2014-11-15
4   4        Gunjan    729.00      2014-05-11
5   5        Sumit     843.25      2015-03-27
6   6        Vaishali  547.00      2015-09-01
employee_idemployee_namesalstarting_date     Address
1   1        Shubham   623.30      2012-01-01     Moradabad
2   2        Arpita    515.20      2013-09-23     Lucknow
3   3        Nishka    611.00      2014-11-15     Etah
4   4        Gunjan    729.00      2014-05-11     Sambhal
5   5        Sumit     843.25      2015-03-27     Khurja
```

Example: Delete Rows and Columns

```
# Creating the data frame.
emp.data<- data.frame(
employee_id = c (1:5),
employee_name = c("Shubham","Arpita","Nishka","Gunjan","Sumit"),
sal = c(623.3,515.2,611.0,729.0,843.25),

starting_date = as.Date(c("2012-01-01", "2013-09-23", "2014-11-15", "2014-05-11",
    "2015-03-27")),
stringsAsFactors = FALSE
)
print(emp.data)

#Delete rows from data frame
emp.data<-emp.data[-1,]
print(emp.data)

#Delete column from the data frame
emp.data$starting_date<-NULL
print(emp.data)
```

Output

```
employee_idemployee_namesalstarting_date
1     1     Shubham623.30  2012-01-01
2     2     Arpita515.20     2013-09-23
3     3     Nishka611.00     2014-11-15
4     4     Gunjan729.00     2014-05-11
5     5     Sumit843.25      2015-03-27
employee_idemployee_namesalstarting_date
2     2     Arpita515.20     2013-09-23
3     3     Nishka611.00     2014-11-15
4     4     Gunjan729.00     2014-05-11
5     5     Sumit843.25      2015-03-27
employee_idemployee_namesal
1     1     Shubham623.30
2     2     Arpita515.20
3     3     Nishka611.00
4     4     Gunjan729.00
5     5     Sumit843.25
```

6.14. Sorting Data Frames

- To sort a data frame in R, the following methods are available. But use the **order ()** function. By default, sorting is ASCENDING.

Methods to Sort a Data Frame

1. **order()** function (increasing and decreasing order)
2. **arrange()** function from dplyr package
3. **setorder()** function from data.table package

Method 1: Using Order() Function

- This function is used to sort the data frame based on the particular column in the data frame
- ***Syntax:*** *order (dataframe$column_name, decreasing = TRUE))*

Where

- Data frame is the input data frame.
- Column name is the column in the data frame such that data frame is sorted based on this column.
- Decreasing parameter specifies the type of sorting order.

If it is TRUE data frame is sorted in descending order. Otherwise, in increasing order.

return type: *Index positions of the elements.*

Example 1: R program to create data frame with 2 columns and order based on particular columns in decreasing order. Display the Sorted data frame based on subjects in decreasing order, display the Sorted data frame based on roll no in decreasing order.

Coding

- # create dataframe with roll no and
- # subjects columns
- data = data.frame(

  rollno = c(1, 5, 4, 2, 3),
- subjects = c("java", "python", "php", "sql", "c")
- print(data)
- print("sort the data in decreasing order based on subjects ")
- print(data[order(data$subjects, decreasing = TRUE),])
- print("sort the data in decreasing order based on rollno ")
- print(data[order(data$rollno, decreasing = TRUE),])

Output

```
roll no  subjects
1  1     java
2  5     python
3  4     php
4  2     sql
5  3     c
[1] "sort the data in decreasing order based on subjects"
roll no  subjects
4  2     sql
2  5     python
3  4     php
1  1     java
5  3     c
```

[1] "sort the data in decreasing order based on rollno"

```
rollno subjects
2   5  python
3   4  php
5   3  c
4   2  sql
1   1  java
```

Example 2: R program to create dataframe with 3 columns named rollno, names, and subjects with a vector, display the Sorted dataframe based on subjects in increasing order, display the Sorted dataframe based on rollno in increasing order, display the Sorted dataframe based on names in increasing order.

Coding

- # create dataframe with roll no, names
- # and subjects columns
- data=data.frame(rollno = c(1, 5, 4, 2, 3),

```
names = c("sravan", "bobby","pinkey", "rohith",
          "gnanesh"),
     subjects = c("java", "python",
                  "php", "sql", "c"))
```

- print(data)
- print("sort the data in increasing order based on subjects")
- print(data[order(data$subjects, decreasing = FALSE),])
- print("sort the data in increasing order based on rollno")
- print(data[order(data$rollno, decreasing = FALSE),])
- print("sort the data in increasing order based on names")
- print(data[order(data$names,decreasing = FALSE),])

Output

```
roll no names   subjects
1   1   sravan  java
2   5   bobby   python
3   4   pinkey  php
4   2   rohith  sql
5   3   gnanesh c
```

[1] **"sort the data in increasing order based on subjects"**

roll	no	names	subjects
5	3	gnanesh	c
1	1	sravan	java
3	4	pinkey	php
2	5	bobby	python
4	2	rohith	sql

[1] **"sort the data in increasing order based on rollno"**

roll	no	names	subjects
1	1	sravan	java
4	2	rohith	sql
5	3	gnanesh	c
3	4	pinkey	php
2	5	bobby	python

[1] **"sort the data in increasing order based on names"**

roll	no	names	subjects
2	5	bobby	python
5	3	gnanesh	c
3	4	pinkey	php
4	2	rohith	sql
1	1	sravan	java

Method 2: Using Arrange() Function from dplyr

Arrange() is used to sort the dataframe in increasing order, it will also sort the dataframe based on the column in the dataframe.

Syntax: arrange(dataframe,column)

Where

- dataframe is the dataframe input.
- column is the column name , based on this column dataframe is sorted.

We need to install dplyr package as it is available in that package.

Syntax: *install.packages("dplyr")*

Example: R program to sort dataframe based on columns.

In this program, we created three columns using the vector and sorted the dataframe based on the subject's column.

Code

- # load the package
- library("dplyr")
- # create dataframe with roll no, names
- # and subjects columns
- data = data.frame(rollno = c(1, 5, 4, 2, 3),
    - names = c("sravan", "bobby", "pinkey",
        - "rohith", "gnanesh"),
    - subjects = c("java", "python", "php",

      "sql", "c"))
- # sort the data based on subjects
- print(arrange(data, subjects))

Output

roll	no	names	subjects
1	3	gnanesh	c
2	1	sravan	java
3	4	pinkey	php
4	5	bobby	python
5	2	rohith	sql

Method 3: Using Setorder() from Data.table Package

- **setorder** is used to sort a dataframe in the set order format.

  Syntax: *setorder(dataframe, column)*
- Where dataframe is the input dataframe
- The column is the column name

Example: R program to sort dataframe based on columns.

In this program, we created the dataframe with three columns using vector and sorted the dataframe using setorder function based on subjects column.

Code

- # load the library
- library("data.table")
- # create dataframe with roll no, names
- # and subjects columns
- data=data.frame(rollno = c(1, 5, 4, 2, 3),
  names = c("sravan", "bobby", "pinkey", "rohith", "gnanesh"),
  subjects = c("java", "python","php", "sql", "c"))
- # sort the data based on subjects
- print(setorder(data,subjects))

Output

roll	no	names	subjects
5	3	gnanesh	c
1	1	sravan	java
3	4	pinkey	php
2	5	bobby	python
4	2	rohith	sql

6.15. Lists

- A list in R can contain many different data types inside it. A list is a collection of data which is ordered and changeable.
- A list is a vector but with heterogeneous data elements. A list in R is created with the use of **list()** function. R allows accessing elements of a list with the use of the index value. In R, the indexing of a list starts with 1 instead of 0 like other programming languages.
- In R, lists are the second type of vector. Lists are the objects of R which contain elements of different types such as number, vectors, string and another list inside it. It can also contain a function or a matrix as its elements.
- A list is a data structure which has components of mixed data types. We can say, a list is a generic vector which contains other objects.

Creating a List

- To create a List in R you need to use the function called "list()". In other words, a list is a generic vector containing other objects.
- We want to build a list of employees with the details. So for this, we want attributes such as ID, employee name, and the number of employees.

Example

```
vec<- c(3,4,5,6)
char_vec<-c("shubham","nishka","gunjan","sumit")
logic_vec<-c(TRUE, FALSE,FALSE,TRUE)
out_list<-list(vec,char_vec,logic_vec)
out_list
```

Output

```
[[1]]
[1] 3 4 5 6

[[2]]
[1] "shubham" "nishka"  "gunjan"  "sumit"

[[3]]
[1] TRUE FALSE FALSE TRUE
```

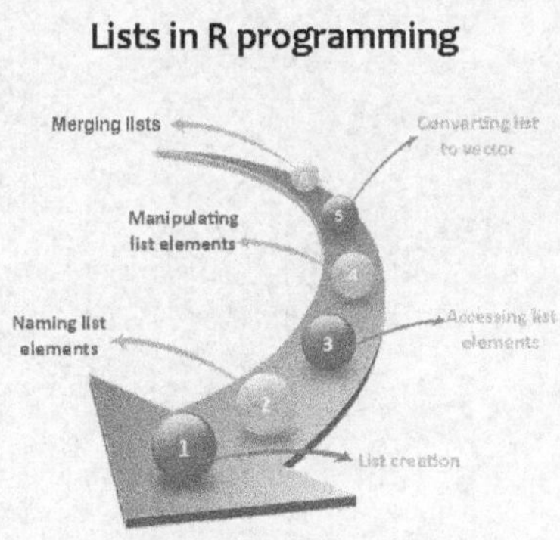

Figure 26: Basics of Lists in R

6.16. Lists Creation

- The process of creating a list is the same as a vector. In R, the vector is created with the help of c() function. Like c() function, there is another function, i.e., list() which is used to create a list in R.
- A list avoids the drawback of the vector which is data type. We can add the elements in the list of different data types.

Syntax

1. ***list()***

Example 1: Creating list with same data type

```
list_1<-list(1,2,3)
list_2<-list("Shubham","Arpita","Vaishali")
list_3<-list(c(1,2,3))
list_4<-list(TRUE,FALSE,TRUE)
list_1
list_2
list_3
list_4
```

Output

```
[[1]]
[1] 1
[[2]]
[1] 2
[[3]]
[1] 3

[[1]]
[1] "Shubham"
[[2]]
[1] "Arpita"
[[3]]
[1] "Vaishali"

[[1]]
[1] 1 2 3

[[1]]
[1] TRUE
[[2]]
[1] FALSE
[[3]]
[1] TRUE
```

Example 2: Creating the list with different data type

```
list_data<-list("Shubham","Arpita",c(1,2,3,4,5),TRUE,FALSE,22.5,12L)
print(list_data)
```

In the above example, the list function will create a list with character, logical, numeric, and vector element. It will give the following output.

Output

```
[[1]]
[1] "Shubham"
[[2]]
[1] "Arpita"
[[3]]
[1] 1 2 3 4 5
[[4]]
[1] TRUE
[[5]]
[1] FALSE
[[6]]
[1] 22.5
[[7]]
[1] 12
```

6.17. Giving a Name to List Elements

- R provides a very easy way for accessing elements, i.e., by giving the name to each element of a list. By assigning names to the elements, we can access the element easily. There are only three steps to print the list data corresponding to the name:
    - Creating a list.
    - Assign a name to the list elements with the help of names() function.
    - Print the list data.

Example

```
# Creating a list containing a vector, a matrix and a list.
list_data <- list(c("Shubham","Nishka","Gunjan"), matrix(c(40,80,60,70,90,80), nrow = 2),
 list("BCA","MCA","B.tech"))
 # Giving names to the elements in the list.
names(list_data) <- c("Students", "Marks", "Course")
 # Show the list.
print(list_data)
```

Output

```
$Students
[1] "Shubham" "Nishka"  "Gunjan"

$Marks
     [,1] [,2] [,3]
[1,]  40   60   90
[2,]  80   70   80

$Course
$Course[[1]]
[1] "BCA"

$Course[[2]]
[1] "MCA"

$Course[[3]]
[1] "B. tech."
```

Accessing List Elements

- R provides two ways through which we can access the elements of a list.
- First one is the indexing method performed in the same way as a vector.
- In the second one, we can access the elements of a list with the help of names.
- It will be possible only with the named list.
- we cannot access the elements of a list using names if the list is normal.

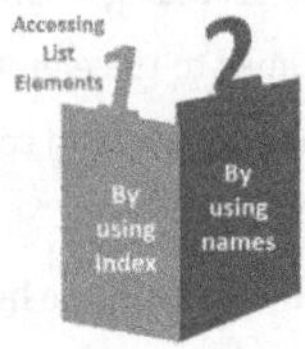

Figure 27: Shows Accessing List Elements

Example 1: Accessing elements using index

```
# Creating a list containing a vector, a matrix and a list
list_data <- list(c("Shubham","Arpita","Nishka"), matrix(c(40,80,60,70,90,80), nrow = 2),
list("BCA","MCA","B.tech"))
 # Accessing the first element of the list.
print(list_data[1])
# Accessing the third element. The third element is also a list, so all its elements will be prin
ted.
print(list_data[3])
```

```
[1]]

[1] "Shubham" "Arpita"  "Nishka"


[[1]]

[[1]][[1]]

[1] "BCA"


[[1]][[2]]

[1] "MCA"


[[1]][[3]]

[1] "B.tech"
```

Example 2: Accessing elements using names

```
# Creating a list containing a vector, a matrix and a list

list_data <-

list(c("Shubham","Arpita","Nishka"), matrix(c(40,80,60,70,90,80), nrow = 2),list("BCA","MCA","B.tech"))

    # Giving names to the elements in the list.

names(list_data) <- c("Student", "Marks", "Course")

    # Accessing the first element of the list.

print(list_data["Student"])

print(list_data$Marks)

print(list_data)
```

Output

```
$Student
[1] "Shubham" "Arpita"  "Nishka"


     [,1] [,2] [,3]
[1,]  40   60   90
[2,]  80   70   80

$Student
[1] "Shubham" "Arpita"  "Nishka"


$Marks
    [,1] [,2] [,3]
[1,] 40   60   90
[2,] 80   70   80


$Course
$Course[[1]]
[1] "BCA"
$Course[[2]]
[1] "MCA"
$Course[[3]]
[1] "B. tech."
```

6.18. Manipulation of List Elements

- R allows us to add, delete, or update elements in the list.
- We can update an element of a list from anywhere, but elements can add or delete only at the end of the list.
- To remove an element from a specified index, we will assign it a null value. We can update the element of a list by overriding it from the new value. Example to understand how we can add, delete, or update the elements in the list.

Example

```
# Creating a list containing a vector, a matrix and a list
list_data <-
list(c("Shubham","Arpita","Nishka"), matrix(c(40,80,60,70,90,80), nrow = 2),
list("BCA","MCA","B.tech"))

# Giving names to the elements in the list.
names(list_data) <- c("Student", "Marks", "Course")
# Adding element at the end of the list.
list_data[4] <- "Moradabad"
print(list_data[4])
# Removing the last element.
list_data[4] <- NULL
# Printing the 4th Element.
print(list_data[4])
# Updating the 3rd Element.
list_data[3] <- "Masters of computer applications"
print(list_data[3])
```

Output

```
[[1]]
[1] "Moradabad"


$<NA>
NULL


$Course
[1] "Masters of computer applications"
```

6.19. Converting List to Vector

- There is a drawback with the list, i.e., we cannot perform all the arithmetic operations on list elements.
- To remove this, drawback R provides unlist() function.
- This function converts the list into vectors. In some cases, it is required to convert a list into a vector so that we can use the elements of the vector for further manipulation.
- The unlist() function takes the list as a parameter and change into a vector.

Example

```
# Creating lists.
list1 <- list(10:20)
print(list1)
 list2 <-list(5:14)
print(list2)
 # Converting the lists to vectors.
v1 <- unlist(list1)
v2 <- unlist(list2)
 print(v1)
print(v2)
 adding the vectors
result <- v1+v2
print(result)
```

Output

```
[[1]]
[1] 1 2 3 4 5

[[1]]
[1] 10 11 12 13 14

[1] 1 2 3 4 5
[1] 10 11 12 13 14
[1] 11 13 15 17 19
```

6.20. Merging Lists

- R allows us to merge one or more lists into one list. Merging is done with the help of the list() function also.
- To merge the lists, we have to pass all the lists into list function as a parameter, and it returns a list which contains all the elements which are present in the lists.

Example

```
# Creating two lists.
Even_list <- list(2,4,6,8,10)
Odd_list <- list(1,3,5,7,9)
  # Merging the two lists.
merged.list <- list(Even_list,Odd_list)
   # Printing the merged list.
print(merged.list)
```

Output

```
[[1]][[1]]
[[1]][[1]]
[1] 2

[[1]][[2]]
[1] 4

[[1]][[3]]
[1] 6

[[1]][[4]]
[1] 8

[[1]][[5]]
[1] 10

[[2]]
[[2]][[1]]
[1] 1

[[2]][[2]]
[1] 3

[[2]][[3]]
[1] 5

[[2]][[4]]
[1] 7

[[2]][[5]]
[1] 9
```

Note

The only difference between vectors, matrices, and arrays are:

- Vectors are uni-dimensional arrays.
- Matrices are two-dimensional arrays.
- Arrays can have more than two dimensions.

6.21. R Arrays

- In R, arrays are the data objects which allow us to store data in more than two dimensions. In R, an array is created with the help of the **array()** function. This array() function takes a vector as an input and to create an array it uses vectors values in the **dim** parameter.
- **For example** - if we will create an array of dimension (2, 3, 4) then it will create 4 rectangular matrices of 2 row and 3 columns.

R Array Syntax

There is the following syntax of R arrays:

```
1. array_name <-
   array(data, dim= (row_size, column_size, matrices, dim_names))
```

- **data**

The data is the first argument in the array() function. It is an input vector which is given to the array.

- **matrices**

In R, the array consists of multi-dimensional matrices.

- **row_size**

This parameter defines the number of row elements which an array can store.

- **column_size**

This parameter defines the number of columns elements which an array can store.

- **dim_names**

This parameter is used to change the default names of rows and columns.

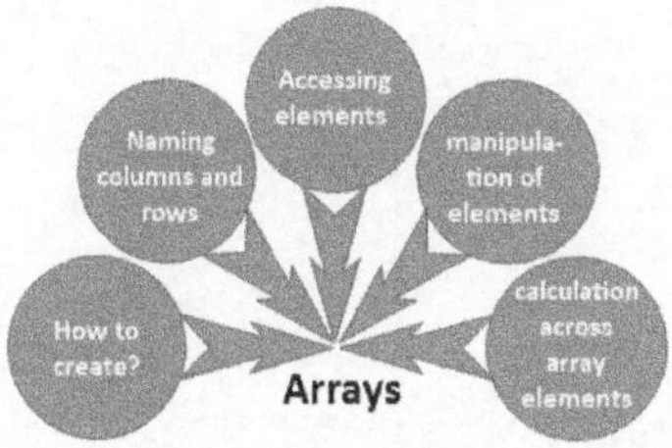

Figure 28: Shows Concept of Array in R

TYPES

Uni-Dimensional Array

- A vector is a uni-dimensional array, which is specified by a single dimension, length. A Vector can be created using '**c()**' function. A list of values is passed to the c() function to create a vector.

Example

```
vec1 <- c(1, 2, 3, 4, 5, 6, 7, 8, 9)
print (vec1)
  # cat is used to concatenate
  # strings and print it.
  cat ("Length of vector : ", length(vec1))
```

Output

```
[1] 1 2 3 4 5 6 7 8 9
Length of vector :  9
```

Multi-Dimensional Array

- A two-dimensional matrix is an array specified by a fixed number of rows and columns, each containing the same data type. A matrix is created by using **array()** function to which the values and the dimensions are passed.

Example 1

```
# arranges data from 2 to 13
# in two matrices of dimensions 2x3
arr = array(2:13, dim = c(2, 3, 2))
print(arr)
```

Output

```
, , 1

     [,1] [,2] [,3]
[1,] 2    4    6
[2,] 3    5    7

, , 2

     [,1] [,2] [,3]
[1,] 8    10   12
[2,] 9    11   13
```

6.22. Creation of Arrays

- In R, array creation is quite simple. We can easily create an array using vector and array() function. In array, data is stored in the form of the matrix. There are only two steps to create a matrix which are as follows.

1. In the first step, we will create two vectors of different lengths.
2. Once our vectors are created, we take these vectors as inputs to the array.

Example

```
#Creating two vectors of different lengths
vec1 <-c(1,3,5)
vec2 <-c(10,11,12,13,14,15)
 #Taking these vectors as input to the array
res <- array(c(vec1,vec2))
res[1]
print(res)
```

Output

```
[1] 1
[1] 1 3 5 10 11 12 13 14 15
```

Naming Rows and Columns

- In R, we can give the names to the rows, columns, and matrices of the array. This is done with the help of the dim name parameter of the array() function.
- It is not necessary to give the name to the rows and columns. It is only used to differentiate the row and column for better understanding.

Example 1

```
#Creating two vectors of different lengths
vec1 <-c(1,3,5)
vec2 <-c(10,11,12,13,14,15)
#Initializing names for rows, columns and matrices
col_names <- c("Col1","Col2","Col3")
row_names <- c("Row1","Row2","Row3")
matrix_names <- c("Matrix1","Matrix2")
#Taking the vectors as input to the array
Res<-
array(c(vec1,vec2),dim=c(3,3,2),dimnames=list(row_names,col_names,matrix_names))
print(res)
```

Output

```
, , Matrix1

     Col1 Col2 Col3
Row1 1    10   13
Row2 3    11   14
Row3 5    12   15

, , Matrix2

     Col1 Col2 Col3
Row1 1    10   13
Row2 3    11   14
Row3 5    12   15
```

Accessing Arrays

- The arrays can be accessed by using indices for different dimensions separated by commas. Different components can be specified by any combination of elements' names or positions.

Accessing Uni-Dimensional Array

The elements can be accessed by using indexes of the corresponding elements.

Example 1

```
vec <- c(1:10)
 # accessing entire vector
cat ("Vector is : ", vec)
 # accessing elements
cat ("Third element of vector is : ", vec[3])
```

Output

```
Vector is :  1 2 3 4 5 6 7 8 9 10 Third element of vector is :  3
```

Access Entire Row or Column

Example 1

```
# create a two 2 by 3 matrix
array1 <- array(c(1:12), dim = c(2,3,2))

print(array1)

# access entire elements at 2nd column of 1st matrix
cat("\n2nd Column Elements of 1st matrix:", array1[,c(2),1])

# access entire elements at 1st row of 2nd matrix
cat("\n1st Row Elements of 2nd Matrix:", array1[c(1), ,2])
```

Output

```
, , 1

     [,1] [,2] [,3]
[1,]    1    3    5
[2,]    2    4    6

, , 2

     [,1] [,2] [,3]
[1,]    7    9   11
[2,]    8   10   12

2nd Column Elements of 1st matrix: 3 4
1st Row Elements of 2nd Matrix: 7 9 11
```

6.23. Manipulating Array Elements

- As array is made up matrices in multiple dimensions, the operations on elements of array are carried out by accessing elements of the matrices.

Example 1

```
# Create two vectors of different lengths.

vector1 <- c(5,9,3)

vector2 <- c(10,11,12,13,14,15)

# Take these vectors as input to the array.

array1 <- array(c(vector1,vector2),dim = c(3,3,2))

array1

# Create two vectors of different lengths.

vector3 <- c(9,1,0)

vector4 <- c(6,0,11,3,14,1,2,6,9)

array2 <- array(c(vector1,vector2),dim = c(3,3,2))

array2

# create matrices from these arrays.

matrix1 <- array1[,,2]

matrix2 <- array2[,,2]

# Add the matrices.

result <- matrix1+matrix2

print(result)
```

Output

```
, , 1

     [,1] [,2] [,3]
[1,]    5   10   13
[2,]    9   11   14
[3,]    3   12   15

, , 2

     [,1] [,2] [,3]
[1,]    5   10   13
[2,]    9   11   14
[3,]    3   12   15

, , 1

     [,1] [,2] [,3]
[1,]    5   10   13
[2,]    9   11   14
[3,]    3   12   15

, , 2

     [,1] [,2] [,3]
[1,]    5   10   13
[2,]    9   11   14
[3,]    3   12   15

     [,1] [,2] [,3]
[1,]   10   20   26
[2,]   18   22   28
[3,]    6   24   30
```

Calculations Across Array Elements

- For calculation purpose, r provides **apply()** function. This apply function contains three parameters i.e., x, margin, and function.
- This function takes the array on which we have to perform the calculations.

Using Apply() Function

- 'apply()' is one of the R packages which have several functions that helps to write code in an easier and efficient way. You'll see the example below where it can be used to calculate the sum of two different arrays.

The syntax for apply() is : apply(x, margin, function)

The argument above indicates that: x: An array or two-dimensional data as matrices. margin: Indicates a function to be applied as margin value to be c(1) for rows, c(2) for columns, and c(1,2) for both rows and columns. function: Indicates the R- built-in or user-defined function to be applied over the given data.

Example 1

```
#Creating two vectors of different lengths
vec1 <-c(1,3,5)
vec2 <-c(10,11,12,13,14,15)

#Taking the vectors as input to the array1
res1 <- array(c(vec1,vec2),dim=c(3,3,2))
print(res1)

#using apply function
result <- apply(res1,c(1),sum)
print(result)
```

Output

```
, , 1

      [,1] [,2] [,3]
[1,]   1   10   13
[2,]   3   11   14
[3,]   5   12   15

, , 2

      [,1] [,2] [,3]
[1,]  1   10   13
[2,]  3   11   14
[3,]  5   12   15

[1] 48 56 64
```

Output

```
, , 1

      [,1]  [,2]  [,3]
[1,]  1     10    13
[2,]  3     11    14
[3,]  5     12    15

, , 2

      [,1]  [,2]  [,3]
[1,]  1     10   13
[2,]  3     11   14
[3,]  5     12   15

[1]   18   66   84
```

Example 2

```
#Creating two vectors of different lengths
vec1 <-c(1,3,5)
vec2 <-c(10,11,12,13,14,15)

#Taking the vectors as input to the array1
res1 <- array(c(vec1,vec2),dim=c(3,3,2))
print(res1)
#using apply function
result <- apply(res1,c(1,2),sum)
print(result)
```

Output

```
, , 1

     [,1] [,2] [,3]
[1,]  1   10   13
[2,]  3   11   14
[3,]  5   12   15

, , 2

     [,1] [,2] [,3]
[1,]  1   10   13
[2,]  3   11   14
[3,]  5   12   15

     [,1] [,2] [,3]
[1,]  2   20   26
[2,]  6   22   28
[3,]  10  24   30
```

Important Questions

1) Vectors
2) Factors
3) Data Frames
4) Lists
5) Arrays
6) Matrices
7) CLASS

The may ask any subpart of the above concepts for short questions/ big questions.

UNIT - 4

CHAPTER 7

7.1. Operator

- In **computer programming**, an operator is a symbol which represents an action. An operator is a symbol which tells the compiler to perform specific **logical** or **mathematical** manipulations. R programming is very rich in built-in operators.
- In **R programming**, there are different types of operator, and each operator performs a different task. For data manipulation, There are some advance operators also such as model formula and list indexing.

There are the Following Types of Operators Used in R

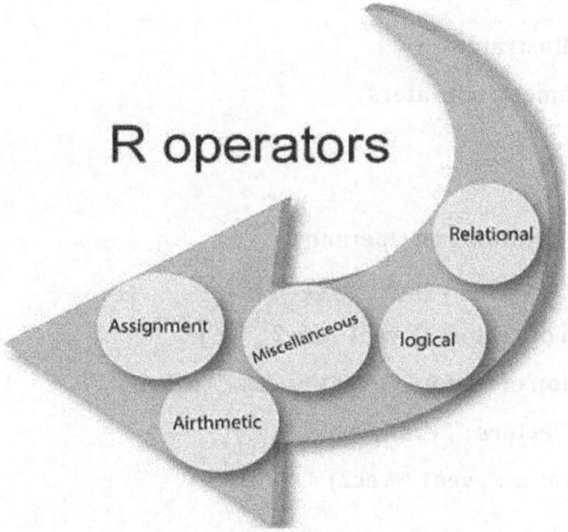

Figure 29: Shows Types of Operators Used in R

1. Arithmetic Operators
2. Relational Operators
3. Logical Operators
4. Assignment Operators
5. Miscellaneous Operators

R Arithmetic Operators

These operators are used to carry out mathematical operations like addition and multiplication. Here is a list of arithmetic operators available in R.

Arithmetic Operators in R	
Operator	Description
+	Addition
–	Subtraction
*	Multiplication
/	Division
^	Exponent
%%	Modulus (Remainder from division)
%/%	Integer Division

Note: cat converts its arguments to character strings, concatenates them, separating them by the given sep= string, and then prints them.

```
# R program to illustrate
# the use of Arithmetic operators
vec1 <- c(0, 2)
vec2 <- c(2, 3)
  # Performing operations on Operands
cat ("Addition of vectors :", vec1 + vec2, "\n")
cat ("Subtraction of vectors :", vec1 - vec2, "\n")
cat ("Multiplication of vectors :", vec1 * vec2, "\n")
cat ("Division of vectors :", vec1 / vec2, "\n")
cat ("Power operator :", vec1 ^ vec2)
```

Output

```
Addition of vectors: 2 5
Subtraction of vectors: -2 -1
Multiplication of vectors: 0 6
Division of vectors: 0 0.6666667
Power operator: 0 8
```

7.2. Logical Operators

- Logical operations simulate element-wise decision operations, based on the specified operator between the operands, which are then evaluated to either a True or False boolean value.

- Any non-zero integer value is considered as a TRUE value, be it a complex or real number.

Element-wise Logical AND Operator (&)

Returns True if both the operands are True.

```
Input : list1 <- c(TRUE, 0.1)
        list2 <- c(0,4+3i)
        print(list1 & list2)
Output : FALSE  TRUE
```

Any non zero integer value is considered as a TRUE value, be it complex or real number.

Element-wise Logical OR Operator (|)

Returns True if either of the operands is True.

```
Input : list1 <- c(TRUE, 0.1)
        list2 <- c(0,4+3i)
        print(list1|list2)
Output : TRUE  TRUE
```

NOT Operator (!)

A unary operator that negates the status of the elements of the operand.

```
Input : list1 <- c(0,FALSE)
        print(!list1)
Output : TRUE  TRUE
```

Logical AND Operator (&&)

Returns True if both the first elements of the operands are True.

```
Input : list1 <- c(TRUE, 0.1)
        list2 <- c(0,4+3i)
        print(list1 && list2)
Output : FALSE
```

Compares just the first elements of both the lists.

Logical OR Operator (||)

Returns True if either of the first elements of the operands is True.

Input : list1 <- c(TRUE, 0.1)

list2 <- c(0,4+3i)

print(list1||list2)

Output : TRUE

7.3. Relational Operators

R Relational Operators

- Relational operators are used to compare between values. Here is a list of relational operators available in R.

Relational Operators in R	
Operator	Description
<	Less than
>	Greater than
<=	Less than or equal to
>=	Greater than or equal to
==	Equal to
!=	Not equal to

Example

```
> x <- 5
> y <- 16
> x<y
[1] TRUE
> x>y
[1] FALSE
> x<=5
[1] TRUE
> y>=20
[1] FALSE
> y == 16
[1] TRUE
> x != 5
[1] FALSE
```

7.4. Operation on Vectors

- The above mentioned operators work on vectors. The variables used above were in fact single element vectors.
- We can use the function c() (as in concatenate) to make vectors in R.

All operations are carried out in element-wise fashion. Here is an example.

```
> x <- c(2,8,3)
> y <- c(6,4,1)
> x+y
[1] 8 12 4
> x>y
[1] FALSE TRUE TRUE
```

- When there is a mismatch in length (number of elements) of operand vectors, the elements in shorter one is recycled in a cyclic manner to match the length of the longer one.
- R will issue a warning if the length of the longer vector is not an integral multiple of the shorter vector.

```
> x <- c(2,1,8,3)
> y <- c(9,4)
> x+y # Element of y is recycled to 9,4,9,4
[1] 11 5 17 7
> x-1 # Scalar 1 is recycled to 1,1,1,1
[1] 1 0 7 2
> x+c(1,2,3)
[1] 3 3 11 4
Warning message:
In x + c(1, 2, 3) :
longer object length is not a multiple of shorter object length
```

7.5. R Logical Operators

- Logical operators are used to carry out Boolean operations like AND, OR etc.

Logical Operators in R	
Operator	Description
!	Logical NOT
&	Element-wise logical AND
&&	Logical AND
|	Element-wise logical OR
||	Logical OR

Operators & and | perform element-wise operation producing result having length of the longer operand.

But && and || examines only the first element of the operands resulting into a single length logical vector.

Zero is considered FALSE and non-zero numbers are taken as TRUE.

```
> x <- c(TRUE,FALSE,0,6)
> y <- c(FALSE,TRUE,FALSE,TRUE)
> !x
[1] FALSE  TRUE  TRUE FALSE
> x&y
[1] FALSE FALSE FALSE  TRUE
> x&&y
[1] FALSE
> x|y
[1]  TRUE  TRUE FALSE  TRUE
> x||y
[1] TRUE
```

7.6. R Assignment Operators

- These operators are used to assign values to variables.

Assignment Operators in R	
Operator	Description
<-, <<-, =	Leftwards assignment
->, ->>	Rightwards assignment

- The operators <- and = can be used, almost interchangeably, to assign to variable in the same environment.
- The <<- operator is used for assigning to variables in the parent environments (more like global assignments). The rightward assignments, although available are rarely used.

```
> x <- 5
> x
[1] 5
> x = 9
> x
[1] 9
> 10 -> x
> x
[1] 10
```

7.7. Conditional Statements

- A conditional expression or a conditional statement is a programming construct where a decision is made to execute some code based on a boolean (true or false) condition.
- A more commonly used term for conditional expression in programming is an 'if-else' condition. In plain English, this is stated as 'if this test is true then do this operation; otherwise do this different operation'.

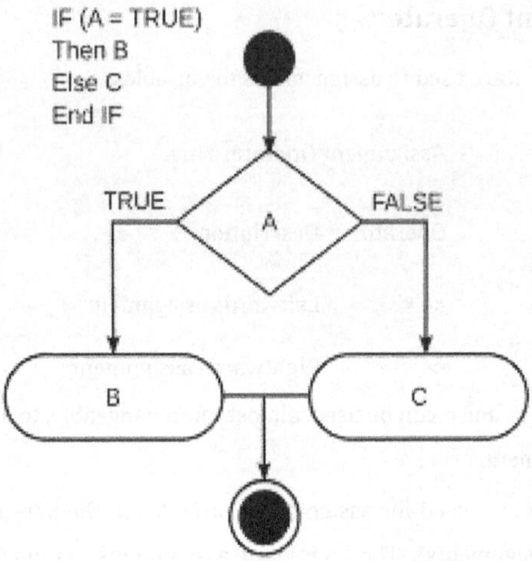

Figure 30: Shows Conditional Statements (if...statement) in R

1. if Statement

- The if statement consists of the Boolean expressions followed by one or more statements.
- The if statement is the simplest decision-making statement which helps us to take a decision on the basis of the condition.
- The if statement is a conditional programming statement which performs the function and displays the information if it is proved true.
- The block of code inside the if statement will be executed only when the boolean expression evaluates to be true.
- If the statement evaluates false, then the code which is mentioned after the condition will run.

The **syntax of if** statement in R is as follows:

```
1. if(boolean_expression) {
2.     // If the boolean expression is true, then statement(s) will be executed.
3. }
```

Flow Chart

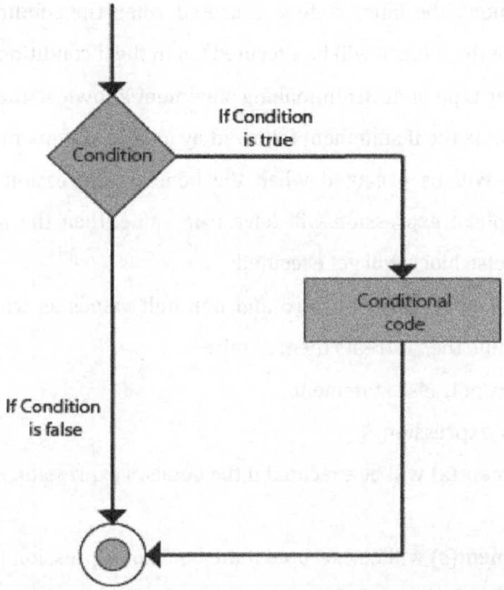

Example 1

```
x <-24L
if(is.integer(x))
{
    print("x is an Integer")
}
```

Output

```
[1] "x is an Integer"
```

Example 2

```
x <- 100
if(x > 10){
print(paste(x, "is greater than 10"))
}
```

Output

```
[1] "100 is greater than 10"
```

2. If-else Statement

- In the if statement, the inner code is executed when the condition is true. The code which is outside the if block will be executed when the if condition is false.
- There is another type of decision-making statement known as the if-else statement. An if-else statement is the if statement followed by an else statement. An if-else statement, else statement will be executed when the boolean expression will false. In simple words, If a Boolean expression will have true value, then the if block gets executed otherwise, the else block will get executed.
- R programming treats any non-zero and non-null values as true, and if the value is either zero or null, then it treats them as false.
- The basic syntax of If-else statement

```
if(boolean_expression) {
   // statement(s) will be executed if the boolean expression is true.
} else {
   // statement(s) will be executed if the boolean expression is false.
}
```

Flow Chart

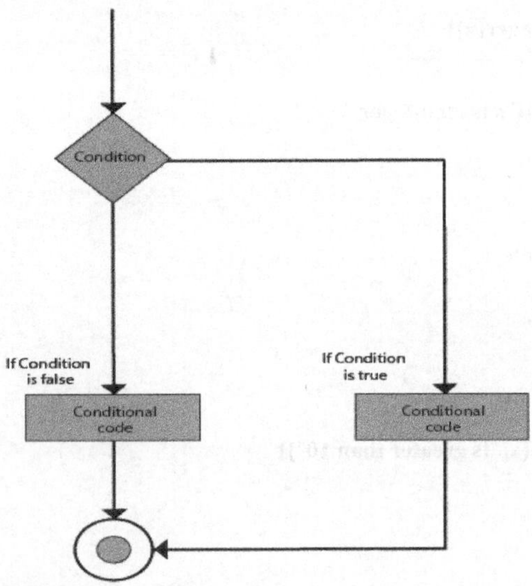

Figure 31: Shows Conditional Statements (if...Else statement) in R

NOTE: paste() will take multiple elements as inputs and concatenate those inputs into a single string. The elements will be separated by a space as the default option.

Example 1

```
if(x > 10){
  print(paste(x, "is greater than 10"))
}else{
  print(paste(x, "is less than 10"))
}
```

Output

```
[1] "5 is less than 10"
```

3. else if statement

- This statement is also known as nested if-else statement.
- The if statement is followed by an optional else if..... else statement.
- This statement is used to test various condition in a single if......else if statement.
- There are some key points which are necessary to keep in mind when we are using the if.....else if.....else statement. These points are as follows:
    1. **if** statement can have either zero or one **else** statement and it must come after any **else if's** statement.
    2. **if** statement can have many **else if's** statement and they come before the else statement.
    3. Once an **else if** statement succeeds, none of the remaining **else if's** or **else's** will be tested.

The basic syntax of If-else statement is as follows:

```
1. if(boolean_expression 1) {
2.   // This block executes when the boolean expression 1 is true.
3. } else if( boolean_expression 2) {
4.   // This block executes when the boolean expression 2 is true.
5. } else if( boolean_expression 3) {
6.   // This block executes when the boolean expression 3 is true.
7. } else {
8.   // This block executes when none of the above condition is true. }
```

Flow Chart

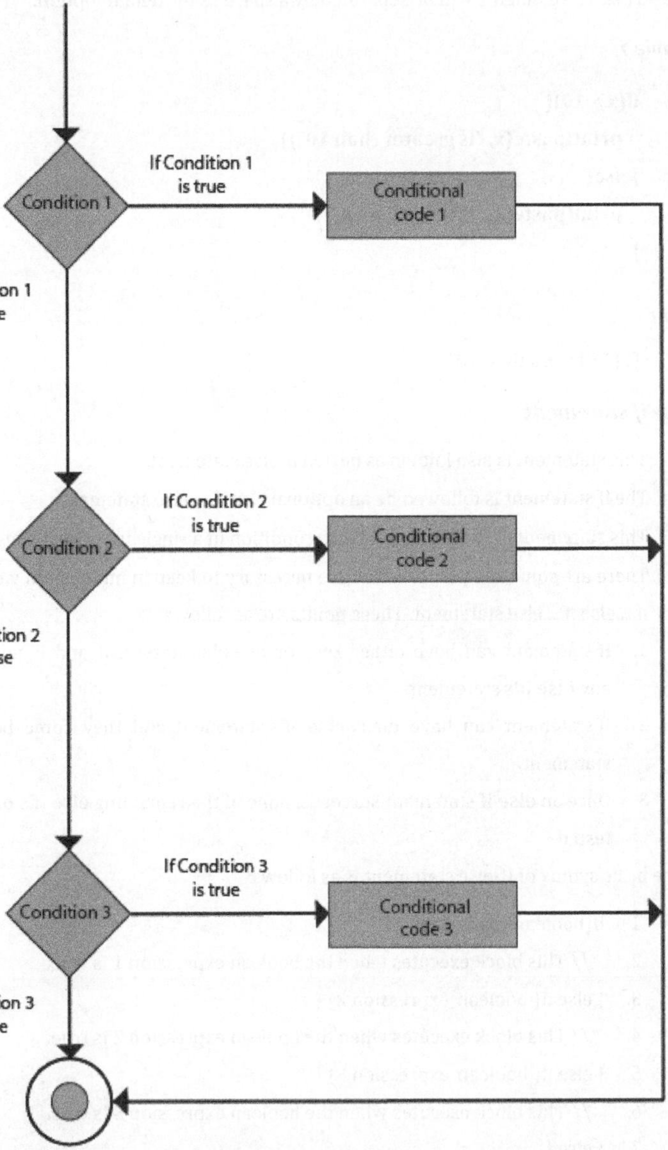

Figure 32: Shows Conditional Statements (Else if statement) in R

Example 1

```
marks<-83;
if(marks>75){
    print("First class")
}else if(marks>65){
    print("Second class")
}else if(marks>55){
    print("Third class")
}else{
    print("Fail")
}
```

Output

```
[1] "First class"
```

Example 2

```
quantity <-  10
# Create multiple condition statement
if (quantity <20) {
      print('Not enough for today')
} else if (quantity > 20  &quantity <= 30) {
     print('Average day')
} else {
      print('What a great day!')
}
```

Output

```
[1] "Not enough for today"
```

Example 3

VAT has different rate according to the product purchased. Imagine we have three different kind of products with different VAT applied:

Categories	Products	VAT
A	Book, magazine, newspaper, etc.	8%
B	Vegetable, meat, beverage, etc.	10%
C	Tee-shirt, jean, pant, etc.	20%

We can write a chain to apply the correct VAT rate to the product a customer bought.

```
category <- 'A'
price <- 10
if (category =='A'){
  cat('A vat rate of 8% is applied.','The total price is',price *1.08)
} else if (category =='B'){
    cat('B vat rate of 10% is applied.','The total price is',price *1.10)
} else {
    cat('C vat rate of 20% is applied.','The total price is',price *1.20)
}
```

Output

A vat rate of 8% is applied. The total price is 10.8.

7.8. Iterative Programming in R

- In R programming, we require a control structure to run a block of code multiple times.
- Loops come in the class of the most fundamental and strong programming concepts.
- A loop is a control statement that allows multiple executions of a statement or a set of statements.
- The word 'looping' means cycling or iterating.
- Loops are used to repeat the process until the expression (condition) is TRUE. R uses three keywords **for, while and repeat** for looping purpose. **Next and break**, provide additional control over the loop.
- The break statement exits the control from the innermost loop.
- The next statement immediately transfers control to return to the start of the loop and statement after next is skipped.
- The value returned by a loop statement is always NULL and is returned invisibly.

There are Three Types of Loop in R Programming

- For Loop
- While Loop
- Repeat Loop

1. For Loop in R

- It is a type of control statement that enables one to easily construct a loop that has to run statements or a set of statements multiple times.
- For loop is commonly used to iterate over items of a sequence. It is an entry-controlled loop, in this loop the test condition is tested first, then the body of the loop is executed, the loop body would not be executed if the test condition is false.

R – For Loop Syntax

```
for (value in sequence)
{
   statement
}
```

For Loop Flow Diagram

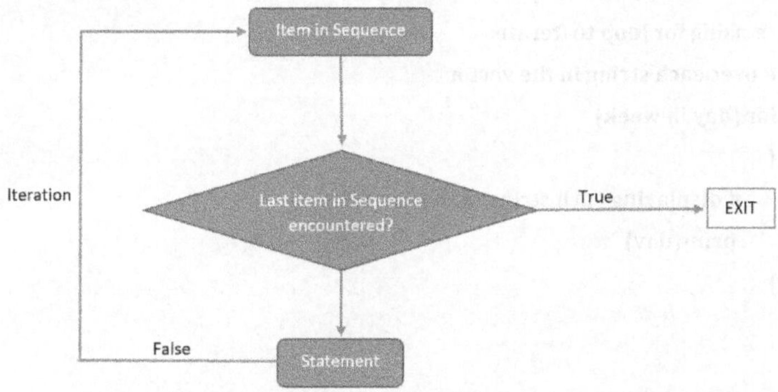

Figure 33: Shows Conditional Statements (For statement) in R

Example 1: Program to display numbers from 1 to 5 using for loop in R.

```
R program to demonstrate the use of for loop
 # using for loop
for (val in 1: 5)
{
   # statement
   print(val)
}
```

Output

```
[1] 1
[1] 2
[1] 3
[1] 4
[1] 5
```

Example 2: Program to display days of a week.

```
# R program to illustrate
# application of for loop
 # assigning strings to the vector
week < - c('Sunday', 'Monday', Tuesday',
      'Wednesday', 'Thursday',
      'Friday', 'Saturday')
 # using for loop to iterate
# over each string in the vector
for (day in week)
{
    # displaying each string in the vector
    print(day)
}
```

Output

```
[1] "Sunday"
[1] "Monday"
[1] "Tuesday"
[1] "Wednesday"
[1] "Thusrday"
[1] "Friday"
[1] "Saturday"
```

2. Repeat Statement

- The repeat statement executes the body of the loop until a break occurs. Be careful while using it because of the infinite nature of the loop.

- We must use the **break statement** to terminate the loop. The syntax of the repeat loop is:

For exiting, we include a **break statement** with a user-defined condition. This property of the loop makes it different from the other loops.

A repeat loop constructs with the help of the repeat keyword in R. It is very easy to construct an infinite loop in R.

The basic syntax of the repeat loop is as follows:

```
1. repeat {
2.   commands
3.   if(condition) {
4.     break
5.   }
6. }
```

Flowchart

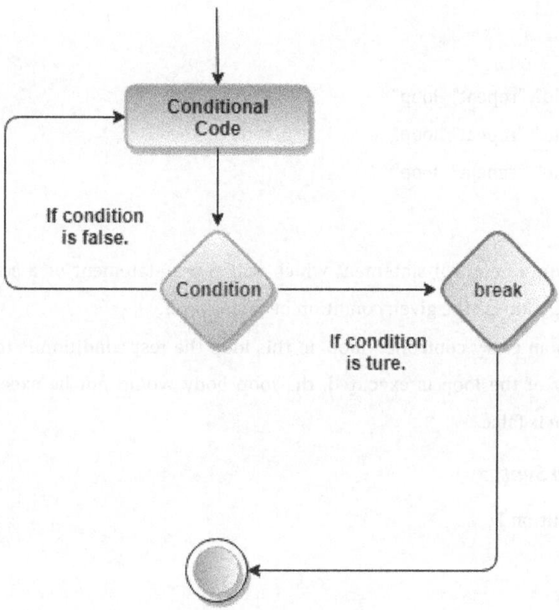

Figure 34: Shows Conditional Statements (break statement) in R

1. First, we have to initialize our variables than it will enter into the Repeat loop.
2. This loop will execute the group of statements inside the loop.
3. After that, we have to use any expression inside the loop to exit.
4. It will check for the condition. It will execute a break statement to exit from the loop.
5. If the condition is true.
6. The statements inside the repeat loop will be executed again if the condition is false.

Example 1

```
v <- c("Hello","repeat","loop")
cnt <- 2
repeat {
   print(v)
   cnt <- cnt+1
      if(cnt > 4) {
    break
  }
}
```

Output

```
[1] "Hello"  "repeat" "loop"
[1] "Hello"  "repeat" "loop"
[1] "Hello"  "repeat" "loop"
```

3. While Loop

- It is a type of control statement which will run a statement or a set of statements repeatedly unless the given condition becomes false.
- It is also an entry controlled loop, in this loop the test condition is tested first, then the body of the loop is executed, the loop body would not be executed if the test condition is false.

R – While Loop Syntax

```
while ( condition )
{
  statement
}
```

While Loop Flow Diagram

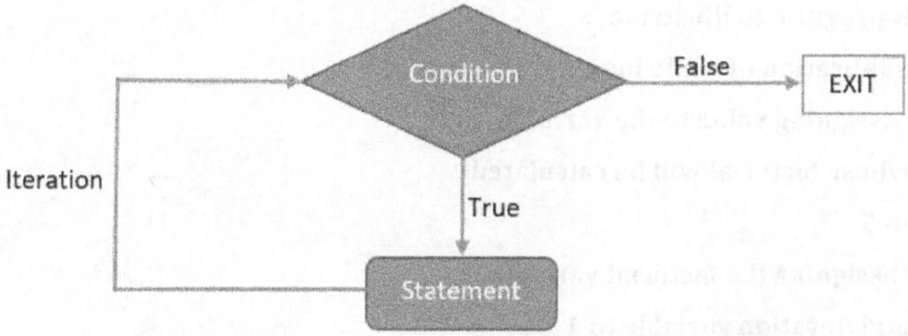

Figure 35: Shows Conditional Statements (While statement) in R

Example 1: Program to display numbers from 1 to 5 using while loop in R.

```
# R program to demonstrate the use of
# while loop
  val = 1
  # using while loop
while (val <= 5)
{
  # statements
  print(val)
  val = val + 1
}
```

Output

```
[1] 1
[1] 2
[1] 3
[1] 4
[1] 5
```

- Initially, the variable value is initialized to 1. In each iteration of the while loop the condition is checked and the value of val is displayed and then it is incremented until it becomes 5 and the condition becomes false, the loop is terminated.

Example 2: Program to Calculate Factorial of a Number

```
# R program to illustrate
# application of while loop
 # assigning value to the variable
# whose factorial will be calculated
n <- 5
 # assigning the factorial variable
# and iteration variable to 1
factorial <- 1
i <- 1
 # using while loop
while (i <= n)
{
   # multiplying the factorial variable
  # with the iteration variable
  factorial = factorial * i
   # incrementing the iteration variable
  i = i + 1
}
 # displaying the factorial
print(factorial)
```

Output

```
[1] 120
```

- Here, at first, the variable n is assigned to 5 whose factorial is going to be calculated, then variable i and factorial are assigned to 1. i will be used for iterating over the loop, and factorial will be used for calculating the factorial.
- In each iteration of the loop, the condition is checked i.e. i should be less than or equal to 5, and after that factorial is multiplied with the value of i, then i is incremented.
- When i becomes 5, the loop is terminated and the factorial of 5 i.e. 120 is displayed beyond the scope of the loop.

4. Jump Statements in Loop

- We use a jump statement in loops to terminate the loop at a particular iteration or to skip a particular iteration in the loop.
- The two most commonly used jump statements in loops are:
- **Break Statement:** The break keyword is a jump statement that is used to terminate the loop at a particular iteration.

Example

```
# R program to illustrate
# the use of break statement
 # using for loop
# to iterate over a sequence
for (val in 1: 5)
{
  # checking condition
  if (val == 3)
  {
    # using break keyword
    break
  }
   # displaying items in the sequence
  print(val)
}
```

Output

```
[1] 1
[1] 2
```

In the above program, if the value of val becomes 3 then the break statement will be executed and the loop will terminate.

Next Statement: The next keyword is a jump statement which is used to skip a particular iteration in the loop.

Example

```
# R program to illustrate
# the use of next statement
 # using for loop
# to iterate over the sequence
for (val in 1: 5)
{
  # checking condition
  if (val == 3)
  {
    # using next keyword
    next
  }
   # displaying items in the sequence
  print(val)
}
```

Output

```
[1] 1
[1] 2
[1] 4
[1] 5
```

- In the above program, if the value of Val becomes 3 then the next statement will be executed hence the current iteration of the loop will be skipped. So 3 is not displayed in the output.
- As we can conclude from the above two programs the basic difference between the two jump statements is that the **break** statement terminates the loop and the **next** statement skips a particular iteration of the loop.

7.9. Loop Over a List

- Looping over a list is just as easy and convenient as looping over a vector. There are again two different approaches here.

```
primes_list <- list(2, 3, 5, 7, 11, 13)

# loop version 1
for (p in primes_list) {
  print(p)
}

# loop version 2
for (i in 1:length(primes_list)) {
  print(primes_list[[i]])
}
```

Notice that you need double square brackets - [[ ]] - to select the list elements in loop version 2.

Output

```
[1] 2
[1] 3
[1] 5
[1] 7
[1] 11
[1] 13
[1] 2
[1] 3
[1] 5
[1] 7
[1] 11
[1] 13
```

CHAPTER 8

8.1. Functions in R Programming

- A set of statements which are organized together to perform a specific task is known as a function.
- R provides a series of in-built functions, and it allows the user to create their own functions.
- Functions are used to perform tasks in the modular approach.
- Functions are used to avoid repeating the same task and to reduce complexity.
- To understand and maintain our code, we logically break it into smaller parts using the function.
- A function should be,
    - Written to carry out a specified task.
    - May or may not have arguments
    - Contain a body in which our code is written.
    - May or may not return one or more output values.

"An R function is created by using the keyword function."

- There is the following syntax of R function:

1. **func_name <- function(arg_1, arg_2, ...) {**
2. **Function body**
3. **}**

Components of Functions

There are four components of function, which are as follows:

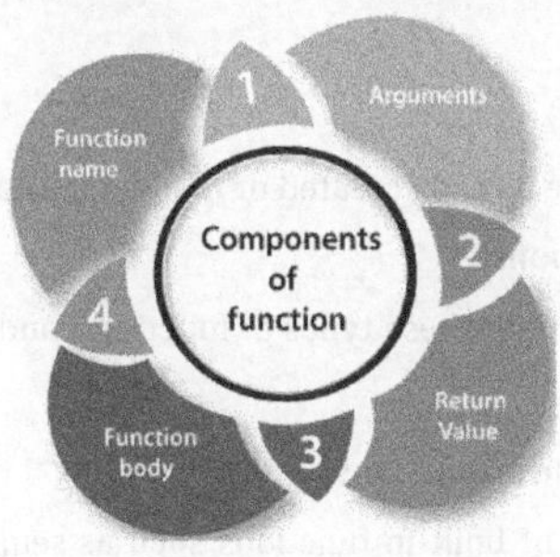

Figure 36: Shows Components of an Function in R

Function Name

- The function name is the actual name of the function.
- In R, the function is stored as an object with its name.

Arguments

- In function, arguments are optional means a function may or may not contain arguments, and these arguments can have default values also.
- We pass a value to the argument when a function is invoked.

Function Body

- The function body contains a set of statements which defines what the function does.

Return Value

- It is the last expression in the function body which is to be evaluated.

Function Types

- Similar to the other languages, R also has two types of function, i.e. **Built-in Function** and **User-defined Function**.
- In R, there are lots of built-in functions which we can directly call in the program without defining them. R also allows us to create our own functions.

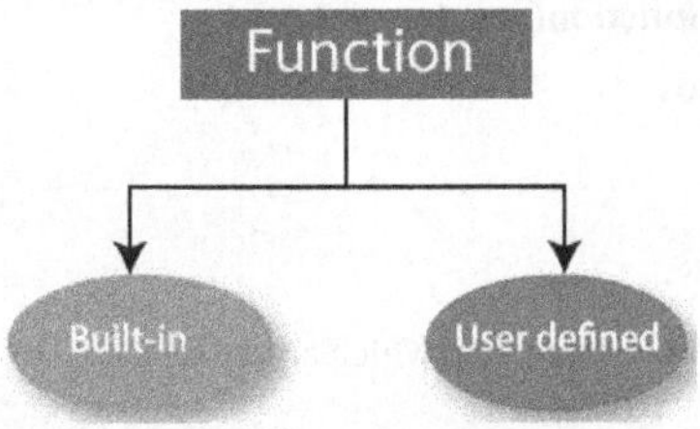

8.2. Built-in Function

- The functions which are already created or defined in the programming framework are known as built-in functions.
- User doesn't need to create these types of functions, and these functions are built into an application.
- End-users can access these functions by simply calling it.
- R have different types of built-in functions such as seq(), mean(), max(), and sum(x) etc.

1. **# Creating sequence of numbers from 32 to 46.**
2. **print(seq(32,46))**
3. **# Finding the mean of numbers from 22 to 80.**
4. **print(mean(22:80))**
5. **# Finding the sum of numbers from 41 to 70.**
6. **print(sum(41:70))**

Output

```
[1] 32 33 34 35 36 37 38 39 40 41 42 43 44 45 46
[1] 51
[1] 1665
```

Example 1

```
# sequence of number from 44 to 55 both including incremented by 1
x_vector <- seq(45,55, by = 1)
#logarithm
log(x_vector)
```

Output

```
## [1] 3.806662 3.828641 3.850148 3.871201 3.891820 3.912023 3.931826
## [8] 3.951244 3.970292 3.988984 4.007333
```

Math Functions

R has an array of mathematical functions.

Operator	Description
abs(x)	Takes the absolute value of x
log(x,base=y)	Takes the logarithm of x with base y; if base is not specified, returns the natural logarithm
exp(x)	Returns the exponential of x
sqrt(x)	Returns the square root of x
factorial(x)	Returns the factorial of x (x!)

Basic Statistic Functions

Operator	Description
mean(x)	Mean of x
median(x)	Median of x
var(x)	Variance of x
sd(x)	Standard deviation of x
quantile(x)	The quartiles of x
summary(x)	Summary of x: mean, min, max etc.

Example 1

```
speed <- dt$speed
speed
# Mean speed of cars dataset
mean(speed)
```

8.3. User-defined Function

- R allows us to create our own function in our program.
- A user defines a user-define function to fulfill the requirement of user.
- Once these functions are created, we can use these functions like in-built function.

Call a Function

- To call a function, use the function name followed by parenthesis, like **my_function()**.

Example

```
my_function <- function()
{
  print("Hello World!")
}

my_function() # call the function named my_function
```

Output

```
[1] "Hello World!"
```

Arguments

- Information can be passed into functions as arguments.
- Arguments are specified after the function name, inside the parentheses.
- You can add as many arguments as you want, just separate them with a comma.
- The following example has a function with one argument (fname).
- When the function is called, we pass along a first name, which is used inside the function to print the full name:

Example

```
my_function <- function(fname)
{
  paste(fname, "Griffin")
}
my_function("Peter")
my_function("Lois")
my_function("Stewie")
```

Output

```
[1] "Peter Griffin"
[1] "Lois Griffin"
[1] "Stewie Griffin"
```

Return Values

- To let a function return a result, use the return() function.

Example

```
my_function <- function(x) {
  return (5 * x)
}
print(my_function(3))
print(my_function(5))
print(my_function(9))
[1] 15
[1] 25
[1] 45
```

Example

```
# A simple R function to check
# whether x is even or odd
evenOdd <- function(x){
  if(x %% 2 == 0)
    return("even")
  else
    return("odd")
}
print(evenOdd(4))
print(evenOdd(3))
```

Output

```
[1] "even"
[1] "odd"
```

Single Input Single Output

- Now create a function in R that will take a single input and gives us a single output.
- Following is an example to create a function that calculates the area of a circle which takes in the arguments the radius.
- So, to create a function, name the function as "areaOfCircle" and the arguments that are needed to be passed are the "radius" of the circle.

```
# A simple R function to calculate
# area of a circle
areaOfCircle = function(radius){
  area = pi*radius^2
  return(area)
}
print(areaOfCircle(2))
```

Output

```
12.56637
```

8.4. Nested Functions

- A **nested function** or the **enclosing function** is a function that is defined within another function. In simpler words, a nested function is a function in another function.
- There are two ways to create a nested function in the R programming language.
  1. **Calling a function within another function we created.**
  2. **Writing a function within another function.**

Calling a Function within another Function

- For this process, we have to create the function with two or more required parameters. After that, we can call the function that we created whenever we want to,

```
# creating a function with two parameters
myFunction <- function(x, y) {
 # passing a command to the function
 a <- x * y
 return(a)
}
# creating a nested function
myFunction(myFunction(2,2), myFunction(3,3))
```

Code Explanation

- **Line 2:** We creatd a function with two parameter values, x and y.
- **Line 4:** The function we created tells x to multiply y and assign the output to a variable a.
- **Line 5:** We return the value of a.
- **Line 9:** We make the first input myFunction (2,2) represent the primary function's x parameter. Likewise, we make the second input myFunction (3,3) represent the y parameter of the main function.

Hence, we get the following expected output: (2 * 2) * (3 * 3) = 36.

Writing a Function within another Function

- In this process, we can't directly call the function because there is an inner function defined inside an outer function. Therefore, we will call the external function to call the function inside.

```
# creating an outer function
outerFunction <- function(x) {
  # creating an inner function
  innerFunction <- function(y) {
    # passing a command to the function
    a <- x * y
    return(a)
  }
  return (innerFunction)
}
# To call the outer functionn
output <- outerFunction(3)
output(5)
```

Code Explanation

- **Line 2:** We create an outer function, outerFunction, and pass a parameter value x to the function.
- **Line 4:** We create an inner function, innerFunction, and pass a parameter value y to the function.
- **Line 6:** We pass a command to the inner function, which tells x to multiply y and assign the output to a variable a.
- **Line 7:** We return the value of a.
- **Line 9:** We return the innerFunction.
- **Line 12:** To call the outer function, we create a variable output and give it a value of 3.
- **Line 13:** We print the output with the desired value of 5 as the value of the y parameter.

Therefore, the output is: (3 * 5 = 15)

8.5. Scopes

- The scope of a variable is nothing more than the place in the code where it is referenced and visible.
- There are two basic concepts of scoping, ***lexical (static)* scoping and is *dynamic* scoping.**
- In R, there is a concept of ***free variables***, which add some spice to the scoping.
- R uses lexical scoping, which says the values of such variables are searched for in the **environment** in which the function was defined.

```
f <- function(a, b) {
      (a * b) / z
}
```

- In this function, you have two formal arguments, a and b.
- You have another symbol, z, in the body of the function, which is a free variable.
- The scoping rules of the language define how value is assigned to free variables.
- R uses lexical scoping, which says the value for z is searched for in the environment where the function was defined.
- **'Z' is called free variable.**

Note: Lexical scoping is also referred to as statical scoping.

- With **dynamic scoping**, the variable is bound to the most recent value assigned to that variable.
- R provides some escape routes to bypass the shortcomings of lexical scoping. The <- operator is called a variable assignment operator.
- **Given the expression a <- 3.14, the value is assigned to the variable in the current environment. If you already had an assignment for the variable before in the same environment, this one will overwrite it.**
- Variable assignments only update in the current environment, and they never create a new scope. When R is looking for a value of a given variable, it will start searching from the bottom.
- This means the **current environment (The top level environment available to us at the R command prompt is the global environment called R_GlobalEnv . Global environment can be referred to as . GlobalEnv in R codes as well. We can use the ls() function to show what variables and functions are defined in the current environment.)** is inspected first, then its enclosing environment **(The enclosing environment is the environment where the function was created. Every function has one and only one enclosing environment)**. The search goes until either the value is found or the empty environment is reached.

```
a <- 3.14
add <- function(x,y)
{
x * y / a
}
add(10,11)
```

The output is the following:

```
1[1] 35.03185
```

- When the function is called, only the two arguments are passed. R tries to look up the a variable's value and first looks at the **scope of the function.**

- Since it cannot be found there, it look for the value in the enclosing scope, where it finally finds it. If you had not defined the a variable, it would give you the following error: Error in b(10, 11) : object 'a' not found, stating that the lookup has failed.
- This brings us to the concept of **environment**. Environments in R are basically mappings from variables to values.
- Every function has a local environment and a reference to the enclosing environment.
- This helps scoping and lookup. You have the option to add, remove, or modify variable mappings and can even change the reference to the enclosing environment.

Math Functions

- R provides the various mathematical functions to perform the mathematical calculation. These mathematical functions are very helpful to find absolute value, square value and much more calculations. In R, there are the following functions which are used.

S. No	Function	Description	Example
1.	abs(x)	It returns the absolute value of input x.	x<- -4 print(abs(x)) **Output** [1] 4
2.	sqrt(x)	It returns the square root of input x.	x<- 4 print(sqrt(x)) **Output** [1] 2
3.	ceiling(x)	It returns the smallest integer which is larger than or equal to x.	x<- 4.5 print(ceiling(x)) **Output** [1] 5
4.	floor(x)	It returns the largest integer, which is smaller than or equal to x.	x<- 2.5 print(floor(x)) **Output** [1] 2
5.	trunc(x)	It returns the truncate value of input x.	x<-c(1.2,2.5,8.1) print(trunc(x)) **Output** [1] 1 2 8
6.	round(x, digits=n)	It returns round value of input x.	x<- -4 print(abs(x)) **Output** 4
7.	cos(x), sin(x), tan(x)	It returns cos(x), sin(x) value of input x.	x<- 4 print(cos(x)) print(sin(x)) print(tan(x)) **Output** [1] -06536436 [2] -0.7568025 [3] 1.157821
8.	log(x)	It returns natural logarithm of input x.	x<- 4 print(log(x)) **Output** [1] 1.386294
9.	log10(x)	It returns common logarithm of input x.	x<- 4 print(log10(x)) **Output** [1] 0.60206
10.	exp(x)	It returns exponent.	x<- 4 print(exp(x)) **Output** [1] 54.59815

Recursive Functions in R Programming

- Recursion, in the simplest terms, is a type of looping technique. It exploits the basic working of functions in R.
- **Recursion is when the function calls itself. This forms a loop, where every time the function is called, it calls itself again and again and this technique is known as recursion.**
- Since the loops increase the memory we use the recursion. The recursive function uses the concept of recursion **to perform iterative tasks they call themselves, again and again, which acts as a loop.**
- These kinds of functions need a stopping condition so that they can stop looping continuously.
- **Recursive functions call themselves.** They break down the problem into smaller components.
- The function() calls itself within the original function() on each of the smaller components. After this, the results will be put together to solve the original problem.

Example: Factorial Using Recursion in R

```
rec_fac <- function(x){
   if(x==0 || x==1)
   {
      return(1)
   }
   else
   {
      return(x*rec_fac(x-1))
   }
}
```

Output

```
[1] 120
```

- Here, rec_fac(5) calls rec_fac(4), which then calls rec_fac(3), and so on until the input argument x, has reached 1.
- The function returns 1 and is destroyed. The return value is multiplied with argument value and returned.

- This process continues until the first function call returns its output, giving us the final result.

Key Features of R Recursion

- The use of recursion, often, makes the code shorter and it also looks clean.
- It is a simple solution for a few cases.
- It expresses in a function that calls itself.

Applications of Recursion in R

- Recursive functions are used in many efficient programming techniques like dynamic programming language (DSL) or divide and conquer algorithms.
- In dynamic programming, for both top-down as well as bottom-up approaches, recursion is vital for performance.
- In divide and conquer algorithms, we divide a problem into smaller sub-problems that are easier to solve. The output is then built back up to the top. Recursion has a similar process, which is why it is used to implement such algorithms.
- In its essence, recursion is the process of breaking down a problem into many smaller problems, these smaller problems are further broken down until the problem left is trivial. The solution is then built back up piece by piece.

Note: We can define looping or iteration as the process where the same set of instructions is repeated multiple times in a single call. In contrast, we can enumerate recursion as the process where the output of one iteration from a function call becomes the input of the next in a separate function call.

8.6. Packages in R

- Packages in R Programming language are a **set of R functions, compiled code, and sample data.**
- These are stored under a directory called "library" within the R environment. By default, R installs a group of packages during installation.
- Once we start the R console, only the default packages are available by default.
- Other packages that are already installed need to be loaded explicitly to be utilized by the R program that's getting to use them.

What are Repositories?

- A repository is a place where packages are located and stored so you can install packages from it.
- Organizations and Developers have a local repository, typically they are online and accessible to everyone.
- Some of the most popular repositories for R packages are:
    - **CRAN: Comprehensive R Archive Network (CRAN)** is the official repository, it is a network of ftp and web servers maintained by the R community around the world.
    - The R community coordinates it, and for a package to be published in CRAN, the Package needs to pass several tests to ensure that the package is following CRAN policies.
    - **Bioconductor:** Bioconductor is a topic-specific repository, intended for open source software for bioinformatics. Similar to CRAN, it has its own submission and review processes, and its community is very active having several conferences and meetings per year in order to maintain quality.
    - **Github:** Github is the most popular repository for open source projects. It's popular as it comes from the unlimited space for open source, the integration with git, a version control software, and its ease to share and collaborate with others.

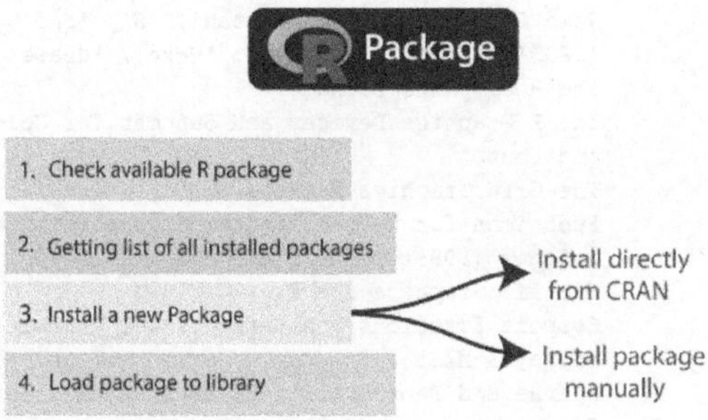

Figure 36: Shows R Packages

1. Check Available R Packages

- To check the available R Packages, we have to find the library location in which R packages are contained. R provides libPaths() function to find the library locations.

libPaths()

- When the above code executes, it produces the following project, which may vary depending on the local settings of our PCs & Laptops.

2. Getting the List of All the Packages Installed

- R provides library() function, which allows us to get the list of all the installed packages.
- library()

When we execute the above function, it produces the following result, which may vary depending on the local settings of our PCs or laptops.

Packages in library 'C:/Program Files/R/R-3.6.1/library':

R packages available

File Edit

```
Packages in library 'C:/Program Files/R/R-3.6.1/library':

base                    The R Base Package
boot                    Bootstrap Functions (Originally by Angelo Canty
                        for S)
class                   Functions for Classification
cluster                 "Finding Groups in Data": Cluster Analysis
                        Extended Rousseeuw et al.
codetools               Code Analysis Tools for R
compiler                The R Compiler Package
datasets                The R Datasets Package
foreign                 Read Data Stored by 'Minitab', 'S', 'SAS',
                        'SPSS', 'Stata', 'Systat', 'Weka', 'dBase', ...
graphics                The R Graphics Package
grDevices               The R Graphics Devices and Support for Colours
                        and Fonts
grid                    The Grid Graphics Package
KernSmooth              Functions for Kernel Smoothing Supporting Wand
                        & Jones (1995)
lattice                 Trellis Graphics for R
MASS                    Support Functions and Datasets for Venables and
                        Ripley's MASS
Matrix                  Sparse and Dense Matrix Classes and Methods
methods                 Formal Methods and Classes
mgcv                    Mixed GAM Computation Vehicle with Automatic
```

Like library() function, R provides search() function to get all packages currently loaded in the R environment.

Install a New Package

- In R, there are two techniques to add new R packages. The first technique is installing package directly from the CRAN directory, and the second one is to install it manually after downloading the package to our local system.

Install Directly from CRAN

The following command is used to get the packages directly from CRAN webpage and install the package in the R environment. We may be prompted to choose the nearest mirror. Choose the one appropriate to our location.

1. install.packages("Package Name")

   The syntax of installing XML package is as follows:

   install.packages("XML")

Output

```
Rterm (64-bit)

> install.packages("XML")
Installing package into 'C:/Users/ajeet/OneDrive/Documents/R/win-library/3.6'
(as 'lib' is unspecified)
--- Please select a CRAN mirror for use in this session ---
trying URL 'https://cloud.r-project.org/bin/windows/contrib/3.6/XML_3.98-1.20.zip'
Content type 'application/zip' length 4610084 bytes (4.4 MB)
downloaded 4.4 MB

package 'XML' successfully unpacked and MD5 sums checked

The downloaded binary packages are in
        C:\Users\ajeet\AppData\Local\Temp\Rtmp0qpzbj\downloaded_packages
>
```

Install Package Manually

To install a package manually, we first have to download it from https://cran.r-project.org/web/packages/available_packages_by_name.html

The required package will be saved as a .zip file in a suitable location in the local system.

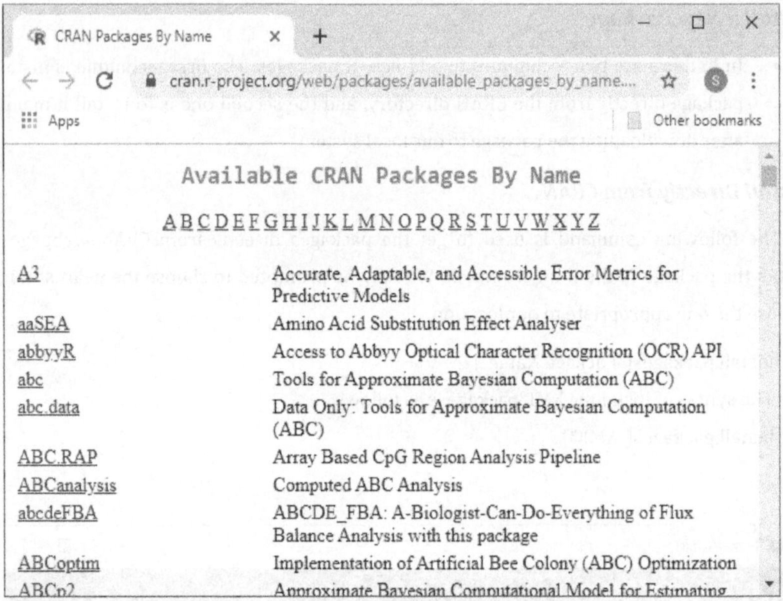

Once the downloading has finished, we will use the following command:

1. install.packages(file_name_with_path, repos = NULL, type = "source")

Install the package named "XML"

1. install.packages("C:\Users\ajeet\OneDrive\Desktop\graphics\xml2_1.2.2.zip", repos = NULL, type = "source")

Load Package to Library

- We cannot use the package in our code until it will not be loaded into the current R environment.
- We also need to load a package which is already installed previously but not available in the current environment.

There is the following command to load a package:

1. library("package Name", lib.loc = "path to library")

Command to load the XML package

1. install.packages("C:\Users\ajeet\OneDrive\Desktop\graphics\xml2_1.2.2.zip", repos = NULL, type = "source")

UNIT - 5

CHAPTER 9

9.1. Data Reduction: Overview of Data Reduction Strategies

- **Data reduction** techniques ensure the **integrity of data** while reducing the data.
- **Data reduction is a process that reduces the volume of original data and represents it in a much smaller volume.**
- Data reduction techniques are used to obtain a reduced representation of the dataset that is much smaller in volume by **maintaining the integrity of the original data**.
- By reducing the data, the efficiency of the data mining process is improved, which produces the same analytical results.
- Data reduction aims to define it more compactly. **When the data size is smaller, it is simpler to apply sophisticated and computationally high-priced algorithms.**
- The reduction of the data may be in terms of the number of **rows (records)** or terms of the number of **columns (dimensions).**

1. Dimensionality Reduction

- Dimensionality reduction eliminates the attributes from the data set under consideration, thereby reducing the volume of original data.
- It reduces data size as **it eliminates outdated or redundant features.** Here are three methods of dimensionality reduction.

9.2. Principal Component Analysis

- Principal Component Analysis is an unsupervised learning algorithm that is used for the dimensionality reduction in machine learning. **It is a statistical process that converts the observations of correlated features into a set of linearly uncorrelated features with the help of orthogonal transformation.** These new transformed features are called the **Principal Components**.
- It is one of the popular tools that is used for exploratory data analysis and predictive modeling. It is a technique to draw strong patterns from the given dataset by reducing the variances.

- PCA works by considering the variance of each attribute because the high attribute shows the good split between the classes, and hence it reduces the dimensionality. Some real-world applications of PCA are ***image processing, movie recommendation system, optimizing the power allocation in various communication channels.*** It is a feature extraction technique, so it contains the important variables and drops the least important variable.
- The PCA algorithm is based on some mathematical concepts such as,
  - Variance and Covariance
  - Eigenvalues and Eigen factors

Some common terms used in PCA algorithm.

- **Dimensionality:** It is the number of features or variables present in the given dataset. More easily, it is the number of columns present in the dataset.
- **Correlation:** It signifies that how strongly two variables are related to each other. Such as if one changes, the other variable also gets changed. The correlation value ranges from -1 to +1. Here, -1 occurs if variables are inversely proportional to each other, and +1 indicates that variables are directly proportional to each other.
- **Orthogonal:** It defines that variables are not correlated to each other, and hence the correlation between the pair of variables is zero.
- **Eigenvectors:** If there is a square matrix M, and a non-zero vector v is given. Then v will be eigenvector if Av is the scalar multiple of v.
- **Covariance Matrix:** A matrix containing the covariance (**Covariance measures the direction of the relationship between two variables. A positive covariance means that both variables tend to be high or low at the same time. A negative covariance means that when one variable is high, the other tends to be low**) between the pair of variables is called the Covariance Matrix.

Principal Components in PCA

- As described above, the transformed new features or the output of PCA are the Principal Components.
- The number of these PCs are either equal to or less than the original features present in the dataset. Some properties of these principal components are given below.

- The principal component must be the linear combination **linear combination is an expression constructed from a set of terms by multiplying each term by a constant and adding the results (e.g. a linear combination of x and y would be any expression of the form ax + by, where a and b are constants)** of the original features.
- These components are orthogonal, i.e., the correlation between a pair of variables is zero.

Steps for PCA Algorithm

- **Getting the dataset**

  Firstly, we need to take the input dataset and divide it into two subparts X and Y, where X is the training set, and Y is the validation set.
- **Representing data into a structure**

  Now we will represent our dataset into a structure. Such as we will represent the two-dimensional matrix of independent variable X. **Here each row corresponds to the data items, and the column corresponds to the Features.** The number of columns is the dimensions of the dataset.
- **Standardizing the data**

  In this step, we will standardize our dataset. Such as in a particular column, the features with high variance are more important compared to the features with lower variance.

  If the importance of features is independent of the variance of the feature, then we will divide each data item in a column with the standard deviation of the column. Here we will name the matrix as Z.
- **Calculating the Covariance of Z**

  To calculate the covariance of Z, we will take the matrix Z, and will transpose it. After transpose, we will multiply it by Z. The output matrix will be the Covariance matrix of Z.
- **Calculating the Eigen Values and Eigen Vectors**

  Now we need to calculate the eigenvalues and eigenvectors for the resultant covariance matrix Z. Eigenvectors or the covariance matrix are the directions of the axes with high information. And the coefficients of these eigenvectors are defined as the eigenvalues.
- **Sorting the Eigen Vectors**

  In this step, we will take all the eigenvalues and will sort them in decreasing order, which means from largest to smallest. And simultaneously sort the eigenvectors accordingly in matrix P of eigenvalues. The resultant matrix will be named as P*.

- **Calculating the new features Or Principal Components**

  Here we will calculate the new features. To do this, we will multiply the P* matrix to the Z. **In the resultant matrix Z*, each observation is the linear combination of original features. Each column of the Z* matrix is independent of each other.**

- **Remove less or unimportant features from the new dataset**

  The new feature set has occurred, so we will decide here what to keep and what to remove. It means, we will only keep the relevant or important features in the new dataset, and unimportant features will be removed out.

Applications of Principal Component Analysis

- PCA is mainly used as the dimensionality reduction technique in various AI applications such **as computer vision, image compression, etc.**
- It can also be used for finding hidden patterns if data has high dimensions. Some fields where PCA is used are Finance, data mining, Psychology, etc.

Application

1. Image compression is a process applied to a graphics file to minimize its size in bytes without degrading image quality below an acceptable threshold.
2. The main idea of using PCA for face recognition is to express the large 1-D vector of pixels constructed from 2-D facial image into the compact principal components of the feature space.
3. PCA has been used on Medical Data to show correlation of Cholesterol with low density lipo-protein.

9.3. Attribute Subset Selection

- Attribute subset Selection is a technique which is used for data reduction in data mining process. Data reduction reduces the size of data so that it can be used for analysis purposes more efficiently.
- **Need of Attribute Subset Selection:** The data set may have a large number of attributes. But some of those attributes can be irrelevant or redundant. The goal of attribute subset selection is to find a minimum set of attributes such that dropping of those irrelevant attributes does not much affect the utility of data and the cost of data analysis could be reduced. Mining on a reduced data set also makes the discovered pattern easier to understand.

- **Process of Attribute Subset Selection:** The brute force approach can be very expensive in which each subset (2^n possible subsets) of the data having *n* attributes can be analyzed.
- **The best way to do the task is to use the statistical significance tests such that best (or worst) attributes can be recognized**. Statistical significance test assumes that attributes are independent of one another.
- This is a kind of **greedy approach** in which a significance level is decided (statistically ideal value of significance level is 5%) and the models are tested again and again until p-value (probability value) of all attributes is less than or equal to the selected significance level. **The attributes having p-value higher than significance level are discarded.**
- **This procedure is repeated again and again until all the attribute in data set has p-value less than or equal to the significance level.** This gives us the reduced data set having no irrelevant attributes.

Methods of Attribute Subset Selection

1. Stepwise Forward Selection.
2. Stepwise Backward Elimination.
3. Combination of Forward Selection and Backward Elimination.
4. Decision Tree Induction.

All the above methods are **greedy** approaches for attribute subset selection.

1. **Stepwise Forward Selection:** This procedure start with an empty set of attributes as the minimal set. The most relevant attributes are chosen (having minimum p-value) and are added to the minimal set. In each iteration, one attribute is added to a reduced set.
2. **Stepwise Backward Elimination:** Here all the attributes are considered in the initial set of attributes. In each iteration, one attribute is eliminated from the set of attributes whose p-value is higher than significance level.
3. **Combination of Forward Selection and Backward Elimination:** The stepwise forward selection and backward elimination are combined so as to select the relevant attributes most efficiently. This is the most common technique which is generally used for attribute selection.

4. **Decision Tree Induction:** This approach uses decision tree for attribute selection. It constructs a flow chart like structure having nodes denoting a test on an attribute. Each branch corresponds to the outcome of test and leaf nodes is a class prediction. The attribute that is not the part of tree is considered irrelevant and hence discarded.

9.4. Numerosity Reduction

Numerosity Reduction is a data reduction technique which replaces the original data by smaller form of data representation. There are two techniques for numerosity reduction.

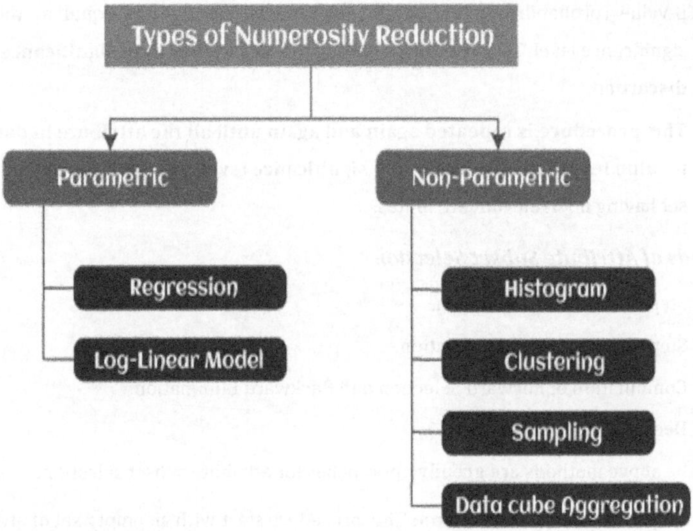

Figure 37: Types of Numerosity Reduction

Parametric and Non-Parametric Methods

Parametric Methods

- For *parametric methods (*Parametric modeling is creating a model from some known facts about a population. These "facts" are called parameters*)*, data is represented using some model.
- The model is used to estimate the data, so that only parameters of data are required to be stored, instead of actual data. Regression and Log-Linear methods are used for creating such models.

Regression

Terms

- **Dependent Variable:** The main factor in Regression analysis which we want to predict or understand is called the dependent variable. It is also called target variable.
- **Independent Variable:** The factors which affect the dependent variables or which are used to predict the values of the dependent variables are called independent variable, also called as a predictor.
- Regression analysis is a statistical method to model the relationship between a dependent (target) and independent (predictor) variables with one or more independent variables.
- More specifically, Regression analysis helps us to understand how the value of the dependent variable is changing corresponding to an independent variable when other independent variables are held fixed. It predicts continuous/real values such as **temperature, age, salary, price,** etc.

  Regression can be a simple linear regression or multiple linear regression. When there is only single independent attribute, such regression model is called simple linear regression and if there are multiple independent attributes, then such regression models are called multiple linear regression.
- In multiple linear regression, y will be modeled as a linear function of two or more predictor (independent) variables.

9.5. Log-Linear Model

Log-linear model can be used to estimate the probability of each data point in a multidimensional space for a set of discretized attributes, based on a smaller subset of dimensional combinations.

- This allows a higher-dimensional data space to be constructed from lower-dimensional attributes.

Regression and log-linear model can both be used on sparse data, although their application may be limited.

Types of Numerosity Reduction

This method uses an alternate, small forms of data representation, thus reducing data volume. There are two types of Numerosity reduction, such as,

Parametric

- This method assumes a model into which the data fits. Data model parameters are estimated, and only those parameters are stored, and the rest of the data is discarded. Regression and Log-Linear methods are used for creating such models. For example, a regression model can be used to achieve parametric reduction if the data fits the Linear Regression model.
    - **Log-Linear Model:** Log-linear model can be used to estimate the probability of each data point in a multidimensional space for a set of discretized attributes based on a smaller subset of dimensional combinations.
    - The Log-Linear model discovers the relationship between two or more discrete attributes. Assume we have a set of tuples in n-dimensional space; the log-linear model helps derive each tuple's probability in this n-dimensional space.

Non-Parametric

1. **Non-Parametric:** A non-parametric numerosity reduction technique does not assume any model. The non-Parametric technique results in a more uniform reduction, irrespective of data size, but it may not achieve a high volume of data reduction like the parametric.
2. There are at least four types of Non-Parametric data reduction techniques, Histogram, Clustering, Sampling, Data Cube Aggregation, and Data Compression.
    - **Histogram**
    - A histogram is used to summarize discrete or continuous data. In other words, it provides a visual interpretation of numerical data by showing the number of data points that fall within a specified range of values (called "bins"). It is similar to a vertical bar graph. However, a histogram, unlike a vertical bar graph, shows no gaps between the bars.

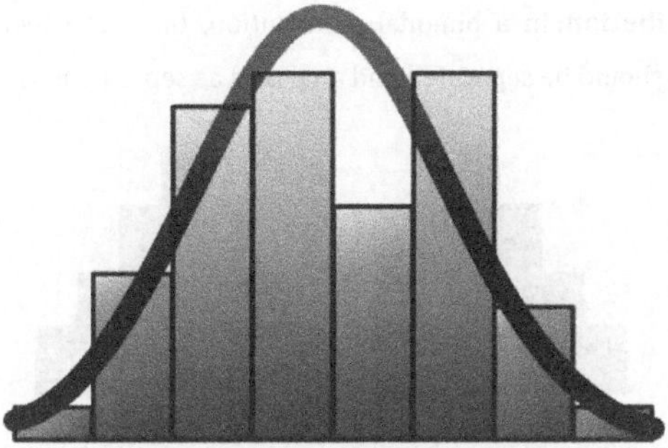

Figure 38: Shows Histogram

Parts of a Histogram

1. **The Title:** The title describes the information included in the histogram.
2. **X-axis:** The X-axis are intervals that show the scale of values which the measurements fall under.
3. **Y-axis:** The Y-axis shows the number of times that the values occurred within the intervals set by the X-axis.
4. **The Bars:** The height of the bar shows the number of times that the values occurred within the interval, while the width of the bar shows the interval that is covered. For a histogram with equal bins, the width should be the same across all bars.

Note: The bar graph is the graphical representation of categorical data. A histogram is the graphical representation of quantitative data.

Importance of a Histogram

1. Creating a histogram provides a visual representation of data distribution. Histograms can display a large amount of data and the frequency of the data values.
   - E.G

Distributions of a Histogram

A Normal Distribution: In a normal distribution, points on one side of the average are as likely to occur as on the other side of the average.

A Bimodal Distribution: In a bimodal distribution, there are two peaks. In a bimodal distribution, the data should be separated and analyzed as separate normal distributions.

- Uncle Bruno owns a garden with 30 black cherry trees. Each tree is of a different height. The height of the trees (in inches): 61, 63, 64, 66, 68, 69, 71, 71.5, 72, 72.5, 73, 73.5, 74, 74.5, 76, 76.2, 76.5, 77, 77.5, 78, 78.5, 79, 79.2, 80, 81, 82, 83, 84, 85, 87. We can group the data as follows in a frequency distribution table by setting a range.

Height Range (ft)	Number of Trees (Frequency)
60 - 75	3
66 - 70	3
71 - 75	8
76 - 80	10
81 - 85	5
86 - 90	1

This data can be now shown using a histogram. We need to make sure that while plotting a histogram, there shouldn't be any gaps between the bars.

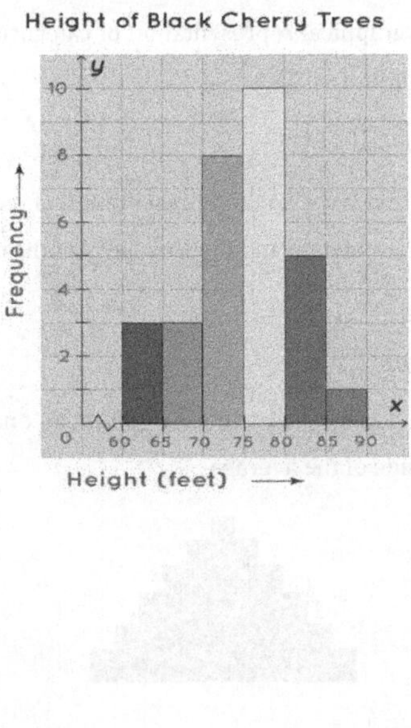

CHAPTER 10

10.1. Clustering

- **Clustering** is the task of dividing the population or data points into a number of groups such that data points in the same groups are more similar to other data points in the same group and dissimilar to the data points in other groups. It is basically a collection of objects on the basis of similarity and dissimilarity between them.
- **For ex:** The data points in the graph below clustered together can be classified into one single group. We can distinguish the clusters, and we can identify that there are 3 clusters in the below picture.

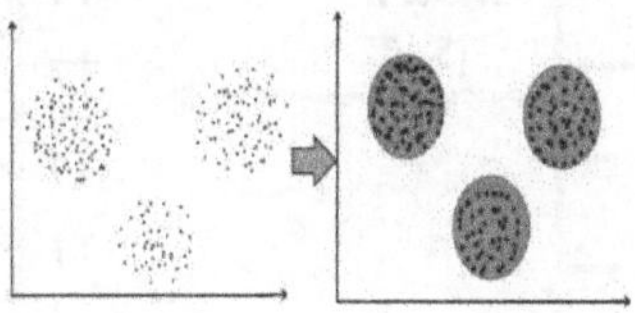

Figure 39: Shows Clustering concept

Applications of Clustering in Different Fields

- **Marketing:** It can be used to characterize & discover customer segments for marketing purposes.
- **Biology:** It can be used for classification among different species of plants and animals.
- **Libraries:** It is used in clustering different books on the basis of topics and information.
- **Insurance:** It is used to acknowledge the customers, their policies and **identifying** the frauds.

10.2. Sampling

- **Sampling:** One of the methods used for data reduction is sampling, as it can reduce the large data set into a much smaller data sample. Below we will discuss the different methods in which we can sample a large data set D containing N tuples.
  a. **Simple Random Sample without Replacement (SRSWOR) of Size s:** In this s, some tuples are drawn from N tuples such that in the data set D (s<N). The probability of drawing any tuple from the data set D is 1/N. This means all tuples have an equal probability of getting sampled.

b. **Simple Random Sample with Replacement (SRSWR) of Size s:** It is similar to the SRSWOR, but the tuple is drawn from data set D, is recorded, and then replaced into the data set D so that it can be drawn again.

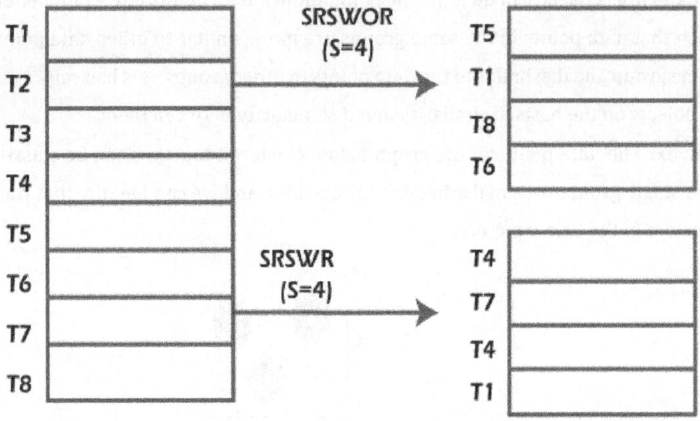

c. **Cluster Sample:** The tuples in data set D are clustered into M mutually disjoint subsets. The data reduction can be applied by implementing SRSWOR on these clusters. A simple random sample of size s could be generated from these clusters where s<M.

d. **Stratified Sample:** The large data set D is partitioned into mutually disjoint sets called 'strata'. A simple random sample is taken from each stratum to get stratified data. This method is effective for skewed data.

10.3. Data Cube Aggregation

- This technique is used to aggregate data in a simpler form. Data Cube Aggregation is a multidimensional aggregation that uses aggregation at various levels of a data cube to represent the original data set, thus achieving data reduction.
- For example, suppose you have the data of All Electronics sales per quarter for the year 2018 to the year 2022. If you want to get the annual sale per year, you just have to aggregate the sales per quarter for each year. In this way, aggregation provides you with the required data, which is much smaller in size, and thereby we achieve data reduction even without losing any data.

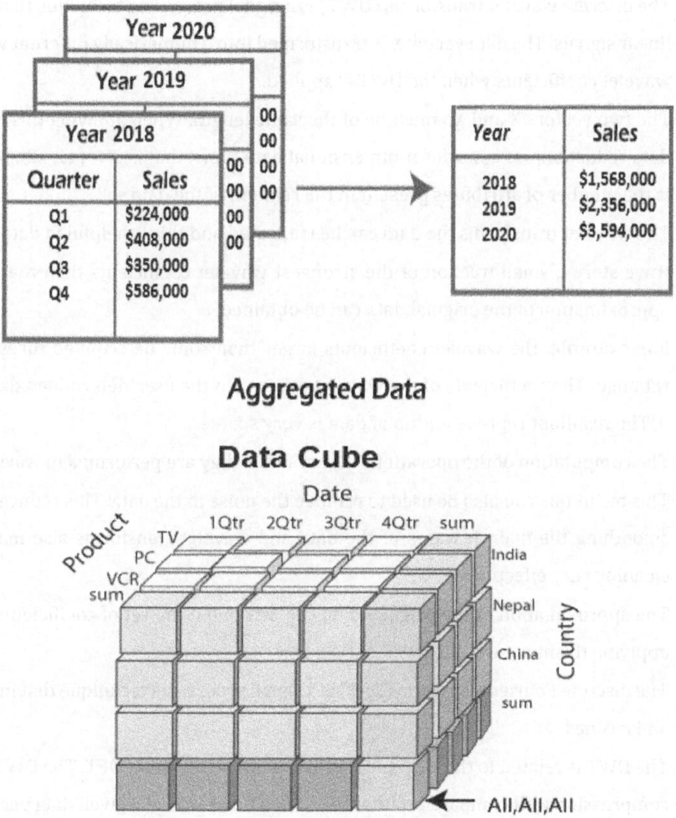

Figure 40: Shows the Data Cube Aggregation Concept

The data cube aggregation is a multidimensional aggregation that eases multidimensional analysis. The data cube present precomputed and summarized data which eases the data mining into fast access.

10.4. Wavelet Transform

Wavelet Transform: In the wavelet transform, suppose a data vector A is transformed into a numerically different data vector A' such that both A and A' vectors are of the same length. Then how it is useful in reducing data because the data obtained from the wavelet transform can be truncated.

- The discrete wavelet transforms (DWT) is a signal processing technique that transforms linear signals. The data vector X is transformed into a numerically different vector, Xo, of wavelet coefficients when the DWT is applied.
- The two vectors X and Xo must be of the same length. When applying this technique to data reduction, we consider n-dimensional data tuple, that is, X = (x1, x2...,xn), where n is the number of attributes present in the relation of the data set.
- The wavelet transforms the data can be truncated and this is helpful in data reduction.
- If we store a small fraction of the strongest wavelet coefficients then the compressed approximation of the original data can be obtained.
- **For example**, the wavelet coefficients larger than some determined threshold can be retained. The coefficients of the wavelet other than the user-determined data are set to 0. The resultant representation of data is very sparse.
- The computation of the operations is very fast if they are performed in wavelet space.
- This technique can also be used to remove the noise in the data. This reduces the task of smoothing the main features of the data and wavelet transforms also make the data cleaning very effective.
- The approximation of the original data can be done if the set of coefficients is given by applying the inverse of the DWT.
- The discrete Fourier transform (DFT) is a signal processing technique that involves sines and cosines.
- The DWT is related to the DFT and it is based on the results of DFT. The DWT gains lossy compression well compared to the DFT. If DWT and DFT of a given data vector have the same number of coefficients then the DWT provides more accurate wavelet coefficients and appropriation of the data. The DWT occupies less space compared to the DFT. There is only one group of DFT but DWT has many groups of it. The most Popular wavelet transforms are Haar-2 and Daubechies-4. The discrete wavelet transform uses a hierarchical pyramid algorithm that halves the data at each iteration, the data is reduced to half, and thus speed of computation of data increases.
- The method of the hierarchical pyramid is as follows.
- The input data vector is of length L and L is an integer and is the power of 2. If length L is not the power of 2 then we can append the zeroes at the end of input data vector to make it as power of 2.

- We apply two functions for each transform of the data vector. The first function is to perform the data smoothing, like finding the weighted average of the data vectors. The second function is to find the weighted difference and this retrieves the important features of the input vector.
- We apply the two functions to the X axis pairs of the data points (x2i,x2i+1). Two different data sets of length L/2 are obtained after applying the two functions. The first data set is the low-frequency version of the original data and the second one is the high frequency data set of it.
- These two functions are applied to the data vectors recursively until the obtained resultant data vectors are of length 2.
- The wavelet coefficients are assigned to the transformed data vectors finally.

10.5. Data Visualization

It is said that a picture is worth a thousand words, and this is especially true for data analytics. Data visualization is all about presenting data in a visual format, using charts, graphs, and maps to tell a meaningful story. It's a crucial step in the data analysis process and a technique that all areas of business can benefit from.

A Definition

Data visualization is the communication of data in a visual manner, or turning raw data into insights that can be easily interpreted by the readers.

Other Definitions Include

Wikipedia's definition of Data Visualization: Data visualization refers to the techniques used to communicate data or information by encoding it as visual objects (points, lines or bars) contained in graphics.

Techopedia's definition of Data Visualization: Data visualization is the process of displaying data or information in graphical charts, figures and bars.

Data visualization is the graphical or visual representation of data. It helps to highlight the most useful insights from a dataset, making it easier to spot trends, patterns, outliers, and correlations. Data visualization convert large and small data sets into visuals, which is easy to understand and process for humans (Figure 1).

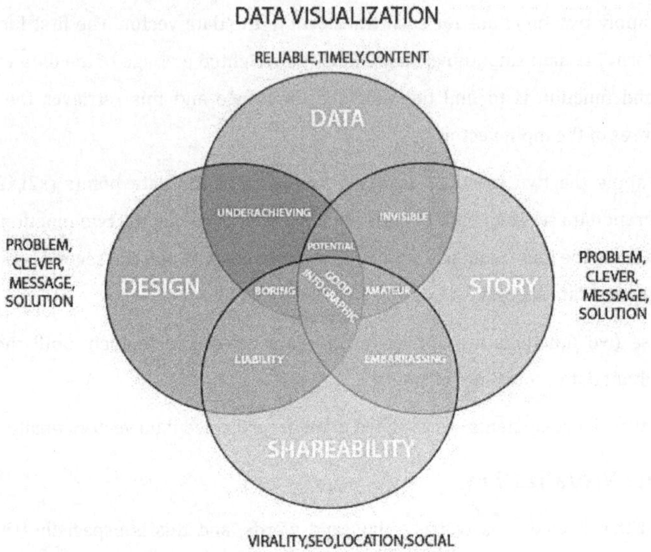

Figure 40: Data Visualization Process

Data visualization tools provide accessible ways to understand outliers, patterns, and trends in the data. In the world of Big Data, the data visualization tools and technologies are required to analyze vast amounts of information. Data visualizations are common in our everyday life, but they always appear in the form of graphs and charts. The combination of multiple visualizations and bits of information are referred to as Infographics.

Data visualizations are used to discover unknown facts and trends. It can be observed that visualizations in the form of line charts to display change over time. Bar and column charts are useful for observing relationships and making comparisons. A pie chart is a great way to show parts-of-a-whole. And maps are the best way to share geographical data visually. Today's data visualization tools go beyond the charts and graphs used in the Microsoft Excel spreadsheet, which displays the data in more sophisticated ways such as dials and gauges, geographic maps, heat maps, pie chart, and fever chart.

10.6. Importance of Data Visualization

Data visualization is important because of the processing of information in human brains. Using graphs and charts to visualize a large amount of the complex data sets is more comfortable in comparison to studying the spreadsheet and reports.

Data visualization is an easy and quick way to convey concepts universally. Within the broader goal of conveying key insights, different visualizations can be used to tell different stories. Data visualizations can be used to:

- **Convey Changes Over Time:** For example, a line graph could be used to present how the value of Bitcoin changed over a certain time period.
- **Determine the Frequency of Events:** You could use a histogram to visualize the frequency distribution of a single event over a certain time period (e.g. number of internet users per year from 2007 to 2021).
- **Highlight Interesting Relationships or Correlations between Variables:** If you wanted to highlight the relationship between two variables (e.g. marketing spend and revenue, or hours of weekly exercise vs. cardiovascular fitness), you could use a scatter plot to see, at a glance, if one increases as the other decreases (or vice versa).
- **Examine a Network:** If you want to understand what's going on within a certain network (for example, your entire customer base), network visualizations can help you to identify (and depict) meaningful connections and clusters within your network of interest.
- **Analyze Value and Risk:** If you want to weigh up value versus risk in order to figure out which opportunities or strategies are worth pursuing, data visualizations—such as a color-coded system—could help you to categorize and identify, at a glance, which items are feasible.

Data Visualization have some more Specialties such as

- Identifying areas that need improvement or modifications.
- Clarifying which factor influences customer behavior.
- Understanding which products to place where.
- Predicting sales volumes.

Data visualization tools have been necessary for democratizing data, analytics, and making data-driven perception available to workers throughout an organization. They are easy to operate in comparison to earlier versions of BI software or traditional statistical analysis software.

10.7. Exploration Versus Explanation

Generally speaking, there are two categories of data visualization: *exploration* and *explanation*. The two serve different purposes, and so there are tools and approaches that may be appropriate only for one and not the other. For this reason, it is important to understand the distinction, so that you can be sure you are using tools and approaches appropriate to the task at hand.

In a nutshell, exploratory data visualization helps you figure out what's in your data, while explanatory visualization helps you to communicate what you've found. Exploration takes place while you're still analyzing the data, while explanation comes towards the end of the process.

Explanatory visualizations are author-driven with a predefined path through the visualization, they rely more heavily on messaging, and include more curated interactivity. This approach works best when the goal is to tell a story or to communicate efficiently. Explanatory visualizations can be used to communicate the key results of an analysis, in which data to be displayed is determined in advance and the way it is presented is informed by the end user's needs.

Explanatory data visualization is appropriate when the data scientist already knows what the data has to say, and he is *trying to tell that story to somebody else*. It could be the head of a department, a grant committee, or the general public.

Whoever the audience is, the story the data scientist is trying to tell (or the answer he is trying to share) is *known to the data scientist at the outset*, and therefore he can design to specifically accommodate and highlight that story. In other words, he can make certain *editorial decisions* about which information stays in, and which is distracting or irrelevant to be removed. This is a process of selecting focused data that will support the story the scientistis trying to tell.

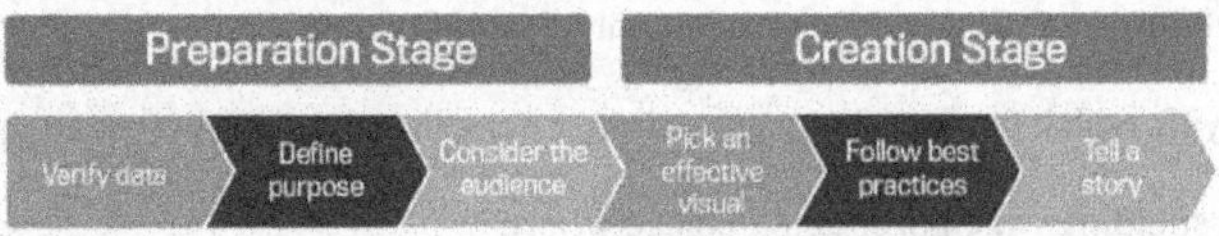

Figure 42: Depicts Explanatory Visualization

Stephen Few, in his book *Show Me the Numbers* (Analytics Press, El Dorado Hills, Calif., 2004), identifies four purposes for tables and graphs of quantitative business information.

1. Analyzing
2. Communicating
3. Monitoring
4. Planning

Think about your purpose and choose only the visualizations that align with that purpose.

When preparing visualizations, always keep in mind the audience that will be viewing the visualization: Who will be consuming the information? How much background do they have regarding the topic? Will they be the decision maker?

Picking an effective visual is easier said than done. Most of us have never been trained in data visualization and have little knowledge as to what type of visual is most effective. It helps to break this down into the following:

- Consider the purpose of your analysis.
- Identify visuals that will meet that purpose.
- Understand the data that's needed to create the visual you would like.
- Match the purpose and the data to the appropriate visual.
- Be sure to follow best practices for your chosen visual.

Determining the purpose of the analysis is critical so that you can pick an effective visual. There are many potential purposes for data analysis. Below is a decision tree that provides a way to identify appropriate visualizations if the purpose of the analysis is to show composition, relationships, or distributions. Following figure provides guidance when the purpose is to show trends or comparisons.

Once you have identified your purpose, you can then narrow down to the types of appropriate visualizations. At this point, you'll need to be sure you understand the type of data required for the possible visualizations. The best visualization will be the one that matches the purpose and works with the data that you need to visualize. Finally, you should follow best practices for the type of visualization that you decide to use.

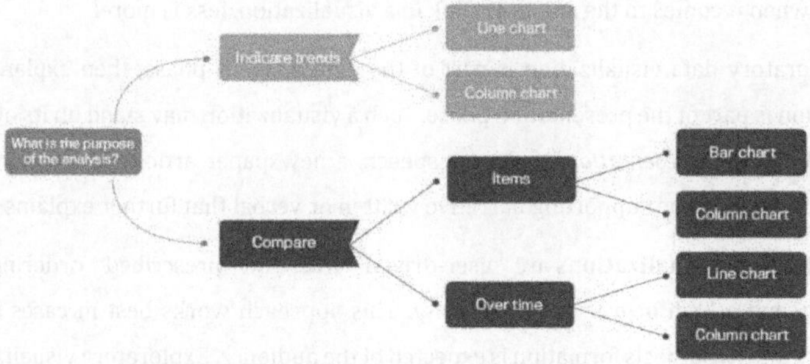

Figure 43: Visual Tools Used to Present Comparisons and Trends

Source: Ann C. Dzuranin, Guido Geerts, and Margarita Lenk, *Data and Analytics in Accounting: An Integrated Approach,* John Wiley & Sons, Hoboken, N.J., forthcoming.

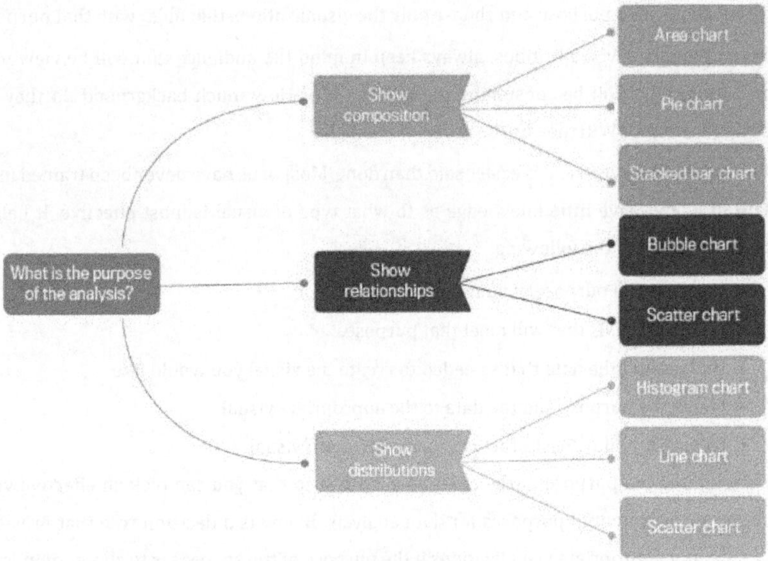

Figure 44: Visual Tools Used to Present Compositions, Relationships and Distributions

Source: Ann C. Dzuranin, Guido Geerts, and Margarita Lenk, *Data and Analytics in Accounting: An Integrated Approach,* John Wiley & Sons, Hoboken, N.J., forthcoming.

Along with the best practices based on the type of visualization, there are a couple of other important practices to consider. The first is to avoid cluttering your visual with nonessential information. Clutter is the enemy of a good visualization. Tufte recommends maximizing the data-to-ink ratio, meaning you should remove any nondate-related ink and any redundant ink. Basically, when it comes to the amount of ink in a visualization, less is more.

If exploratory data visualization is part of the data analysis phase, then explanatory data visualization is part of the presentation phase. Such a visualization may stand on its own, or *may be part of a larger presentation*, such as a speech, a newspaper article, or a report. In these scenarios, there is some supporting narrative written or verbal that further explains things.

Exploratory visualizations are user-driven with no prescribed ordering, limited messaging, and a high degree of interactivity. This approach works best in cases when data diagnostics and hypothesis formation is expected of the audience. Exploratory visualizations can be used to allow users to independently discover patterns and unravel connections by presenting different perspectives onto the data to be analyzed.

Exploratory data visualizations are appropriate when a whole bunch of data is available and the data scientist is *not sure what is in it*. When he needs to get a sense of what is inside the data set, translating it into a visual medium can help in quickly identify its features, including interesting curves, lines, trends, or anomalous outliers.

Exploration is generally best done at a high level of granularity. There may be a whole lot of noise in the data, but if it is oversimplified or strip out too much information, the analyst could end up missing something important. This type of visualization is typically part of the *data analysis* phase, and is used to find *the story the data has to tell the data scientist*.

Hybrids: Exploratory Explanation

It is worth noting that there is also a kind of hybrid category, which involves a *curated dataset* that is nonetheless presented with the intention to allow some exploration on the reader's part. These visualizations are usually interactive via some kind of graphical interface that lets the reader choose and constrain certain parameters, thereby discovering for themselves whatever insights the dataset may have to offer. These might even be insights the creator of the visualization has not come across yet.

So, in these hybrid designs there is a certain freedom-of-discovery aspect to the information presented, but it is usually not totally raw; it has been distilled and facilitated to some extent.

Differences in Visualizations

So, let's see how the differences between exploratory and explanatory analyses manifest in their visualizations.

Exploratory

- Don't use heavy annotations such arrows or explanatory texts, to encourage unbiased exploration and original thinking.
- Have filters/filter actions in order to aid in digging through data and seeing from different perspectives.
- Do not phrase titles as call to actions or explanatory insights.
- Usually have more than one type of visualizations to view the same data from different perspectives.
- Usually not used for data storytelling/presentations until the explanatory phase is complete.
- Sharing is limited to internal teams/research groups and not published or presented to larger groups.

Explanatory

- Use annotations and attributes (such as color and size) to focus the audience's attention to a particular insight and/or to explain observations.
- Optionally, have some filters/filter actions.
- Optimize titles to highlight insights or be a call to action.
- Use for data storytelling/presentations.

10.8. The Designer-Reader-Data Trinity

It is useful to think of an effective explanatory data visualization as being supported by a three-legged stool consisting of the designer, the reader, and the data. Each of these exerts a force, or contributes a separate perspective, that must be taken into consideration for a visualization to be stable and successful.

Each of the three legs of the stool has a unique relationship to the other two. While it is necessary to account for the needs and perspective of all three in each visualization project, the dominant relationship will ultimately determine which category of visualization is needed.

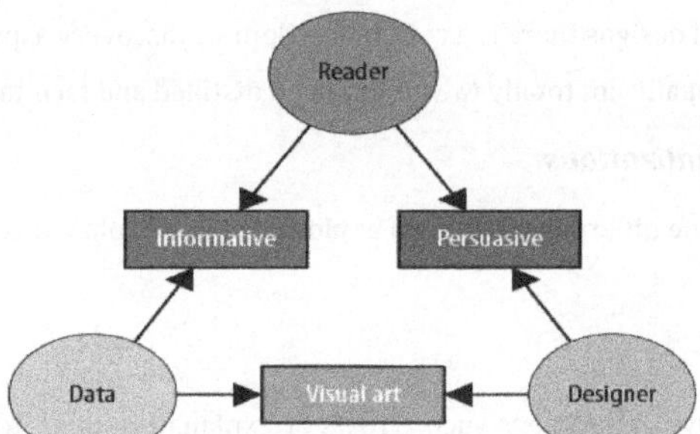

Figure 45: Designer-Reader-Data Trinity

Informative

An *informative visualization* primarily serves the relationship *between the reader and the data.* It aims for a neutral presentation of the facts in such a way that will educate the reader (though not necessarily persuade him). Informative visualizations are often associated with broad data sets, and seek to distill the content into a manageably consumable form. Ideally, they form the bulk of visualizations that the average person encounters on a day-to-day basis whether that is at work, in the newspaper, or on a service-provider's website. The Burning Man Info graphicis an example of informative visualization.

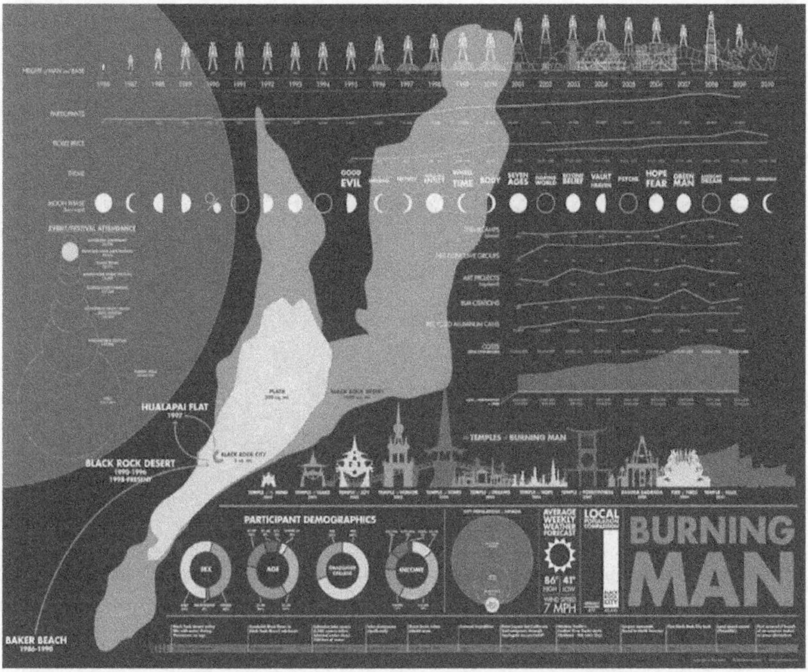

Figure 46: The Burning Man Infographic

Persuasive

A *persuasive visualization* primarily serves the relationship *between the designer and the reader*. It is useful when the designer wishes to change the reader's mind about something. It represents a very specific point of view, and advocates a change of opinion or action on the part of the reader. In this category of visualization, the data represented is specifically chosen for the purpose of supporting the designer's point of view, and is presented carefully so as to convince the reader of same.

A good example of persuasive visualization is the Joint Economic Committee minority's rendition of the proposed Democratic health care plan in 2010 shown below. While an informative visualization may not have an intentional point of view in the manner that a persuasive visualization does, all visualizations are going to be biased to some degree, based on the fact that designers are human and have to make choices.

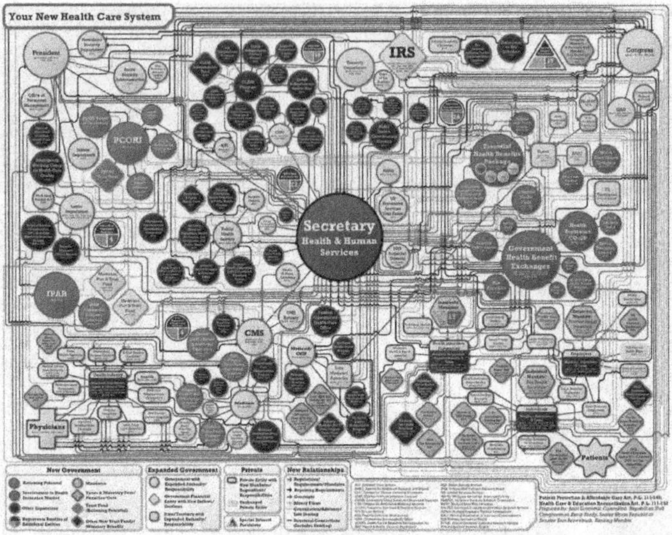

Figure 47: Joint Economic Committee Minority's Rendition of the Proposed Democratic Health Care Plan in 2010

Visual Art

The third category, *visual art*, primarily serves the relationship *between the designer and the data*. Visual art is unlike the previous two categories in that it often entails *unidirectional* encoding of information, meaning that the reader may not be able to decode the visual presentation to understand the underlying information.

Whereas both informative and persuasive visualizations are meant to be easily decodable *bidirectional* in their encoding visual art merely translates the data into a visual form. The designer may intend only to condense it, translate it into a new medium, or make it beautiful; she may not intend for the reader to be able to extract anything from it other than enjoyment.

This category of visualization is sometimes more easily recognized than others. For example, Nora Ligorano and Marshall Reese designed a project that converts Twitter streams into a woven fiber-optic tapestry shown below. A project like this is abstract enough that most people intuitively recognize it as art: something to be appreciated rather than explicitly decoded.

Participants address the Fiber Optic Tapestry by tweeting #optic tapestry and a primary color of the tapestry displays the colors in algorithmically-determined patterns.

Figure 48: Fiber Optic Tapestry

General tools used for visualization are charts, tables, graphs, geospatial representation, infographics and dashboards. All of these are explained below.

Chart

A chart is a representation of data in the form of a graph, diagram, map, or tabular format. This could make the other two families, Geospatial and Tables, subfamilies of it. We distinguish between them to help you identify when one works better for your data. Consider the most common Charts: Scatterplots, Bar Charts, Line Graphs, and Pie Charts. These chart types, or a combination of them, provide answers to most questions with relational data. They are the backbone of performing visual analysis on non-geospatial data.

Visualizing data with Charts relies on drawing points using cartesian coordinates (Ex. X, Y, Z) based on a set of dimensions and measures. Dimensions (Ex. categories, dates, etc.) group the measures (Ex. profit, deaths, temperature, etc.) for analysis. The measures are then rendered on the corresponding coordinates to create a visualization. Some types of visualizations excel at displaying many dimensions (Ex. Ordered Bar Charts), while others can only support a few with clarity (Ex. Pie Charts).

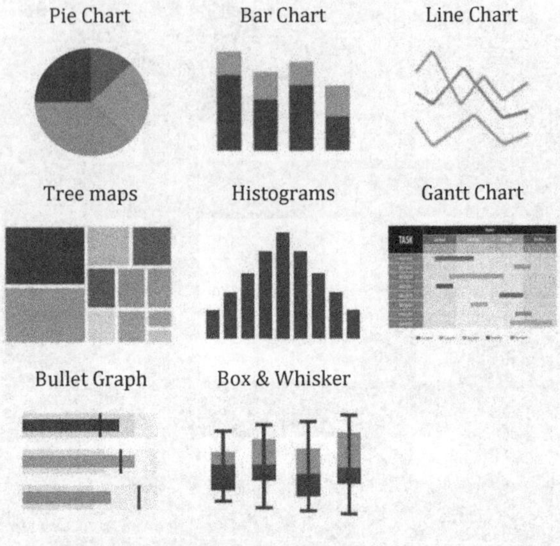

Figure 48: Shows different Types of Charts

1. **Pie Chart:** A common, but limited, visualization used to show how a few dimensions compare to one another and the whole.
2. **Bar Chart:** Used to categorize elements based on size. Can be ordered or unordered based on the nature of the dimensions.
3. **Line Chart:** Best used to show trends across time intervals. Multiple lines can be used to compare categories within a dimension.
4. **Treemaps:** A treemap breaks the whole into its parts using a quantitative measure to determine the size of each square.
5. **Histogram:** Histograms split a single continuous measure into bins, or groups, to analyze distribution.
6. **Gantt Chart:** A Gantt chart is a project management tool that illustrates work completed over a period of time in relation to the time planned for the work. A Gantt chart can include the start and end dates of tasks, milestones, dependencies between tasks, assignees, and more.
7. **Bullet Graph:** A bullet graph takes a bar chart and adds additional elements to create a compact way to analyze performance against a goal or threshold.
8. **Box & Whisker:** A box and whisker plot shows the range of values along with the average and interquartile ranges.

Table: Like most charts, a table organizes data by axis. The rows are the x-axis and columns are the y-axis. Common convention, because tables are read, uses the x-axis to display the categories. The y-axis displays the values within each measure, with the columns being labeled to clearly indicate their meaning. Unlike most charts, tables can display qualitative data in an organized manner and highlight relationships between them.

1. **Highlight Table:** A form of table that uses color to categorize similar data, allowing the viewer to read it more easily and intuitively.
2. **Heat Map:** A heatmap uses color and size to show the values of a measure. A type of geospatial visualization in map form which displays specific data values as different colors (this doesn't need to be temperatures, but that is a common use).
3. **Contingency table:** A contingency table (also known as a cross tabulation or crosstab) is a type of table in a matrix format that displays the (multivariate) frequency distribution of the variables. They are heavily used in survey research, business intelligence, engineering, and scientific research.

Highlight Table | Heatmap | Contingency table

Graph: Graph visualization is concerned with visual representations of graph or network data. Effective graph visualization reveals structures that may be present in the graphs and helps the users to understand and analyze the underlying data.

A graph consists of nodes and edges. It is a mathematical structure describing relations among a set of entities, where a node represents an entity, and an edge exists between two nodes if the two corresponding entities are related. A graph can be described by writing down the nodes and the edges.

Graph visualization, also called link analysis or network visualization, is a way to visually represent connections between entities in data. The most effective way to visualize graphs is through a node-link model, where nodes represent entities and links represent connections. These nodes and links can be anything – transactions between accounts, devices on a network, or phone calls between friends.

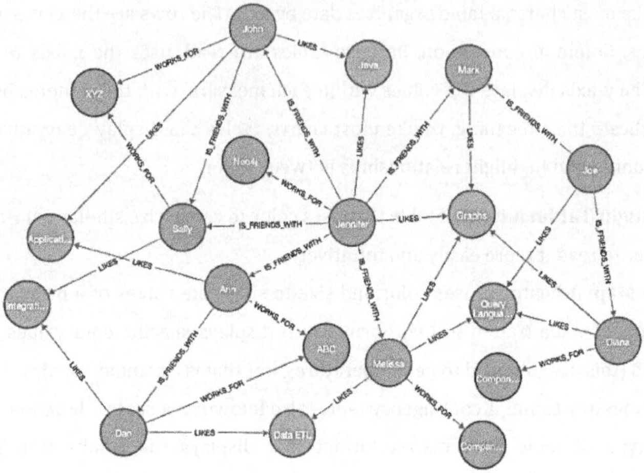

Figure 49: Example of Graph Visualization

Geospatial: A visualization that shows data in map form using different shapes and colors to show the relationship between pieces of data and specific locations. These visualizations focus on the relationship between data and its physical location to create insight. Any positional data works for spatial analysis. What makes geospatial visualizations unique is the scale.

Geospatial or spatial data visualizations relate to real life physical locations, overlaying familiar maps with different data points. These types of data visualizations are commonly used to display sales or acquisitions over time, and can be most recognizable for their use in political campaigns or to display market penetration in multinational corporations.

The following are the types of geospatial maps:

Proportional Symbol Maps: Symbols placed at locations represent events of interest. Measures are represented by shapes using size and color to display values.

Choropleth, Isopleth, Area Maps: These area maps represent values by different shades of color over a geographic region. Choropleths rely on boundaries, while isopleths rely on density to display the data.

Flow Map: A flow map is a type of thematic map that uses linear symbols to represent movement. It may thus be considered a hybrid of a map and a flow diagram. The movement being mapped may be that of anything, including people, highway traffic, trade goods, water, ideas, or even telecommunications data.

Density Map: Density mapping is simply **a way to show where points or lines may be concentrated in a given area**. Often, such maps utilize interpolation methods to estimate, across a given surface, where concentration of a given feature might be (e.g., population).

Cartogram: A **cartogram** (also called a **value-area map** or an **anamorphic map**, the latter common among German-speakers) is a thematic map of a set of features (countries, provinces, etc.), in which their geographic size is altered to be directly proportional to a selected ratio-level variable, such as travel time, population. Geographic space itself is thus warped, sometimes extremely, in order to visualize the distribution of the variable. It is one of the most abstract types of map; in fact, some forms may more properly be called diagrams.

Heat Map: A heat map (or heatmap) is a graphical representation of data where values are depicted by color. Heat maps make it easy to visualize complex data and understand it at a glance. Website heatmaps visualize the most popular (hot) and unpopular (cold) elements of a webpage using colors on a scale from red to blue.

Proportional Symbol Maps	Choropleth, Isopleth, Area Maps

Flow Map	Density Map

Cartogram	Heat Map
	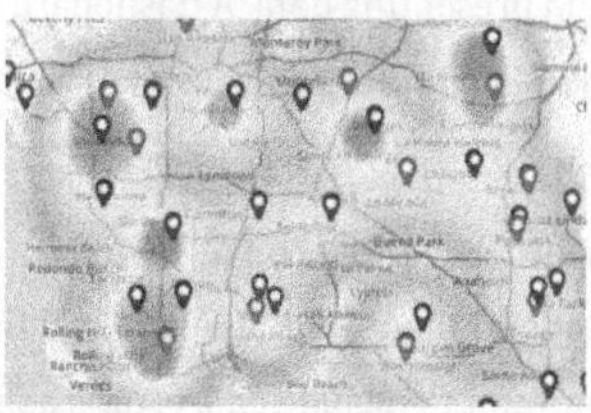

Infographic

An infographic is a collection of imagery, data visualizations like pie charts and bar graphs, and minimal text that gives an easy-to-understand overview of a topic. According to the Oxford English Dictionary, an infographic (or information graphic) is "a visual representation of information or data". But the meaning of an infographic is something much more specific. An infographic is a big picture that summarizes a topic. It is a one-page publication that presents **info**rmation in a **graphic** way. Simple icons, symbols, maps, and charts combine to explain the data. Text is only used as labels or to briefly describe facts. The viewer explores the content by studying each section of cartoon-like images. An example is shown in the below figure.

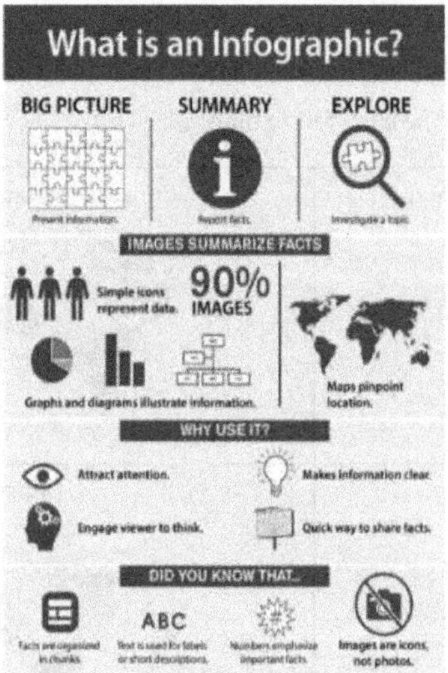

Figure 50: Example of Inforgraph

Dashboards: A collection of visualizations and data displayed in one place to help with analyzing and presenting data. A dashboard is a visual display of all of your data. While it can be used in all kinds of different ways, its primary intention is to provide information at-a-glance, such as KPIs.

A dashboard usually sits on its own page and receives information from a linked database. In many cases it's configurable, allowing you the ability to choose which data you want to see and whether you want to include charts or graphs to visualize the numbers.

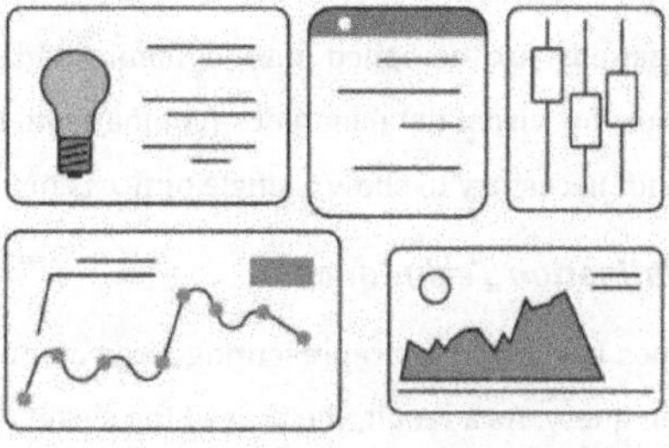

Figure 51: Dashboard

10.9. Data Visualization Techniques

The type of data visualization technique you leverage will vary based on the type of data you're working with, in addition to the story you're telling with your data. The variety of Data visualization techniques is given in figure 11.

5 factors that influence data visualization choices:

Audience: It's important to adjust data representation to the specific target audience. For example, fitness mobile app users who browse through their progress can easily work with uncomplicated visualizations. On the other hand, if data insights are intended for researchers and experienced decision-makers who regularly work with data, you can and often have to go beyond simple charts.

Content: The type of data you are dealing with will determine the tactics. For example, if it's time-series metrics, you will use line charts to show the dynamics in many cases. To show the relationship between two elements, scatter plots are often used. In turn, bar charts work well for comparative analysis.

Context: You can use different data visualization approaches and read data depending on the context. To emphasize a certain figure, for example, significant profit growth, you can use the shades of one color on the chart and highlight the highest value with the brightest one. On the contrary, to differentiate elements, you can use contrast colors.

Dynamics: There are various types of data, and each type has a different rate of change. For example, financial results can be measured monthly or yearly, while time series and tracking data are changing constantly. Depending on the rate of change, you may consider dynamic representation (steaming) or static data visualization techniques in data mining.

Purpose: The goal of data visualization affects the way it is implemented. In order to make a complex analysis, visualizations are compiled into dynamic and controllable dashboards equipped with different tools for visual data analytics (comparison, formatting, filtering, etc.). However, dashboards are not necessary to show a single or occasional data insight.

1. *Pixel Oriented Visualization Techniques*

Pixel-oriented techniques have used for representing large amounts of high - dimensional data with respect to a given query. As a result, the user of the system is able to refine his query based on the knowledge gathered from the visual representation of the data. The basic idea of pixel-oriented techniques is to represent each attribute value as a single colored pixel, mapping the range of possible attribute values to a fixed color map and displaying different attributes in different sub windows. Pixel-oriented visualization techniques maximize the amount of information represented at one time without any overlap. They effectively preserve the perception of small regions of interest while still maintaining the global view. These properties making them suitable for various data mining tasks.

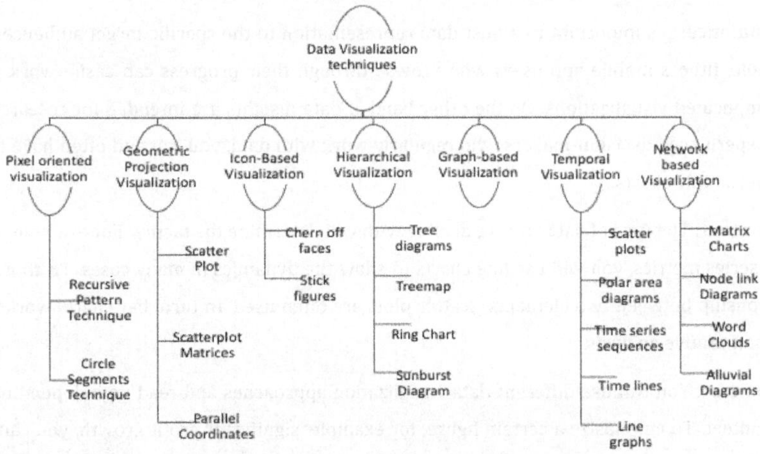

Figure 52: Categories of Data Visualization Techniques

Several pixel-oriented visualization techniques have been proposed two of which we present in this section, the recursive pattern technique and the circle segments technique. Others are the spiral technique or techniques relying on space-filling curves like the Morton and Z-order techniques. We will take the stock market application as a running example for illustrating the techniques.

For a data set of m dimensions pixel-oriented techniques create m windows on the screen, one for each dimension. The m dimension values of a record are mapped to m pixels at the corresponding position in the windows. The color of the pixel reflects other corresponding values. Inside a window, the data values are arranged in some global order shared by all windows Eg: All Electronics maintains a customer information table, which consists of 4 dimensions: income, credit limit, transaction volume and age. We analyze the correlation between income and other attributes by visualization. We sort all customers in income in ascending order and use this order to layout the customer data in the 4 visualization windows as shown in below figure. The pixel colors are chosen so that the smaller the value, the lighter the shading. Using pixel-based visualization we can easily observe that credit limit increases as income increases customer whose income is in the middle range are more likely to purchase more from All Electronics, these is no clear correlation between income and age.

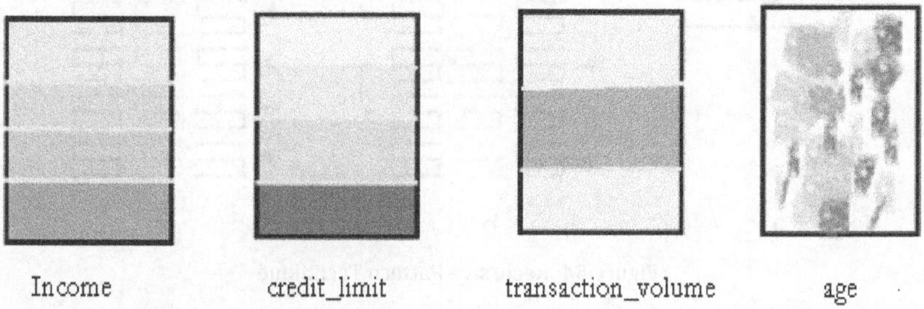

Figure 53: Pixel Oriented Visualization of 4 Attributes by Sorting all Customers in Income Ascending Order

The Recursive Pattern Technique

The recursive pattern technique is based on a generic recursive schema and is in particular aimed at representing datasets having a natural order according to one attribute (e.g. time series data). With parameters for each recursive schema, it allows the user to control the semantically meaningful substructures which determine the arrangement of the attribute values.

The recursive pattern technique visualizes each attribute in a separate sub window. Within a sub window, each attribute value is represented by one colored pixel with the color reflecting the attribute value. In order to enable the user to relate attribute values of different attributes but at the same positions, the order of the objects is reflected by the same arrangement of pixels in each sub window.

The recursive pattern technique is based on a back and forth arrangement. The recursive base element is a pattern of height h1 and width w1 as specified by the user. First, the elements of the pattern correspond to single pixels which are arranged within a rectangle of height h1 and width w1 from left to right, then below backwards from right to left, then again forward from left to right, and so on (cf. figure 13a). The same basic arrangement is done on all recursion levels with the only difference that the basic elements which are arranged on level i are the patterns resulting from the level (i-1)-arrangements (cf. figure 13b for w2 = 3, h2 = 7 and figure 13c for w2 = 3, h2 = 1 and w3 = 1, h3 = 7).

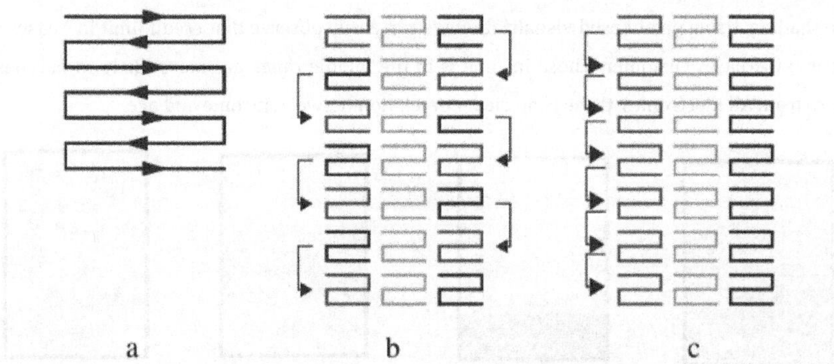

Figure 54: Recursive Pattern Technique

The Circle Segments Technique

The circle segments technique has been used for visualizing large high-dimensional datasets. The idea is not to represent different attributes in sub windows any more, instead the whole dataset is represented by a circle which is divided into segments, one for each attribute. Within the segments each attribute value is again visualized by a single colored pixel. The arrangement of the pixels starts at the center of the circle and continues to the outside by plotting on a line orthogonal to the segment-halving line in a back and forth manner (see figure14). The rationale of this approach is that close to the center all attributes are close to each other enhancing the visual comparison of their values. Besides, users involved in a highly interactive exploration process based on different pixel-oriented techniques have reported the circle segments technique to be less tedious than other techniques since they have a "visual anchor point" in the center. However, a more extensive usuability test has to be made to draw conclusions about advantages or biases.

Figure 55: Circle Segments Technique

2. *Geometric Projection Visualization Techniques*

A drawback of pixel-oriented visualization techniques is that they cannot help us much in understanding the distribution of data in a multidimensional space.

Geometric projection techniques are a good choice for finding outliers and correlation between attributes in multivariate data. A geometric projection technique does this by using transformations and projections of the data. When using large data sets a clustering algorithm is usually necessary to apply before the visualization technique to avoid cluttered and unclear data caused by the too much information. Geometric projection techniques help users find interesting projections of multidimensional data sets. Some widely used geometric projection techniques are: Scatter plot, Scatter plot matrix, parallel coordinates.

Scatter Plot

A scatter plot is one of the most common visualization techniques and can be visualized both in 3D and 2D. The scatter plot visualizes different attributes of the data on the x, y axis for 2D visualizations and also along the z-axis in 3D. A scatter plot displays 2-D data point using Cartesian co-ordinates. A third dimension can be added using different colors of shapes to represent different data points.

Scatter plots are usable to find correlations between attributes in arbitrary small data sets. If the data set gets too big or contains too many attributes the scatter plot gets cluttered and hard to interpret.

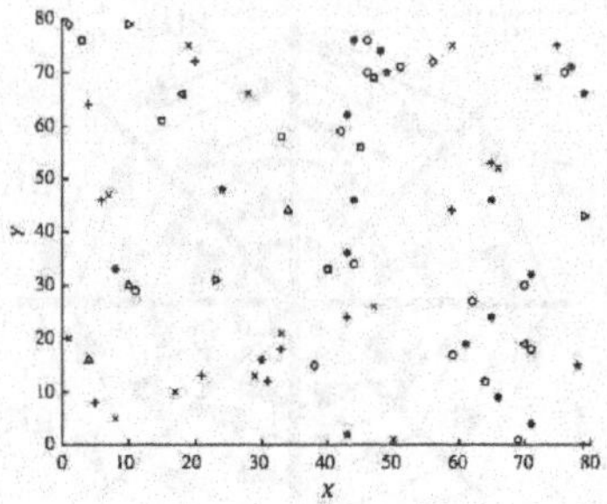

Figure 56: Visualization of 2D Data set Using Scatter Plot

Scatterplot Matrices

The scatter-plot matrix is an extension to the scatter plot. For k-dimensional data a minimum of (k2-k)/2 scatterplots of 2D will be required. There can be maximum of k2 plots of 2D in the adjoining figure, there are k2 plots. Out of these, k are X-X plots, and all X-Y plots (where X, Y are distinct dimensions) are given in 2 orientations (X vs Y and Y vs, X).

Parallel Coordinates

The scatter-plot matrix becomes less effective as the dimensionality increases. Another technique, called parallel coordinates, can handle higher dimensionality n equidistant axes which are parallel to one of the screen axes and correspond to the attributes (i.e. n dimensions). If the data contains many attributes you will need several scatter plots to visualize all attributes and it might become hard to see patterns. A technique often used for multivariate data is parallel coordinates. They work by visualizing each attribute on a vertical axis and connecting each individual data with lines between the axis (as in figure 16). Parallel coordinates strength is the possibility to find correlations between a high number of attributes. The weakness of parallel coordinates is the same as with scatter plots, if the data set is too large it easily gets cluttered.

The axes are scaled to the [minimum, maximum]: range of the corresponding attribute.

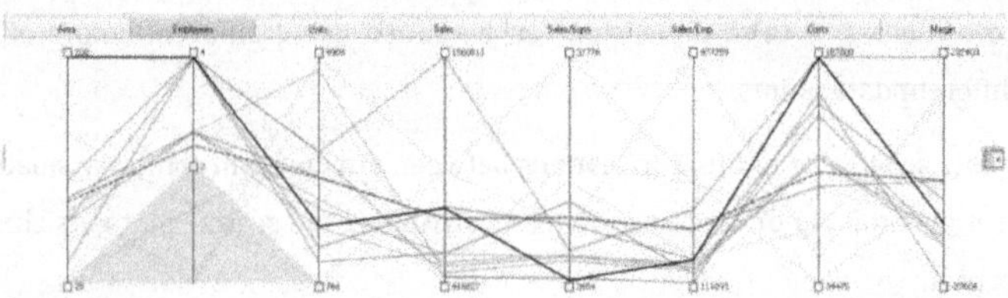

Figure 57: Visualization of 2D Data set Using Parallel Coordinates

3. *Icon-based Visualization Techniques*

Icon-based techniques visualize data by changing the properties of an icon or glyph according to the data. An early version was Chernoff faces where data is mapped to different face parts as nose, mouth, eyes and more. For example, how rich people are can be mapped to the mouth of the Chernoff face. Rich people represented by a happy mouth and poor people by a sad mouth. It uses small icons to represent multidimensional data values. Icon-based methods have the strength of being easily interpreted if icons/glyphs are chosen wisely. A poor choice can make it difficult to distinguish differences.

The popular icon-based techniques:

Chern off Faces

Chernoff faces were introduced in 1973 by statistician Herman Chernoff. They display multidimensional data of up to 18 variables (or dimensions) as a cartoon human face (See figure 17). Chernoff faces help reveal trends in the data. Components of the face, such as the eyes, ears, mouth, and nose, represent values of the dimensions by their shape, size, placement, and orientation. For example, dimensions can be mapped to the following facial characteristics: eye size, eye spacing, nose length, nose width, mouth curvature, mouth width, mouth openness, pupil size, eyebrow slant, eye eccentricity, and head eccentricity.

Chernoff faces make use of the ability of the human mind to recognize small differences in facial characteristics and to assimilate many facial characteristics at once.

Furthermore, facial features vary in perceived importance. This means that the similarity of two faces (representing two multidimensional data points) can vary depending on the order in which dimensions are assigned to facial characteristics. Therefore, this mapping should be carefully chosen. Eye size and eyebrow slant have been found to be important.

Asymmetrical Chernoff faces were proposed as an extension to the original technique. Since a face has vertical symmetry (along the y-axis), the left and right side of a face are identical, which wastes space. Asymmetrical Chernoff faces double the number of facial characteristics, thus allowing up to 36 dimensions to be displayed.

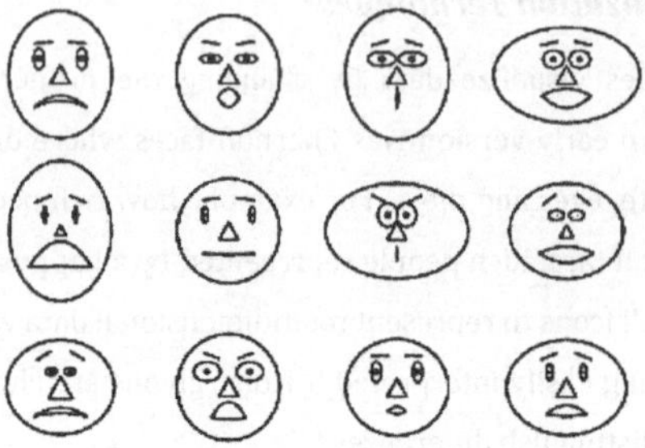

Figure 58: Chern off Faces Each Face Represents an 'n' Dimensional Data Points (n<18)

Stick Figures

The stick figure visualization technique maps multidimensional data to five-piece stick figures, where each figure has four limbs and a body. Two dimensions are mapped to the display (x and y) axes and the remaining dimensions are mapped to the angle and/or length of the limbs as in below figure. shows census data, where age and income are mapped to the display axes, and the remaining dimensions (gender, education, and so on) are mapped to stick figures. If the data items are relatively dense with respect to the two display dimensions, the resulting visualization shows texture patterns, reflecting data trends.

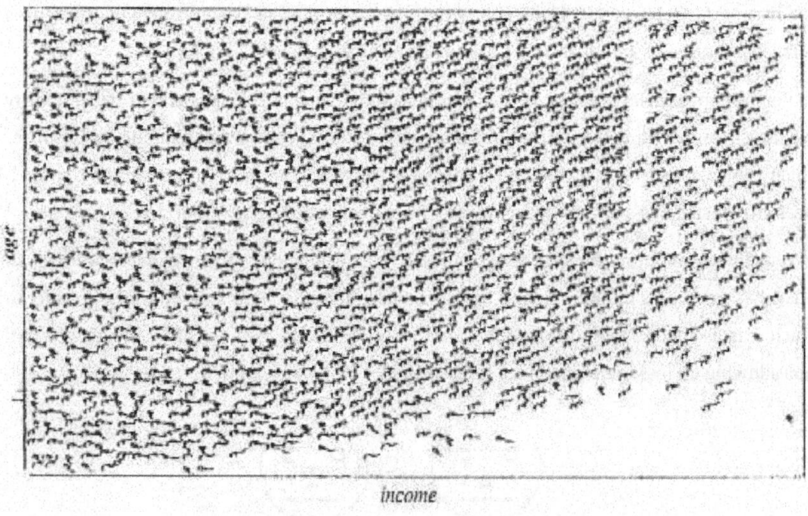

Figure 59: Stick Figure Visualization Technique

4. *Hierarchical Visualization Techniques*

Data visualizations that belong in the hierarchical category are those that order groups within larger groups. The visualization techniques discussed so far focus on visualizing multiple dimensions simultaneously. However, for a large data set of high dimensionalities, it would be difficult to visualize all dimensions at the same time. Hierarchical visualization techniques partition all dimensions into subsets (i.e., subspaces). The subspaces are visualized in a hierarchical manner.

Hierarchical visualizations are best suited if you're looking to display clusters of information, especially if they flow from a single origin point.

"Worlds-within-Worlds," also known as n-Vision, is a representative hierarchical visualization method. Suppose we want to visualize a 6-D data set, where the dimensions are F, X1, : : :, X5. We want to observe how dimension F changes with respect to the other dimensions. We can first fix the values of dimensions X3, X4, X5 to some selected values, say, c3, c4, c5. We can then visualize F, X1, X2 using a 3-D plot, called a world, as shown in figure. The position of the origin of the inner world is located at the point. c3, c4, c5/ in the outer world, which is another 3-D plot using dimensions X3, X4, X5. A user can interactively change, in the outer world, the location of the origin of the inner world.

The user then views the resulting changes of the inner world. Moreover, a user can vary the dimensions used in the inner world and the outer world. Given more dimensions, more levels of worlds can be used, which is why the method is called "worlds-within worlds." As another example of hierarchical visualization methods, tree-maps display hierarchical data as a set of nested rectangles. For example, figure shows a tree-map visualizing Google news stories. All news stories are organized into seven categories, each shown in a large rectangle of a unique color. Within each category (i.e., each rectangle at the top level), the news stories are further partitioned into smaller subcategories. The downside to these graphs is that they tend to be more complex and difficult to read, which is why the tree diagram is used most often. It is the simplest to follow due to its linear path.

Examples of Hierarchical Data Visualizations Include

1. Tree diagrams
2. Treemap
3. Ring charts
4. Sunburst diagrams

Tree Diagrams

A tree diagram is a tool in the fields of general mathematics, probability, and statistics that helps calculate the number of possible outcomes of an event or problem, and to cite those potential outcomes in an organized way.

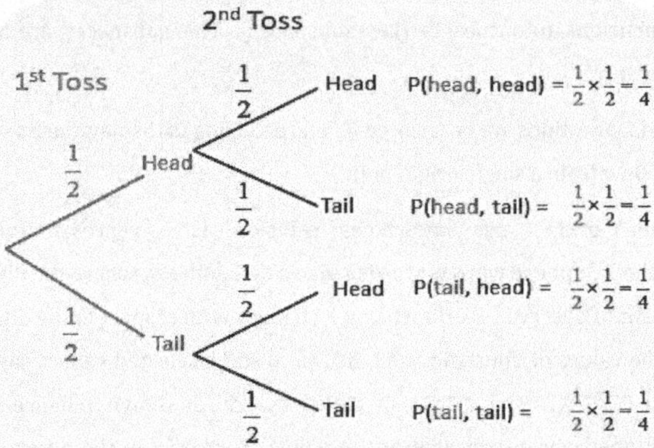

Figure 60: Tree Diagram Presenting Probabilities When a Coin is Tossed Twice

Treemap

Treemaps display hierarchical data using rectangles. Each branch of the tree is assigned a rectangle. Then each sub-branch gets assigned to a rectangle and this continues recursively until a leaf node is found. Depending on choice the rectangle representing the leaf node is colored, sized or both according to chosen attributes. This is a good way to spot relevant data and is good for categorized data, although the result can be cluttered when dealing with large data sets.

Ring Charts

Ring charts: a ring chart data visualization, or sunburst diagram, depicts hierarchy with a series of concentric rings, in which each ring corresponds to a level in the hierarchy as in figure 20. However, Ring Charts have a slight advantage over Pie Charts, which are sometimes criticized for focusing on the relative sizes of the pieces to one another and to the chart as a whole, giving no indication of changes as a whole when compared to other Pie Charts. A Ring Chart partly addresses this problem by de-emphasizing the use of area, to make the viewer focus more on the changes in overall values. You are focused on reading the length of the arcs, rather than comparing the proportions between slices.

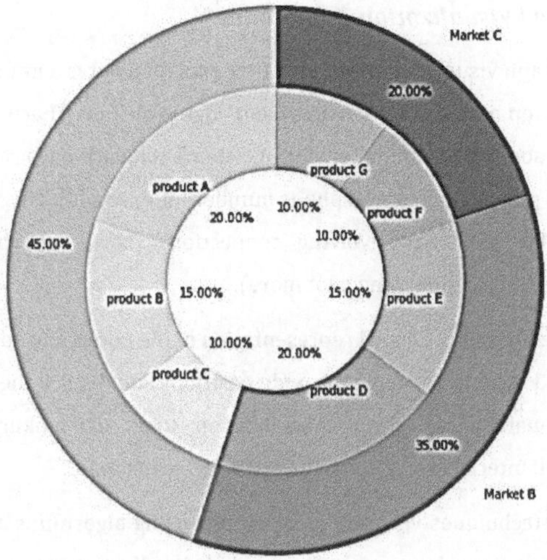

Figure 61: Ring Chart Presenting Different Products and their Markets

Sunburst Diagrams

A Sunburst Diagram is used to visualize hierarchical data, depicted by concentric circles. The circle in the centre represents the root node, with the hierarchy moving outward from the center. A sunburst chart without any hierarchical data (one level of categories), looks similar to a doughnut chart or ring chart.

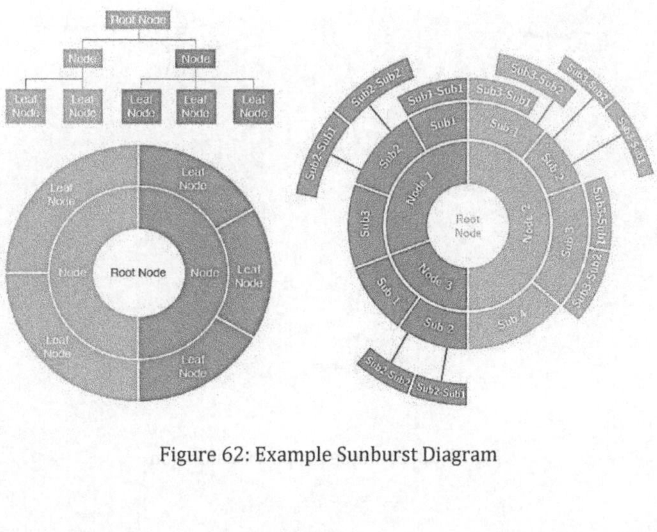

Figure 62: Example Sunburst Diagram

5. *Graph-based Visualization Techniques*

To present graph visualization we must first explain what is a graph. Also called network, a graph is a collection of nodes (or vertices) and edges (or links). Each node represents a single data point (a person, a phone number, a transaction) and each edge represents how two nodes are connected (a person possesses a phone number for example). This way of representing data is well suited for scenarios involving connections (social networks, telecommunication networks, protein interactions, and a lot more).

Graph visualization is the visual representation of the nodes and edges of a graph. Dedicated algorithms, called layouts, calculate the node positions and display the data on two (sometimes three) dimensional spaces. Graph visualization tools like Linkurious Enterprise provide user-friendly web interfaces to interact and explore graph data.

Graph-based techniques visualize large graphs using algorithms and abstraction layers to present a clear overview of the graph. This kind of visualization is less intuitive when searching in large data sets but has the advantage of being able to see relations and large amounts of data in a single graph.

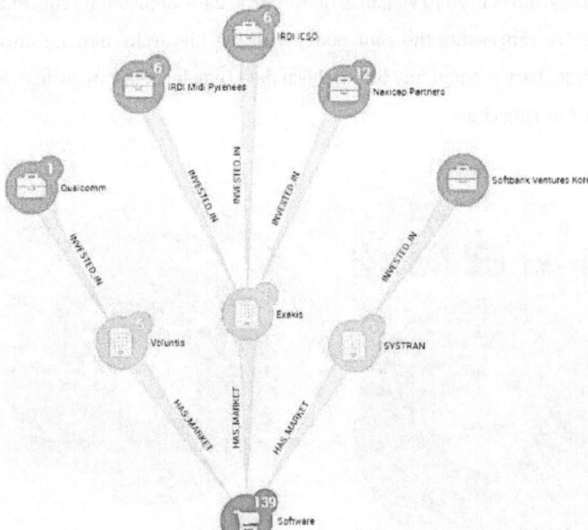

Figure 63: Example Graph Visualization

6. *Temporal*

Data visualizations belong in the temporal category if they satisfy two conditions: that they are linear, and that they are one-dimensional. Temporal visualizations normally feature lines that either stand alone or overlap with each other, with a start and finish time.

1. Scatter plots
2. Polar area diagrams
3. Time series sequences
4. Time lines
5. Line graphs

Examples of Temporal Data Visualization Include

Scatter Plots: A scatter plot (also called a scatterplot, scatter graph, scatter chart, scatter gram, or scatter diagram) is a type of plot or mathematical diagram using Cartesian coordinates to display values for typically two variables for a set of data.

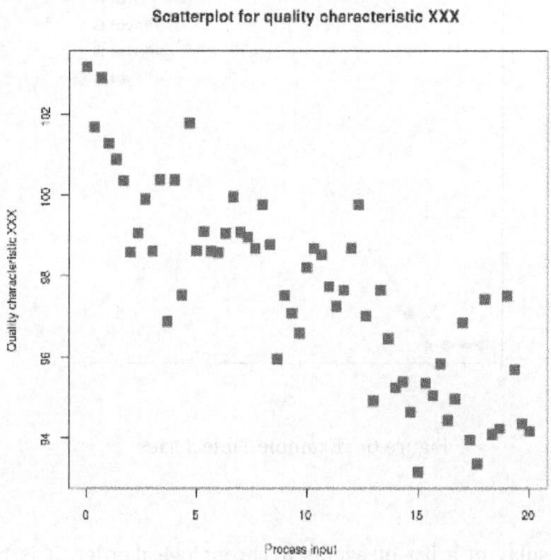

Figure 64: Example Scatter Plot

Polar Area Diagrams: Polar area diagrams are a mix of pie charts and histograms. They have identical angles and extend from the plot's center depending on the magnitude of the values that are plotted.

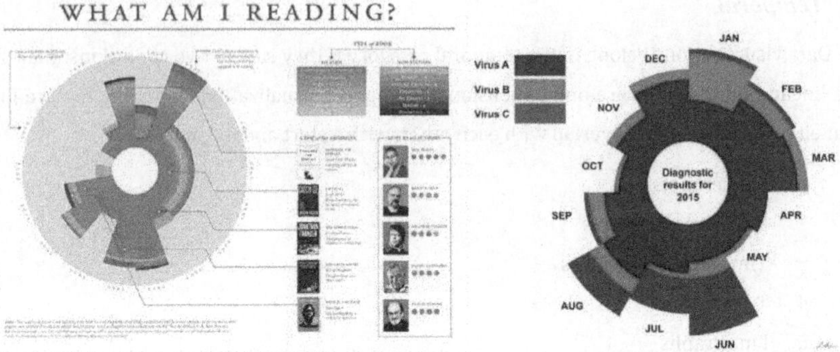

Figure 65: Example Polar Area Diagrams

Time Series Sequences: A time series is a sequence of data points that occur in successive order over some period of time. This can be contrasted with cross-sectional data, which captures a point-in-time.

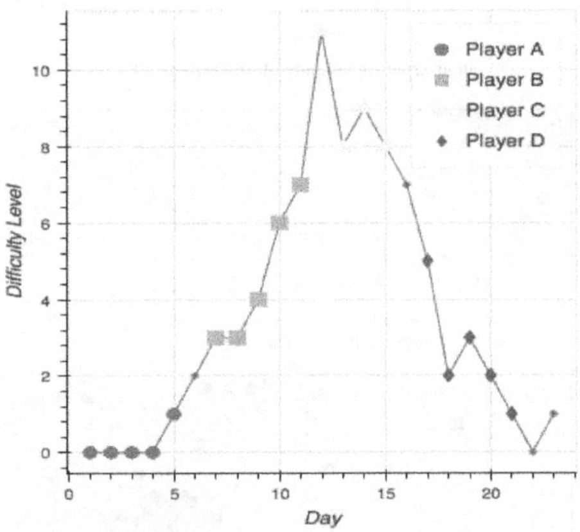

Figure 66: Example Time Series

Timelines

A **timeline** is a display of a list of events in chronological order. It is typically a graphic design showing a long bar labelled with dates paralleling it, and usually contemporaneous events. It's a graphical representation of a period of time, on which important events are marked.

They are a chronological arrangement of events in the order of their occurrence and can also be a schedule for when a process or procedure will be carried out.

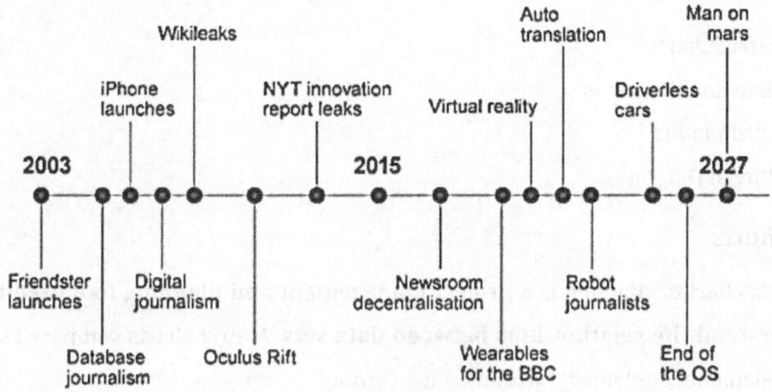

Figure 67: Timeline Representation

Line Graphs

A line graph is a type of chart used to show information that changes over time. We plot line graphs using several points connected by straight lines. We also call it a line chart. The line graph comprises of two axes known as 'x' axis and 'y' axis.

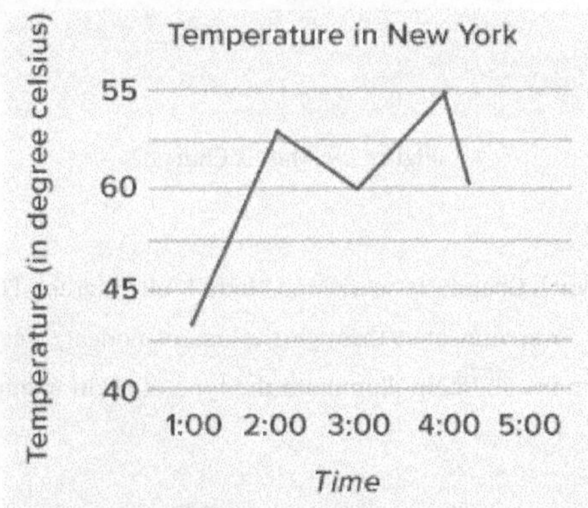

Figure 68: Line Graph Denoting Time

7. *Network*

Datasets connect deeply with other datasets. Network data visualizations show how they relate to one another within a network.

In other words, demonstrating relationships between datasets without wordy explanations.

Examples of Network Data Visualizations Include

1. Matrix Charts
2. Node link Diagrams
3. Word Clouds
4. Alluvial Diagrams

Matrix Charts

A matrix chart or diagram is **a project management and planning tool used to analyze and understand the relationships between data sets**. Matrix charts compare two or more groups of elements or elements within a single group.

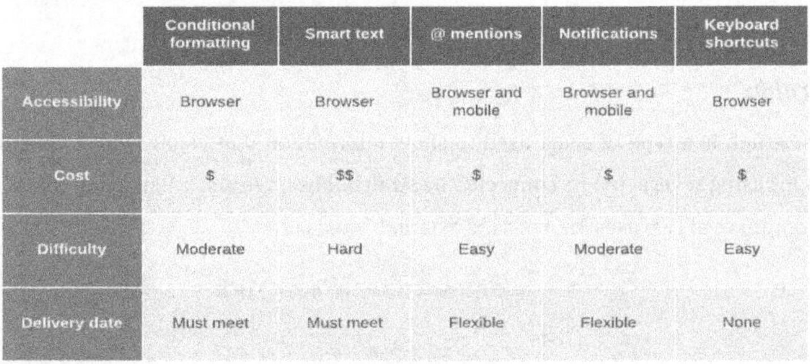

	Conditional formatting	Smart text	@ mentions	Notifications	Keyboard shortcuts
Accessibility	Browser	Browser	Browser and mobile	Browser and mobile	Browser
Cost	$	$$	$	$	$
Difficulty	Moderate	Hard	Easy	Moderate	Easy
Delivery date	Must meet	Must meet	Flexible	Flexible	None

Figure 69: Matrix Charts

Node-link Diagrams

Also known as **Network Graph**, Network Map, Node-Link Diagram. This type of visualisation shows how things are interconnected through the use of nodes / vertices and link lines to represent their connections and help illuminate the type of relationships between a group of entities.

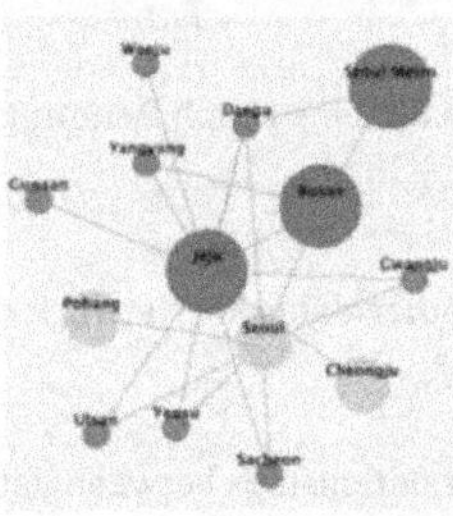

Figure 70: Node-link Representation

Word Clouds

Word clouds (also known as text clouds or tag clouds) work in a simple way: the more a specific word appears in a source of textual data (such as a speech, blog post, or database), the bigger and bolder it appears in the word cloud.

A word cloud is a collection, or cluster, of words depicted in different sizes. The bigger and bolder the word appears, the more often it's mentioned within a given text and the more important it is.

Also known as tag clouds or text clouds, these are ideal ways to pull out the most pertinent parts of textual data, from blog posts to databases. They can also help business users compare and contrast two different pieces of text to find the wording similarities between the two.

Figure 71: Word-Cloud Representation

Alluvial Diagrams

Alluvial diagrams are **a type of flow diagram originally developed to represent changes in network structure over time.** In allusion to both their visual appearance and their emphasis on flow, alluvial diagrams are named after alluvial fans that are naturally formed by the soil deposited from streaming water.

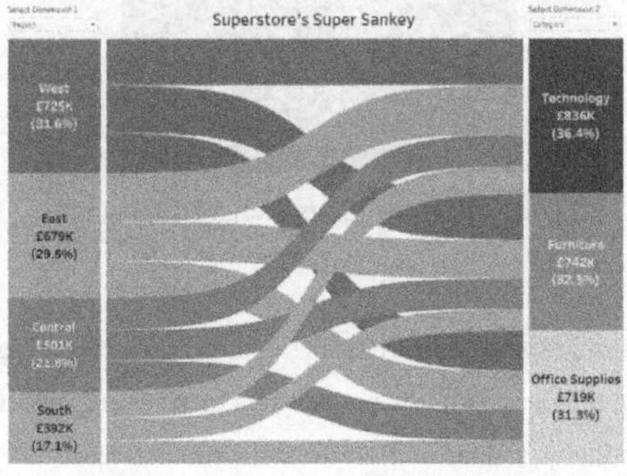

Figure 72: Example Alluvial Diagram

8. *Multidimensional*

Just like the name, multidimensional data visualizations have multiple dimensions. This means that there are always 2 or more variables in the mix to create a 3D data visualization.

Because of the many concurrent layers and datasets, these types of visualizations tend to be the most vibrant or eye-catching visuals. The same visualization tools escribed earlier may be used to present data visually for multi-dimensional data also.

These visuals can break down a ton of data down to key take aways.

Examples of Multidimensional Data Visualizations Include

1. Scatter plots
2. Pie charts
3. Venn Diagrams
4. Stacked bar graphs
5. Histograms

Scatter Plots

A scatter plot (also called a scatterplot, scatter graph, scatter chart, scatter gram, or scatter diagram) is **a type of plot or mathematical diagram using Cartesian coordinates to display values for typically two variables for a set of data.**

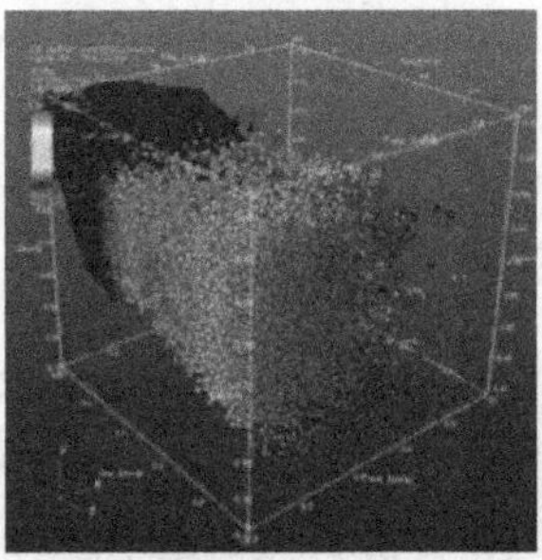

Figure 73: Multi-dimensional Scatter Plot

Pie Charts

A **pie chart** is a type of graph that represents the data in the circular graph. The slices of pie show the relative size of the data, and it is a type of pictorial representation of data. A pie chart requires a list of categorical variables and numerical variables. Here, the term "pie" represents the whole, and the "slices" represent the parts of the whole.

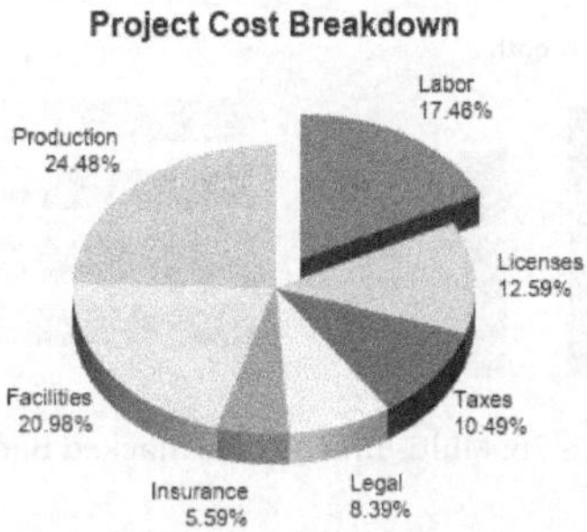

Figure 74: Multi-dimensional Pie Chart

Venn Diagrams

A Venn diagram is an illustration that uses circles to show the relationships among things or finite groups of things. Circles that overlap have a commonality while circles that do not overlap do not share those traits.

Venn diagrams help to visually represent the similarities and differences between two concepts. They have long been recognized for their usefulness as educational tools. Since the mid-20th century, Venn diagrams have been used as part of the introductory logic curriculum and in elementary-level educational plans around the world.

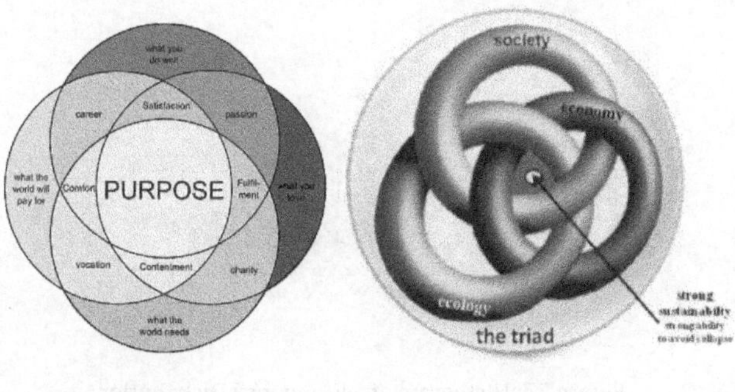

Figure 75: Multi-dimensional Venn Diagram

Stacked Bar Graphs

A stacked bar chart, also known as a stacked bar graph, is **a graph that is used to break down and compare parts of a whole**. Each bar in the chart represents a whole, and segments in the bar represent different parts or categories of that whole.

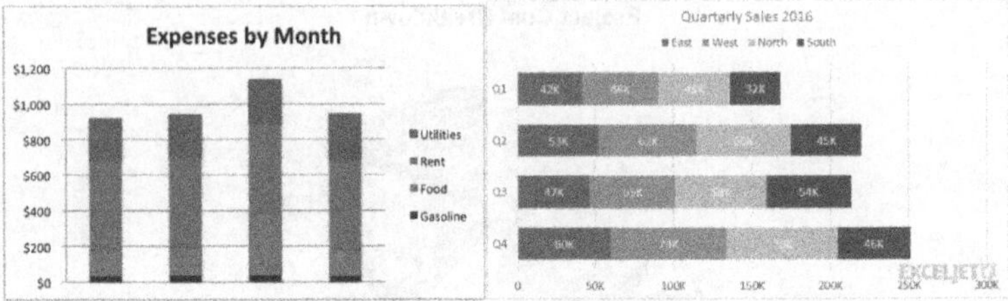

Figure 76: Multi-dimensional Stacked Bar Graphs

Histograms

A **histogram** is a graphical representation of a grouped frequency distribution with continuous classes. It is an area diagram and can be defined as a set of rectangles with bases along with the intervals between class boundaries and with areas proportional to frequencies in the corresponding classes. In such representations, all the rectangles are adjacent since the base covers the intervals between class boundaries. The heights of rectangles are proportional to corresponding frequencies of similar classes and for different classes, the heights will be proportional to corresponding frequency densities.

When numerals are repeated in statistical data, this repetition is known as Frequency and which can be written in the form of a table, called a frequency distribution. A Frequency distribution can be shown graphically by using different types of graphs and a Histogram is one among them.

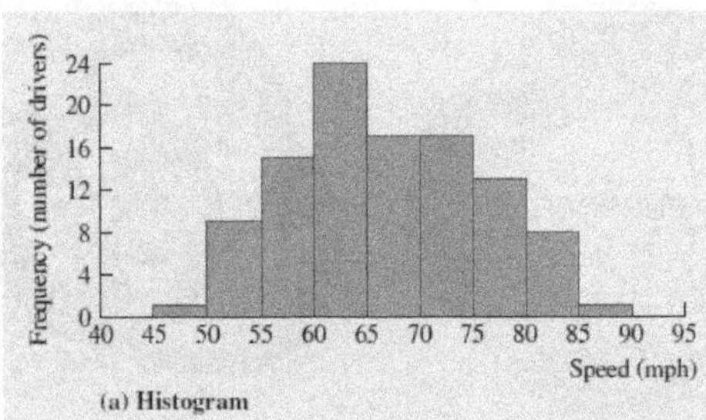

Figure 77: Histogram of a Frequency Distribution

10.10. Visualizing Complex Data and Relations

In early days, visualization techniques were mainly for numeric data. Recently, more and more non-numeric data, such as text and social networks, have become available.

Visualizing and analyzing such data attracts a lot of interest.

There are many new visualization techniques dedicated to these kinds of data. For example, many people on the Web tag various objects such as pictures, blog entries, and product reviews. A tag cloud is a visualization of statistics of user-generated tags. Often, in a tag cloud, tags are listed alphabetically or in a user-preferred order. The importance of a tag is indicated by font size or color. Figure shows a tag cloud for visualizing the popular tags used in a Web site.

Figure 78: Using a Tag Cloud to Visualize Popular Web Site Tags

Tag clouds are often used in two ways. First, in a tag cloud for a single item, we can use the size of a tag to represent the number of times that the tag is applied to this item by different users. Second, when visualizing the tag statistics on multiple items, we can use the size of a tag to represent the number of items that the tag has been applied to, that is, the popularity of the tag.

In addition to complex data, complex relations among data entries also raise challenges for visualization. For example, Figure uses a disease influence graph to visualize the correlations between diseases. The nodes in the graph are diseases, and the size of each node is proportional to the prevalence of the corresponding disease.

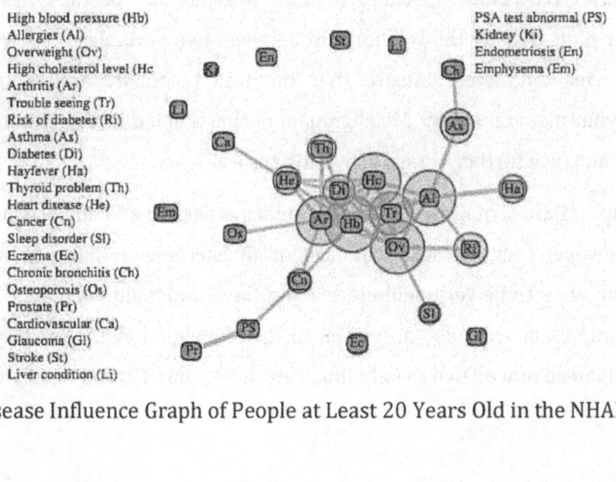

Figure 79: Disease Influence Graph of People at Least 20 Years Old in the NHANES Data Set

Two nodes are linked by an edge if the corresponding diseases have a strong correlation.

The width of an edge is proportional to the strength of the correlation pattern of the two corresponding diseases.

Data Visualization Best Practices

With so many data visualization tools readily available, there has also been a rise in in effective information visualization. Visual communication should be simple and deliberate to ensure that your data visualization helps your target audience arrive at your intended insight or conclusion. The following best practices can help ensure your data visualization is useful and clear:

Set the Context: It's important to provide general background information to ground the audience around why this particular data point is important. For example, if e-mail open rates were underperforming, we may want to illustrate how a company's open rate compares to the overall industry, demonstrating that the company has a problem within this marketing channel. To drive an action, the audience needs to understand how current performance compares to something tangible, like a goal, benchmark, or other key performance indicators (KPIs).

Know your Audience(s): Think about who your visualization is designed for and then make sure your data visualization fits their needs. What is that person trying to accomplish? What kind of questions do they care about? Does your visualization address their concerns? You'll want the data that you provide to motivate people to act within their scope of their role. If you're unsure if the visualization is clear, present it to one or two people within your target audience to get feedback, allowing you to make additional edits prior to a large presentation.

Choose an Effective Visual: Specific visuals are designed for specific types of datasets. For instance, scatter plots display the relationship between two variables well, while line graphs display time series data well. Ensure that the visual actually assists the audience in understanding your main takeaway. Misalignment of charts and data can result in the opposite, confusing your audience further versus providing clarity.

Keep it Simple: Data visualization tools can make it easy to add all sorts of information to your visual. However, just because you can, it doesn't mean that you should! In data visualization, you want to be very deliberate about the additional information that you add to focus user attention. For example, do you need data labels on every bar in your bar chart? Perhaps you only need one or two to help illustrate your point. Do you need a variety of colors to communicate your idea? Are you using colors that are accessible to a wide range of audiences (e.g. accounting for color blind audiences)? Design your data visualization for maximum impact by eliminating information that may distract your target audience.

In summary, visualization provides effective tools to explore data. We have introduced several popular methods and the essential ideas behind them. There are many existing tools and methods. Moreover, visualization can be used in data mining in various aspects. In addition to visualizing data, visualization can be used to represent the data mining process, the patterns obtained from a mining method, and user interaction with the data. Visual data mining is an important research and development direction.